S0-ASF-190

WITHDRAWN

ARKAD'S WORLD

ARKAD'S WORLD

James L. Cambias

Mount Laurel Library
100 Walt Whitman Avenue
Mount Laurel, NJ 08054-9539
856-234-7319
www.mountlaurellibrary.org

ARKAD'S WORLD

This is a work of fiction. All the characters and events portrayed in this book are fictional, and any resemblance to real people or incidents is purely coincidental.

Copyright © 2019 by James L. Cambias

All rights reserved, including the right to reproduce this book or portions thereof in any form.

A Baen Books Original

Baen Publishing Enterprises
P.O. Box 1403
Riverdale, NY 10471
www.baen.com

ISBN: 978-1-4814-8370-4

Cover art by Dave Seeley

First printing, January 2019

Distributed by Simon & Schuster
1230 Avenue of the Americas
New York, NY 10020

Library of Congress Cataloging-in-Publication Data

Names: Cambias, James L., author.
Title: Arkad's world / James L. Cambias.
Description: Riverdale, NY : Baen, 2019.
Identifiers: LCCN 2018047828 | ISBN 9781481483704 (hardback)
Subjects: | BISAC: FICTION / Science Fiction / Adventure. | FICTION / Science Fiction / Space Opera. | FICTION / Science Fiction / General. | GSAFD: Science fiction.
Classification: LCC PS3603.A4467 A89 2019 | DDC 813/.6—dc23
LC record available at https://lccn.loc.gov/2018047828

10 9 8 7 6 5 4 3 2 1

Pages by Joy Freeman (www.pagesbyjoy.com)
Printed in the United States of America

For my children,
Emily and Robert

CHAPTER 1

THE STREET CALLED THE RING CIRCLES THE CITY OF AYAVIZ just atop the iron walls which hold back the ice sheet and the sea. Two huge machines endlessly follow the street around the edge of the city, using invisible beams of heat to clear fallen snow from a belt a hundred meters wide, all around the city. For that reason nobody can build anything permanent on the Ring, which means that, almost alone among the streets of Ayaviz, it is broad and unobstructed, a natural marketplace.

Traders and vendors put up stalls and tents in the wake of the ice-burners and do business until the second giant crawls along, a little more than eight and a half hours later. The city never rests, but all living things must, so when the Ring empties out and the machines pass, new merchants come afterward to replace the ones who left. On a world where the sun sits immobile in the sky, the passage of the ice-burners gives Ayaviz something like a daily cycle.

When the great machine moves silently into view around the curve of the city, the vendors hurry to pack up their stalls and carts. They toss all their refuse onto the smooth surface of the road, where everything gets swept up as the ice-burner passes. The packing-up time attracts bargain hunters, eager to haggle when the vendors can't linger, and scavengers who pick through the refuse.

A human boy named Arkad picked his way through the clear lane down the middle of the roadway, prodding at trash with his

1

feet and occasionally picking things up. He was thin and very dirty, dressed in a tattered blanket wrapped around his body toga-style, with layers and layers of cloth and plastic sheeting on his feet. His black hair was a mass of tangles, but his face was cheerful and his eyes were bright.

So far he had acquired some string, a couple of sheets of waterproof plastic, and a handful of frozen larvae. Most of the discarded food items—like the larvae thawing in his hand—were things he couldn't eat, but the ones that looked fresh enough might be traded. He had not eaten since the other ice-burner had passed this part of the Ring, and was hoping to find something to fill his stomach.

Nearby a pair of Pfifu loaded trays of fresh seafood on ice into their cart, which was itself built in the shape of a mythical sea creature on wheels, with brightly colored cloth tentacles on top which fluttered in the cold wind. Arkad hadn't seen that cart around before, which suggested they were new in town. One of them was male, the other female, and Arkad guessed they were mates as well as partners; Pfifu typically combined business and reproduction. Their seafood was stuff he could eat, so he lingered nearby, hoping they might discard something.

Arkad looked over his shoulder at the oncoming ice-burner. It was about fifty meters away, sliding forward at a relentless ten centimeters per second. This seemed like a good moment to make his move. He approached the cart.

"You tell me do you need help," he said in the city pidgin, a mishmash of loan words that half a dozen species could pronounce, more or less.

"No," said the female, and went back to work, folding up the tent. A chilly gust made her exposed tentacles go pale for a moment.

"You can not eat all that," said Arkad. "Fish will spoil soon." The ice-burner closed the distance by a couple of meters as they spoke. The machine was big and boxy, its slab sides brushing the buildings on the inner side of the Ring and overhanging the city's edge on the outside. On its flat top, a spherical turret gazed endlessly outward, and sometimes the airborne dust in front of the turret glowed blue-white when the invisible beam caught it. Its base seemed to touch the ground solidly, with no gap at all.

As it moved steadily forward, Arkad could see the front edge conform perfectly to every curve and bump in the road, every scrap of debris. Anything left on the street, living or dead, vanished under the machine, and what happened after that was a mystery. The popular belief in Ayaviz was that the burners used everything they swept up as fuel for their heat beams; it was certainly true that they never needed unloading or recharging.

The most alarming thing about the ice-burner was not its size but its silence. It made no sound as it crept along, and despite its bulk, the road did not tremble. Puddles on the pavement didn't even ripple as it approached. Its movement was barely noticeable if Arkad watched it steadily, but when he glanced away and then looked back, the machine seemed to jump forward in a way that was very disturbing.

Only a few laggards were left in this stretch of the market, and people of the neighborhood were tossing trash and poisonous wastes onto the Ring to be swept up by the burner.

"We have kin, and folk who live near us," said the male, who was already done cleaning off the grill. "They eat what we do not sell. But if you help us move the cart, I will tell you a thing you want to hear."

"*Hurry, spouse, like a rocket ascending into the sky,*" said his mate in the Pfifu language of tentacle gestures and whistles, which Arkad could understand but not speak. "*I urge you to pack up the fish as securely as locking up a treasure, without standing idly wasting irreplaceable time with that ungainly creature.*" The burner had closed to eighteen meters while they spoke.

"You tell me what is that thing I should hear," Arkad asked. What could a couple of back-country Pfifu tell him that he didn't already know?

"I will tell you when we move the cart."

"You tell me and give me two small fish for my help," said Arkad.

"One fish," said the male. "Take down pole and put on cart."

"Fool," said the female in pidgin. She climbed onto the cart and pulled the tent up after her. The ice-burner was only twelve meters off.

"*Gentle companion, I am tired and cold, and if the poor creature can help us accomplish our task swiftly, then I am willing to part with a spare fish or two that would otherwise only return lifeless to the sea which birthed them and some miscellaneous trivia of no*

value to anyone. I encourage you not to leave that rope behind,"
said the male to the female in their own language.

Arkad had no trouble getting the tent pole (it was aluminum,
sculpted like braided vines) out of its base, and found the little
latch where it folded in half, then handed it up to the female.
The male dragged the pole's base aboard, and then the two Pfifu
wrapped their long upper tentacles around the cart ropes and
began pulling the whole thing toward a nearby alley.

The ice-burner was less than five meters away. Its massive
front loomed over them, still approaching in absolute silence.
Arkad threw his shoulder against the back of the cart, pushing
as hard as he could. His feet in their dirty wrappings couldn't
find much purchase on the smooth damp road, but he put all his
weight into it and the cart slipped into the alley with at least four
seconds to spare before the flat side of the ice-burner slid past.

"Fish," said Arkad to the male. "And tell me the thing."

"First you tell me what you are."

"*Human,*" said Arkad, saying the word slowly and carefully.
"From world with name of *Earth.*"

"Feeufa from Eeauf," said the male, unable to manage the
troublesome consonants. He scrambled up onto the cart and
tossed a fish down to Arkad. It smelled a little far gone already,
but cooking would fix that. "A short time past I saw three of
your kind in this town."

In an instant the boy's skepticism was replaced by a desperate
urgency. "You tell me where."

"Here on the Ring, when we set up the cart," said the male
Pfifu, and gestured, *"The city is full of strange creatures, and it is
not worth my time to keep track of them."* Its tentacles were still
forming the last shapes of that remark as Arkad turned and ran.

The alley was narrow and cluttered with debris. The only light
came from the glow of the sky above, a dim band between the
tall towers that stretched up from the city's iron base. Here and
there the sky was blocked altogether by rickety platforms and
nets suspended between the alley walls.

Arkad ran, ducking around pedestrians and hopping over
puddles, barely noticing. Humans! Here in Ayaviz!

He left the alley and turned into one of the main avenues.
The beings in the street were a cross section of the inhabitants of
Ayaviz. Vziim slithered along, usually in groups led by a wealthy

elder on a power-cart. They had long, dark, legless bodies covered in short dense fur, with four thick arms spaced evenly around their heads. Vziim ignored Arkad, or at least pretended to.

Pfifu stumped along on their four lower tentacles if they had anything to carry, or swung along from overhead ropes and girders if their upper tentacles were free. Their bodies were as long and thick as Arkad's leg, and their skin shifted color and pattern.

Itooti flew past, or rode in bunches on overloaded scooters. They were small, with leathery wings wider than Arkad's outstretched arms, and four other limbs. They darted their barbed prehensile tongues at each other. The ones who knew him called out boasts and friendly insults.

A scattering of aliens from offworld moved among the natives: tall Roon traders in elaborate robes, a tentacled being with a barrel-shaped body riding in a wheeled environment tank, a hairy thing with six skinny limbs, and an orderly line of rainbow-feathered bipeds with prehensile tails.

There were no humans. There never were.

Ayaviz was too big and crowded for Arkad to search by himself. If there were other humans in town, someone would know of it. He stopped running long enough to think about where to start.

The closest place to begin finding out was the house of Tatoota, the mother of his friend Tiatatoo. As long as his mother was single, Tiatatoo would likely be there, and Arkad could get all the latest gossip from him. But if Tatoota had a new lover, all her male children would stay far away, and any reminder of their existence—such as Arkad—would be unwelcome.

Arkad ran along the avenue until he found a dangling rope, which he began to climb hand over hand. The rope took him ten meters up to a platform, where a crude ladder extended up to the roof of a low tower. From the top of the tower, he followed a rope bridge across two streets to a broken dome, climbed up another ladder to a gallery lashed to the dark side of a bigger tower, and finally up fifty meters of rope to the home of Tatoota.

Tatoota's house was typical Itooti engineering: a mess of scavenged struts and cord lashed to the side of a much more solid building constructed by somebody else. Layers of tarps and blankets kept out the chill, and heat came from a fire of scraps in a steel drum with a crude flue sticking out the top. Just about all the city's towers had scores of Itooti constructions sticking to their sides, like parasitic growths. Others hung from cables over the streets, and the undersides of all the upper-level streets were thickly encrusted with them. They burned up or fell down fairly often, and from time to time, the owners of the big towers would send out crews to clear them off the exterior, but the Itooti always came back.

Before going in, he looked around as he always did. From up here he could see Ayaviz spread out around him. The base of the city was a perfect circle, walled with steel. Within that ring, the ancient builders—whoever they were—had put up various strange industrial structures: windowless metal towers, giant conduits, big spheres and cubes of gray metal. Those structures were all still active, fulfilling whatever mysterious purpose they had been built for. The machinery extended down kilometers below the city now, still digging new shafts and tunnels.

From time to time the rest of the city felt the effects of whatever those machines were doing. Arkad could remember once when all the metal in Ayaviz had become too hot to touch for nearly an hour. Another time one of the featureless cubes gave off a buzzing sound which shattered windows. Nobody interfered with the ancient machines; the only thing that ever accomplished was the destruction of whoever tried it.

The machines had been there forever, apparently. The Psthao-psthao had come to the planet Syavusa millennia ago, and found the surface of the world dotted with mysterious constructions. A community of them settled in the warm dark tunnels of the city they named Hoasfeoth.

Vziim followed and put up their towers of brick and concrete, overshadowing the ancient machines, and in some cases, incorporating them into the new structures. They renamed the city Ayaviz, which was as close as they could come to the Psthao-psthao word, and built a harbor and spaceport, turning an isolated outpost into the planet's gateway.

Pfifu arrived a few centuries later, building their own low, rambling structures, encrusted with decoration or actually shaped like fantastic monsters, around the bases of the Vziim towers and the old machines. They created factories and workshops, and pronounced the name Ayafif. In recent years the numbers of Pfifu had expanded as they fled their home planet, so that their pronunciation would probably become the standard in another generation.

The Itooti were the most recent arrivals, still living in the shells and crevices of other people's buildings, working for Vziim merchants and Pfifu manufacturers. Among themselves, they called the city Aitateet, and someday that might be the common name for the place.

There were other species—AaaAa in the forests along the edge of the ice cap, silent five-finned beings with pincers down in the ocean, and doubtless many others Arkad had never seen. Exiles fled to Syavusa from all over, because there was nobody to keep them away. Nobody ruled Syavusa. Yet somehow no conquerors ever came, no interstellar powers claimed the world. Arkad didn't know why, and didn't really wonder about it.

Beyond the city to the east, the ice cap stretched away into darkness. A line of lights marked the railway, and on the horizon, Arkad could make out a flickering glow from the refineries and workshops around the spaceport. To the west, between the towers that blocked the sunlight, he could just glimpse the ocean, studded with ice floes. Warm currents and the city's own waste heat kept the bay ice-free, and someone had cut docking slips out of the rocky shores of the inlet near the city. Right on the rim of the ocean, the sun sat unmoving, a shining red half-disk.

As Arkad looked that way, he saw a bright star leap up from the sun's glare, moving swiftly upward until it passed right overhead. It dropped down in the east and winked out just before touching the horizon. A spaceship in orbit—a big one, judging from how brightly it shone in the sunlight.

Arkad's yearning to leave the planet was almost a physical force. For a moment, he wanted to just leap off the tower and follow the spaceship away from Syavusa.

A gust of cold wind out of the eastern darkness nearly blew Arkad off the rope. He turned and poked his head through the entry flap of Tatoota's house and called out in the Itooti language, which he could speak with some fluency. "Friendly Arkad wonders who is in the snug home."

To his relief he heard his friend answer. "Generous Tiatatoo welcomes homeless Arkad."

Tiatatoo dropped down from the spot near the ceiling where he had been hanging. With his wings folded, he could have perched on Arkad's shoulder—Itooti males seldom weighed more than five or ten kilos. "Lonely Tiatatoo suggests gentle Arkad come view the adorable babies."

On one side of the stove, Tiatatoo's mother had created a kind of corral for her latest brood. There were half a dozen of them, small enough to fit in Arkad's hand, their wings still stubby and covered with fuzz.

"Curious Arkad wonders if the healthy babies have personal names," asked Arkad.

"Sensible Tatoota has not given her feeble new babies individual names yet," said Tiatatoo. "When the strong children learn to fly, proud Tatoota will give them impressive names."

One of the baby males darted his sharp little tongue at Tiatatoo, who pressed his own much bigger barb to the little one's belly, forcing him down onto his back.

"Anxious Arkad hopes affectionate Tiatatoo doesn't hurt his tiny brother," said Arkad. He handed Tiatatoo one of the females to distract him, and stroked the male's downy belly to make sure Tiatatoo hadn't pierced the skin.

"The vigorous little male will seduce many adoring females if the annoying infant survives," said Tiatatoo, flicking his tongue at his little half-brother once more. He turned to Arkad. "Proud Tiatatoo has important news!"

"Solitary Arkad is eager to hear well-connected Tiatatoo's interesting news."

For an instant his young Itooti friend cocked his head in puzzlement, but then continued anyway. "Soft-furred Atett flew to meet brightly colored Tiatatoo and hear him recite seductive verses. Vigorous and passionate mating ensued. Soon, fertile Atett will bear a numerous litter of exceptional offspring!"

"Sincere Arkad is glad to hear virile Tiatatoo's wonderful news," he said.

"Devoted Atett will build a secure and comfortable home," said Tiatatoo. "Generous Tiatatoo assures helpful Arkad that he will always be a welcome guest."

"Happy Arkad wishes both affectionate lovers a prolonged pairing." Arkad was genuinely happy for his friend—but it came with a new pang of loneliness. Tiatatoo could pair off with the lovely Atett and raise a brood of fuzzy children, but Arkad would be alone as long as he stayed on Syavusa.

Time to get straight to the point. "Desperate Arkad wonders if wide-ranging Tiatatoo has heard any interesting news concerning exotic humans in smoky Ayaviz."

Tiatatoo looked away in the ancient negative gesture. "All-seeing Tiatatoo has heard no recent report of remarkable humans. Baffled Tiatatoo wonders why excited Arkad asks."

"Two observant Pfifu selling tasty fish claimed to have seen three apparent humans recently."

"Gullible Arkad should remember how often dishonest Pfifu invent false stories."

"Determined Arkad intends to continue searching for the hypothetical humans. Persistent Arkad wonders if handsome Tiatatoo knows where to find shrewd Zvev."

Zvev wasn't exactly Arkad's friend; she was a Vziim and, outside their families, Vziim didn't have friends, only temporary allies. Like him, she was an orphan, surviving on the streets of Ayaviz through scavenging, odd jobs, and petty crime. Her quick wits and sheer muscle made her the de facto boss of the little gang made up of Arkad, Tiatatoo, Zvev, and a Pfifu named Fuee. She always seemed to know about everything going on in the city.

The trick was finding her. Zvev claimed to be the daughter of a wealthy tower-building matriarch, unfairly defrauded of her rightful inheritance and hunted by the minions of her greedy half-sisters. Arkad had his doubts about the story, but kept them to himself. Whatever the real reason, she kept her hiding places secret, and liked to appear and disappear without warning. If Tiatatoo didn't know where she was, Arkad would have to wait until she found him.

A gust of cold wind swept through the little house as Tiatatoo's mother, Tatoota, returned with a basket of food for the babies.

"Tolerant Tatoota is glad to see ever-present Arkad," she told him.

"Grateful Arkad thanks kind Tatoota for her generous hospitality," he answered.

"Harried Tatoota would appreciate some welcome aid in the tiresome feeding of her hungry children," she said, handing him some strips of meat.

"Eager Arkad will help."

"The tough meat must be made soft before the weak babies can eat." She took a strip in her own mouth and rasped it with the sides of her tongue before spitting the chewed meat into the mouth of an eager baby.

Arkad followed suit. The meat was raw, so he was careful not to swallow any. Cooked Itooti food was delicious, but if it wasn't well-done it gave him diarrhea and monumental flatulence. He chewed the strip vigorously and then held it in his teeth for one of the little females to snatch away.

He finished with the first strip and took a second. He could see Tiatatoo watching from where he clung to a support rope over the stove. A young male Itooti would rather cut off his wings than be seen feeding infants.

Chewing the meat for the infants reminded Arkad of how hungry he was. The uneaten fish tucked into his blanket would start to spoil soon—if it wasn't too far gone already. He didn't have enough to share, and didn't want to ask Tatoota for anything—she was a resource he was saving for a real emergency.

So when the last of the meat had gone into the hungry little mouths, and Tiatatoo's half-siblings dozed in a heap next to the stove, Arkad slipped out of the house and descended to the street. Maybe he would find Zvev, maybe he would find the humans. But first he would eat.

As he walked along, Arkad kept his eyes open for scraps which might make a good fire. From uncomfortable experience, he knew that while the Pfifu could happily eat the local seafood raw, his own stomach would only tolerate uncooked fish if it was perfectly fresh.

When he had enough fuel, he climbed onto the stump of a ruined wall in a convenient alley and put the flammable trash into a hollow between the bricks, then squeezed a tiny drop from the bottle of firestarter he'd found many markets ago. The liquid burst into flame on contact with the fuel, and soon he had a steady if smoky fire.

Arkad's only cooking utensil was a skewer—which also served him as a toothpick, personal-defense weapon, and digging tool. He slid the fish onto the skewer and broiled it until the skin was completely blackened and the tips of the fins were starting to catch fire. Then he brushed away the burnt skin and gnawed at the steaming flesh.

He took his time about it, eating all the meat, picking out the edible entrails, and finally sucking the thin bones clean. Only when everything human-edible was in his stomach did he toss the remains into the fire, enjoying the warmth until it burned down to ashes.

Four short but massive arms gripped his torso from behind, and he felt himself hoisted into the air, to dangle helplessly four meters above the ground. He glanced up and recognized Zvev holding him. Her long tail was wrapped securely around a pipe which spanned the alley a couple of meters higher up.

"I have caught prey to eat," she said. "But it is too thin, all bone and no meat. I will toss it back." She lowered him to the ground and then slid down beside him. "Tell me why you seek me."

"I need to know if there are more of my folk here in Ayaviz," he said. "A Pfifu said he saw three."

Zvev reared back and regarded him. Vziim faces were always immobile anyway, but she was even more unreadable than usual. "You tell me why you want to know that."

"I want to meet them."

"You tell me why I should help," she said.

Because you are my friend was what Arkad did not say. "I want to leave this place," he told her. "If I can go with them, you can have all my stuff."

"Small gain for me," she said, "but I will tell you what I learn." She turned to go, then stopped. "You tell me why you wish to leave."

For a moment Arkad had trouble putting it all into words. If she didn't understand, how could he explain it? "There is no one like me here," he said. "I wish to live with folk like me."

"They may look like you but they are not your kin," she said. "You have no kin on or off this world. With no kin, you will have to get by on your own."

"I still want to go. It is hard to be the sole one of my kind."

"You are a fool. There are a lot of Vziim here but none are like me. All who live are the sole one of their kind." She clacked her claws together. "I will tell you if I hear of them." She slid over the wall and, in an instant, Arkad was alone in the alley again.

The fish and his brief rest had restored Arkad's energy, and his encounter with Zvev made him want to demonstrate that he didn't need her help. So he got to his feet and thought. What was the most likely place in Ayaviz for newly arrived humans to be?

They must have come from offworld, which means they had landed at the spaceport, off to the east on the dark ice. From there, all offworlders rode the rail line into Ayaviz, so the neighborhood around the rail terminal was the best place to start.

That part of town was a mix of cheap housing for new arrivals, expensive hotels for rich travelers, and lots of markets selling offworld merchandise to locals and local goods to offworlders. The really important deals were made in the wide streets on either side of the rail line, where road tractors hauling strings of wagons could pull up. There, Vziim and Itooti traders haggled with Roon and other aliens, making bids on cargoes and shouting out what they had to exchange, all while Pfifu crane operators swung containers between the wagons and the trains.

Arkad stood in the square in front of the terminal and turned slowly around. If he was newly arrived on Syavusa, where would he go first? A prudent traveler would find food and a place to sleep before doing anything else.

To his left was a jumble of whimsical-looking Pfifu buildings, all devoted in some way to the road-tractor business—repair shops, fuel stations, and bathing-houses where Pfifu tractor drivers gathered to soak in hot scented seawater and watch satirical puppet shows.

Straight ahead was Eviavo's tower, a smooth, six-sided spire clad in thick glass, which tapered straight up from a broad base to a needle tip three hundred meters above the ground. Six smaller spires only a hundred meters high surrounded it, and graceful bridges connected them to the main tower at their tips. Eviavo and her siblings tolerated the usual clutter of Itooti construction on the subsidiary towers, but had made it clear—with flame-projectors—that the main tower was to remain pristine. Only the wealthiest visitors could afford rooms there.

On the right was Aviiva's tower, a handsome four-sided structure of steel with a skin of thin-sliced white stone. It rose in a series of setbacks to a height of two hundred meters. That was tall enough to catch some direct sunlight at the top, so the upper floors supported a wide flower of solar panels and some twirling wind generators. Below that the building was a random combination of residences, workshops, offices, storage space, and hotel rooms. That was where the more budget-conscious offworlders wound up.

How rich were these visiting humans? Arkad knew that even the cheapest fare aboard a starship, risking cold sleep to save the ruinous life-support charges, cost at least thirty kilos of platinum. Just *being* here meant they were rich. Didn't it?

Well, if nothing else, Eviavo's tower was nicer looking, so he decided to start there. The shabby-looking alien boy attracted a great many odd looks in the market that occupied the two bottom floors of the tower—almost certainly because the vendors here were selling some of the most expensive merchandise on the planet. One could buy genomes from offworld, or sculptures by legendary Pfifu artists, or cargoes of thorium in other star systems, or real estate, or Machine Civilization devices which defied the laws of nature. Buyers and sellers alike were old, well-dressed, and unmistakably rich.

Arkad saw one ancient Vziim female on a power-cart, whose entire body, from her arms to the tip of her tail, was wrapped in helical strands of gold. He also slowed to goggle at a pair of aliens of some species he didn't recognize; they were taller than he was and seemed to consist of nothing but a dozen spindly legs and a small globular head on top.

He heard a flutter of wings and his Itooti friend Tiatatoo landed on his shoulder, then poked him in the ear with his tongue. "Oblivious Arkad is being followed."

The boy didn't react, but kept up his slow strolling pace as they passed a shop selling psychoactive bath salts for Pfifu. "Embarrassed Arkad did not notice, and tense Arkad hopes keen-eyed Tiatatoo will reveal the current location of the mysterious pursuer."

"Reckless Arkad should look between the overpriced claw-trimming parlor and the rapacious gene-buyer office."

He turned around, as if he was watching a passing Pfifu carrying a basket of electronic components, then glanced at the spot Tiatatoo had described. The spot between the two shops was a small alcove lined with deep red tiles, sheltering some thick blue and white pipes carrying water and compressed air up into the tower above. Only because he had been told someone was there could Arkad notice the figure standing in the niche. It was about his own height, wearing a hooded cloak that reached to the floor. The cloak was the same deep red as the tile wall, with wide blue and white stripes that aligned with the pipes. He could just make out the dark opening at the front of the thing's hood, and glimpsed a pale face within.

It was a human face.

CHAPTER 2

ARKAD TOOK A STEP TOWARD THE FIGURE IN THE ALCOVE, AND instantly it snapped into motion, almost too fast for him to see. The cloak changed to a chaotic blur of color as the figure dodged between shoppers. But in that instant, Arkad saw that it was indeed a human underneath the cloak—someone slender, very pale, and no taller than Arkad himself.

He followed, feet pounding on the smooth concrete floor. The pale figure grabbed a post in order to swing around a corner, then sprinted toward the big doors facing the rail terminal. Arkad skidded around that corner himself a second later, but the cloaked human was already at the door.

Tiatatoo shot past Arkad and dove through the doors along with the fleeing human. When Arkad burst out into the square a moment later, the Itooti called down to him, "The swift fugitive turned right!"

He spotted the cloak, which had now gone a neutral gray, as the slim human plunged into a narrow street on the north side of the square. Arkad followed. His quarry was fast, which was a little galling to Arkad. For most of his life in Ayaviz, he had relied on three talents: running fast, throwing things accurately, and noticing things. But this other human wasn't just faster than Arkad, he—she? Arkad wasn't sure—was faster than a flying Itooti.

But Arkad also knew the city, including many secret ways that a stranger wouldn't even see. He turned aside and climbed up to a walkway which ran above the rooftops roughly parallel to the street. Traffic up there was a lot thinner, so he could run at full speed until he was almost level with the cloaked figure in the street below.

She—definitely a she, he decided—looked up at him and ducked into a side passage on her left. Arkad ran to a taut cable which spanned the street, and dashed across with the confidence of long practice, grabbed a hanging cable to swing to a wall where bolted-on rungs allowed him to climb down. He took a narrow alley to the left where the Vziim brokers traded property and loan shares, dodging through the crowd calling apologies over his shoulder.

The cloaked female human disappeared into a dark passage to the right, and Arkad followed. They emerged into a plaza where Itooti tanned fish skins. The place reeked of smoke, sulfur, and rotting flesh, but the smell didn't seem to deter the other human. Arkad followed her between stacks of dried sea plants ready for burning, then under racks of skins drying, and around the big vats of lye and acid, then down a half-hidden passage leading back toward the center of the city.

His side was starting to hurt, but the other human showed no sign of slowing. They reached a wide avenue where a six-wagon road train rumbled along, headed for the north road out of town along the coast. The cloaked figure didn't even slow down. One leap took her to the top of the fourth wagon; she dashed along the top of the train to just behind the tractor, and then jumped off on the far side, thirty meters down the street.

Arkad waited for the last wagon to pass, then ran across, but he couldn't see the other human anymore.

Tiatatoo circled his head. "Heavy-breathing Arkad has lost his elusive prey."

"Frustrated Arkad asks if observant Tiatatoo can find the cloaked being."

His friend rose into the air again, spiraling up on a column of warm air coming from one of the deep shafts which led down hundreds of meters into the bedrock. He dove in a wide loop which brought him back to Arkad's shoulder. "High-flying Tiatatoo can see no running cloaked being nearby. Surprised Tiatatoo asks secretive Arkad if that mysterious fugitive is another uncommon human."

"Uncertain Arkad does not know. The bipedal being looks

like a graceful human, but the high-leaping creature performed physical feats agile Arkad could not."

Just then Tiatatoo dove into the folds of Arkad's blanket, clutching the boy's torso with his claws and pulling his tail in after him. "Worried Tiatatoo begs large Arkad to find a place of effective concealment."

"Baffled Arkad wonders what terrifying thing fearless Tiatatoo wishes to hide from," said Arkad, as he found a narrow alley between two large buildings and slipped in.

"Lovely Atett has jealous suitors who resent handsome Tiatatoo's romantic success. Vicious Utto and brutal Tattat are circling above us and may wish to inflict permanent harm on vulnerable Tiatatoo."

Arkad glanced casually upward, as if checking the weather, and saw a pair of powerful-looking Itooti males. "Perhaps cautious Tiatatoo should seek a willing female who does not have so many dangerous suitors."

"Voluptuous Atett has many ardent lovers because of her matchless desirability. Daring Tiatatoo does not allow those unattractive rivals to deter him—but prudent Tiatatoo hopes helpful Arkad will let him stay hidden until the two impotent bullies leave."

It was difficult for Arkad to walk casually with a nearly full-grown male Itooti clinging to him under his blanket, but he managed as best he could. His pursuit of the cloaked human had taken him about a quarter of the way across the city, so he took a more direct route back to the square by the rail terminal. After a few minutes Tiatatoo poked his head out and anxiously surveyed the sky, then climbed up onto Arkad's shoulder.

"Dirt-encrusted Arkad should bathe more often," he said.

"Poverty-afflicted Arkad cannot afford luxurious baths."

"Cost-conscious Arkad could take a free dip in the cleansing sea."

"Warm-blooded Arkad does not want to take a life-threatening dip in the icy ocean. Fastidious Tiatatoo should not complain about the adequate hygiene of the generous friend who is hiding him."

Just then he stumbled as a long furry body shot across the alley at knee level. Before Arkad could recover his balance, Zvev had wrapped herself around him with her head above his looking down.

"I know where they are," she said.

"You tell me where," said Arkad.

Zvev took her time answering. She uncoiled herself and spent a few seconds cleaning her fur, then said, "I am wise. I do not run through town and try to catch one who is too fast for me. Nor do I let the one I seek know I am here. I go to those I know and ask them. At last I find one who has seen your kind in this town."

"You tell me where," Arkad repeated.

"I spent time in the search," said Zvev. "And now I owe a debt to the one who told me where they are. All this has cost me."

"You tell me what you want," said Arkad.

"They come from space," she said. "To do that is not cheap. They must have wealth. I want you to find out why they are here. What they want—and how much they can pay for it. We can make a lot from them if we are wise."

Arkad thought for a moment before answering. Zvev was probably smarter than he was, but her goals were not his. He decided to be honest, if only because she probably suspected the truth anyway. "I do not want to get some small gain from a quick scam," he said. "I want to leave this world with them."

"You tell me what you will do if they do not want to take you with them."

"I will do what I must to make them want to do it."

"But you may fail. Then you are stuck here as you are now, but with no more than you have."

"Then I will be no worse off."

"You will have no friends," she pointed out. "If you do not help us to gain, you tell me why we should still be your friends."

Arkad looked up at Tiatatoo, who was sitting on his head, and switched to the Itooti language. "Loyal Arkad wonders if honorable Tiatatoo will remain his reliable friend without any material reward."

They both knew that Zvev could understand what he was saying, even if she couldn't manage the precise vowels of Itooti speech. Tiatatoo leaped from Arkad's head and landed neatly on a broken arch which had once spanned the alley. He looked from Arkad to Zvev a couple of times before replying.

"If you go from here, you should help the friends you leave," he said, using the pidgin.

"I will do that," said Arkad quickly.

"If you go," said Zvev.

"Yes."

She groomed herself a little longer, then said, "They are at the spire of Aviiva, four floors up. I do not know which room."

"I thank you," said Arkad. He hesitated for a moment, then took off again at a run back to the plaza by the terminal.

As with most Vziim-built towers in Ayaviz, the lower levels of Aviiva's tower were market space, so even a stray young alien like Arkad could enter freely. Unlike the restrained affluence of Eviavo's tower, the market section of Aviiva's was loud and eclectic. One saw spaceship crew members here, buying souvenirs or trying to work out private deals with merchants. Crafters hawked the goods they made. At least a few of the stalls had goods which were probably stolen, or at least had been "salvaged" before they were quite lost.

The tower boasted two elevators, a pair of big open platforms four meters square that ran next to each other in a single shaft up the center of the building. Their cables were connected at the top, so that the two platforms counterweighted each other. They both went up and down ceaselessly, stopping for five seconds at each floor before continuing.

Arkad waited at the center of the building until one platform landed at the bottom with a bump. Four Pfifu dragged off a small cart loaded with blown glass, and the boy boarded along with a pair of female Vziim who were apparently inspecting the building and taking notes. Itooti never bothered with elevators unless they had a heavy load to move. A couple of them swooped past him to circle up the central shaft. Arkad stood at the edge of the platform and counted four floors, then hopped off and explored the corridors. His mouth was dry. How would he find them? He could just start knocking on doors...

Just then he caught a scent which was unique in Ayaviz, but which struck a chord in his memory. It was the smell of cooking sausage. He couldn't remember when or where he had eaten it, but he knew what it tasted and smelled like. His dry mouth began to water.

The sausage smell led him to a door, where he stood for a moment working up his courage and composing himself before he knocked.

The door opened, and Arkad had a glimpse of a pale figure shrouded in black before she grabbed him by the throat and one arm, lifted him, and yanked him into the room, pinning him against the wall with his feet half a meter off the floor.

"Who are you and why did you follow me?" she asked very calmly.

"My name is Arkad, I'm the only human on the planet, I wanted to meet you," he said.

"Be polite, Baichi. Put him down," said a man, putting his hand gently on the girl's shoulder. He was much taller and heavier than Arkad, with darker skin. His eyebrows and the hair on his face were gray. He wore sturdy-looking clothing with lots of pockets and a wide-brimmed hat, and he smelled like smoke.

The pale girl lowered Arkad to the floor and let go, then stepped back and wrapped her cloak around her, all without saying a word. Now that Arkad could get a good look at her, he could see that she was about a hand's width shorter than he was. Her skin was hairless and white—not the light pinkish-tan of people he had seen in pictures, but an absolutely colorless white, like clouds or new snow. Combined with her slender build, it gave her an appearance of delicacy, almost fragility. Her eyes were all black, and she looked at Arkad without any expression. Her cloak had turned black, so black Arkad couldn't see any folds or wrinkles in it, just the outline.

The third person in the room was a little bit shorter than Baichi, with skin about the same color as Arkad's, and short blue hair. Arkad couldn't tell right away if the individual was male or female, but something in the shape of the face and the narrow shoulders made him guess female. There was no sign of hair on her face, and she wore a spotless white smart-cloth coverall. She looked very surprised.

"Let's start over," said the man. "My name's Jacob Sato." He extended a hand toward Arkad, who wasn't sure what to do with it. "And you are?"

"My name is Arkad," he repeated.

"Pleased to meet you, young man. This is Ree Bright," said the man, gesturing to the blue-haired woman. "It appears you've already met Baichi," he added, nodding at the cloaked girl. "Would you like some dinner? Or breakfast, or whatever you want to call it?"

"Yes...please," said Arkad, remembering the way people in books asked for things.

Jacob went to a corner of the room where a small fire of rubbish was burning in a metal can. He knelt by the can, took up a fork and resumed cooking sausage. "Give me a minute and I'll whip something up. Have a seat."

The room was small, with no windows. Small vent holes near the low ceiling opened into the elevator shaft. The glow of the ceiling was controlled by a small slider switch by the door. There was a water tap in one corner with a drain below it for waste. About half the floor space was covered by luggage and supply boxes. Arkad had seldom seen such luxury.

As Jacob cooked, he and Ree Bright fired questions at Arkad while Baichi sat silently watching him.

"Why are you here?"

"How did you find us?"

"What happened to your parents?"

"How do you survive?"

In the end, he wound up simply telling them his story, or at least as much of it as he could remember.

"My name is Arkad. I was born on this planet, but I think it was far from here. I came to this city with my mother when I was small, and then she died. The Psthao-psthao took her. Since then I have lived here in the city, and a few other places. I find things, I work, I have friends who help me sometimes."

As he talked, Arkad focused his attention on the three humans. For half his life, his survival had depended on being able to read the behavior and emotions of alien beings. Applying his skill to humans was simultaneously easier and more difficult. He could tell some things about them without even thinking, but other things were very confusing.

Jacob Sato was easy to read. The big man was relaxed, confident, and very observant himself. Even as he cooked he was obviously paying attention to everything Arkad said and did. He worked with the ease of skill and long practice. His movements and posture matched his expressions and his words.

Ree Bright was more puzzling. Her curiosity about Arkad was genuine; that was plain to see. But she also seemed nervous; even when speaking with Arkad she kept glancing at the other two. Her speech and her face didn't match her body.

If Bright was a puzzle, Baichi was a complete enigma. Arkad couldn't read her at all. When she moved, she was fluid and graceful, with never a correction or a wasted motion. When she sat still, she was absolutely immobile. Her face was perfectly blank, like a mask carved from ice.

"There!" said Jacob, putting three bowls in front of Arkad. "A proper dinner. I made you some miso, grilled up the last of the hard sausage, and fixed you a little salad of raisins and pickled carrots. Bon appétit!"

Arkad seldom turned down food, and this time he didn't even have to worry about whether he could eat it safely. The soup was hot and salty, with cubes of something soft and flakes of limp green matter floating in it. Arkad sipped it tentatively at first, then drank it in great gulps. The sausage tasted of smoke and salt and spices—almost, but not exactly like what he remembered—and he nibbled it slowly to prolong the experience. The salad also tasted familiar: he had a sudden memory of picking up raisins from a plate and feeding himself. When had that taken place?

Sato shared out soup and salad with the other two. "There's more if anyone wants it," he said. He watched Arkad eat with a look of amusement. "Though I rather doubt we'll have any left once our guest is finished."

Baichi ate her serving gracefully and efficiently, still without any expression. Ree finished her salad but handed off the soup to Arkad. "This poor hungry boy needs it more than I do," she said, and then unwrapped a food bar for herself.

When Arkad had finished his own food, Ree's soup, a third helping of miso and the remains of the salad, Jacob collected the bowls and rinsed them. "Now that we're done with dinner, we can talk more comfortably. We've been asking Arkad about himself, so now it's only fair that we explain ourselves, if that's possible. Ask away," he said, extending a hand toward Arkad.

"Why are you in Ayaviz?" the boy asked.

Jacob didn't answer right away. He glanced over at Ree and raised his eyebrows. She licked her lips nervously and then nodded her head.

"Okay," said Jacob. "We're here looking for a spacecraft called the *Rosetta*, and I'm pretty sure it wound up on this world, about fifty years ago. Fifty Earth years, that is. In local years that would be..."

"Thirty-eight," said Baichi.

Jacob nodded to her. "Thank you, my dear. Anyway..." He paused and looked at Arkad thoughtfully for a moment. "How old are you, by the way?"

"I'm not sure. Nobody here pays much attention to days or years."

"Hmm." Jacob peered at Arkad. "From his voice I'd say he's at least fourteen," said Jacob. "He's got some lip fuzz, too. Maybe fifteen? The lack of height could be malnutrition, or maybe he just comes from a short family. Never mind. Back to *Rosetta*."

Arkad found it hard to keep up with Jacob's shifts of subject. It was like having dozens of tempting dishes put in front of him, but he could only get a bite of each before they were snatched away.

"Anyway, I traced the *Rosetta* from when it left Earth, as far as the Roon merchant station in the Qualaroo system. Just before flipping the ship into hyperspace there, the crew transmitted a message, but they used a code that only a very clever person well versed in Terran literature could figure out. Fortunately, I'm both extremely clever and extremely well educated—not to mention insufferably modest. The message said they were heading for this system next. That was fifty years ago. In all that time, the *Rosetta* hasn't been seen anywhere else, as far as I could find out. So odds are it's still here."

"Why are you looking for it?" asked Arkad.

"I want to liberate Earth, and *Rosetta* is my weapon of choice. Her cargo could do more to free Earth from the invaders than any warship ever built."

"Don't be elliptical, Jacob," said Ree.

"It's the simple truth!" he insisted.

"Who are the invaders?" asked Arkad. The other three looked at him in surprise.

"You don't know?" asked Jacob.

Arkad shrugged. "I've lived here as long as I can remember."

"What do you know about Earth?" asked Jacob.

"I know a lot of things. There are cities called London and Paris and Bristol and Lahore and Oxford and Petersburg and Chang'an and Vulture Peak and Baghdad and Jerusalem and Ithaca. There are oceans and jungles and forests and mountains and islands and a desert called the Sahara, and a river called the Mississippi and another one called the Ganges. Thousands of humans live there, and many different animals."

"There may be some gaps in your knowledge," said Jacob. "In particular, fifty years ago, Earth was invaded by a species called the Elmisthorn."

"I've seen some of them! They come here sometimes to trade. They have four legs and lots of little limbs around their mouths."

"That's them. They rule an empire they call the Family of Species, and wanted to add humans to their collection, so they showed up with a battle fleet. We fought, we lost, and now they control the whole Solar System. A few thousand humans got away and set up refuges in systems where the Elmisthorn couldn't reach. The *Rosetta* was one of the last ships out. It was a good-sized interstellar ship, a hundred meters long, built for planetary landings. Show him, Ree."

She tapped a device on her wrist and the image of a sleek triple-hulled spaceship appeared in the air between her and Arkad. He felt the hair stand up on the backs of his arms when he saw it.

"And that's the one you're looking for," said Arkad.

"Exactly! But I don't know where it is. I paid the Roon who brought us here to do a quick orbital survey, but unfortunately this planet is just *cluttered* with weird masses of metal, electromagnetic emissions, and heat sources. It's like we're trying to find a needle in a haystack made of metal hay."

"We still haven't established that the ship is even on this world," Ree added. "There are four other planets in the system, plus who knows how many asteroids and moons."

"Which is why we're looking here first," said Jacob patiently. "It's the most likely place, and we simply don't have funds to search the whole system. Now, Arkad: your presence here is a bit suggestive, to put it mildly. Do *you* know anything about the *Rosetta*?"

He started to answer, then stopped himself. This was it, the big moment. His whole future depended on how he handled this.

How would Zvev do it? She would be able to get what she wanted from them.

He cleared his throat, took a deep breath, and said, "Yes, but it will cost you."

Jacob raised an eyebrow at that. Ree was looking back and forth between Arkad and Jacob. Baichi was immobile.

"Well?" asked Jacob. "What's your price?"

"I want to leave Syavusa," he said.

Jacob visibly relaxed. He looked inquiringly at Ree. "Can we afford an extra ticket home?"

She tapped at her wrist computer, and Arkad could see flickers of green light from her eyes as it projected text onto her retinas. "I think so," she said. "Knowing where the *Rosetta* is should cut a lot of time off this expedition." She looked up at Arkad and gave him a friendly smile. "Don't worry, Arkad. I'll get you off this planet somehow."

"Will you take me to Earth?"

"No. Not to Earth," said Jacob. "Not yet, anyway. Maybe someday. But you can come back to Hinan with us; that's a space habitat in Machine Civilization space. It's where Baichi and I come from. Or you could go to Invictus, where Ree lives. That's where the government-in-exile is based."

"Are there other humans there?"

"About ten thousand, and there's always room for more."

"When can we go?"

Jacob smiled. "Well, that's up to you now. Take us to the *Rosetta* and we'll be on our way. The quicker we get going, the quicker we can get you civilized—if you can stand it."

There was a moment when nobody said anything, and then Ree asked him, "Where is it? The *Rosetta*."

"I can take you to it," said Arkad.

"Why can't you just tell us?"

Because I don't really know was not the answer Arkad wanted to give, so instead he replied, "I don't want you to leave me here. I want to go with you."

"Don't quite trust us yet?" asked Jacob. "I guess that makes sense. We could be anybody. Of course, that works both ways. You could be lying, too." His gaze was steady, and Arkad realized that here were some beings who could read *his* expressions and body language as well as he could read theirs.

"No, I promise I know where it is. I swear by the River Styx," he said, remembering the most binding oath in any of the stories he had read.

That made Jacob smile. "A hero of the old school, I see. Very well, Arkad Polytropos, I'll take your word for it. Lead us to the *Rosetta* and you can leave the planet with us. Deal?" He extended his hand again.

"Deal," said Arkad, and now he realized what the hand was for. He took it in both of his and shook it.

"I'd suggest a drink but you look a little young."

"Do you need a place for the night, Arkad?" Ree gestured at the foam pads on the floor. "You're welcome to stay."

"No, I—thank you, but there's some stuff I need to do. Before we leave." Arkad stood up.

Jacob got to his feet along with Arkad and offered him his hand once again. "Well, Arkad, it has been a pleasure meeting you. Please come back soon. Is there a way we can get in touch with you?"

His mind was whirling, but Arkad tried to concentrate. "On the other side of the rail terminus there's a big slab of red stone, part of an old wall. Write on that in English. I don't think anyone else on the planet can read it."

"No phone, no comm implant demanding your attention thirty times a day? You don't know how lucky you are. All right, we'll write on the wall. And we'll check it for messages from you. But feel free to stop in whenever you like." They shook hands yet again.

Arkad turned to go, making himself walk to the door before he said something he shouldn't. He looked carefully up and down the corridor to make sure nobody was watching, then slipped out. To see if they were following him, he got on the first elevator going up, and he rode all the way to the top of Aviiva's tower, glad of the chance to think.

The humans wanted to find the *Rosetta*. The humans could take Arkad with them, to a habitat where more humans lived—thousands of them!

The tiny flaw in that arrangement was that Arkad didn't actually know where the *Rosetta* was. He remembered his mother talking about it, and he had vague memories of traveling, but the details were lost in the fog of early childhood. Syavusa was a big place, even with half the planet perpetually covered by darkness and ice.

There was a game the Vziim played, which they called Zom-Zviivazi. Each player had an army, moving on a board of squares, and the goal was to get control of the enemy's fortress. But before starting, each player could put colored dots under some of the other player's men, and reveal those traitorous units at a key moment during the game. When you played, you always had to make sure that your pieces couldn't turn against you.

Arkad felt as though he was playing a game of Zom-Zviivazi, or maybe two games at once, with everything he owned and his life as the bet on the outcome. He had to pick his moves very carefully right now. It was kind of exciting.

By the time the elevator car reached the top of the tower and then began descending, Arkad had worked out a plan. It involved some risks, but after all, what didn't?

CHAPTER 3

H E GOT OFF THE ELEVATOR A FEW FLOORS ABOVE THE GROUND, went out a window into an Itooti house literally glued to the skin of the building, and from there climbed up a rope to a power cable extending across the street. Arkad walked on the power cable, avoiding places where the insulation had peeled away, and hopped down onto the roof where it ended. From there it was a straightforward journey back to the South Shaft where he usually slept.

The South Shaft was a perfectly hexagonal pit about a hundred meters across. Nobody knew how deep it was because the air coming out was hot enough to scald unprotected skin. Supposedly there was something far down that glowed purple-white, but you needed a mirror to see it because you'd go blind if you looked directly at it. Small objects tossed into the shaft were lifted high over the city by the rising air; heavier things caught fire as they fell.

Pfifu had built heat exchangers all around the edge, and suspended turbines in the air flow, so that the neighborhood was full of workshops and the sound of power tools. All the surfaces near the shaft were covered with a thick spongy white growth which left powdery spores on Arkad's hand when he touched it.

The area around the shaft was too busy to be safe for a lone sleeper, but there was a narrow dead-end alley leading off to the seaward side where the inhabitants didn't usually mind Arkad as long as he stayed out of the way. He found a dry spot in front of the kite makers' place, wrapped himself in his blanket, and tried to sleep.

But even though he was very full and very tired, Arkad was too excited to fall asleep. Finally, to calm himself, he pulled his book out of the blanket. The book was called WOL, and it was a plump, bright blue disk ten centimeters across covered with soft cuddly plush designed to be indestructible by any human infant. Two eyes and a stylized mouth made a simple face on one side. It could beam text and images directly into his eyes, or play audio.

WOL had taught Arkad languages, mathematics, science, and history, and it stored hundreds of text works, videos, music, and interactives. But WOL was dying, its memory slowly corrupting from physical abuse, ambient magnetic fields, and sheer age. Every time Arkad turned it on, the list of works available was shorter. He had started rationing it out to himself, going for two or three sleep cycles between taking it out again.

"WOL, tell me a story," he told it.

"What story would you like to hear?" The book's voice was soothing, androgynous.

"I don't know, pick one."

WOL's voice changed to that of a long-dead professor. *"In a hole in the ground there lived a hobbit..."* it began. Arkad listened to the very familiar words and felt himself starting to doze off. The story continued but WOL's voice grew softer and softer until Arkad's pulse and breathing told the little machine he was asleep. Arkad dreamed, as he often did, of his mother. In his dreams, he could never see her face.

He woke up a long time later with a stiff back and a full bladder. After stretching one and emptying the other, he considered the problem at hand. He needed to find the *Rosetta*, but all he really knew was that it was somewhere on Syavusa, and the more he thought about it, the bigger the planet seemed.

Arkad knew more about the city of Ayaviz than nine out of ten others—gossip, secrets, people and places. But he realized he had little understanding of how it really worked. He knew that cargo came down from space to the spaceport, and entered the city via the rail line, and eventually made its way out across the world by ship or road train. In the other direction, bioproducts, refined resources, and craftworks flowed through the city on their way up to ships in orbit. Somehow that all paid for Vziim to build towers and Pfifu to repair machines and Itooti to run grooming parlors and all the other myriad things people did in Ayaviz. The deals of Vziim and Itooti merchants had something to do with it, but beyond that he knew nothing.

Ayaviz had been his home for longer than he could remember, but now he found himself looking at it like a stranger. Suddenly it seemed very *odd* to build a city in and around ancient machines of unknown purpose, and odder still that four major species plus individuals or families from a dozen more could live and work there peacefully. Mostly peacefully, anyway.

When the sense of how big everything was became almost overwhelming, he climbed up to an elevated walkway that wound between towers. On a footbridge spanning the street where mechanics repaired broken vehicles, he stopped at a Pfifu vendor's cart. The cart was a sphere on wheels, painted in a detailed globe of the planet. The bottom half was all black, except for the burner controls, but the top was a patchwork of bright blue ocean and continents in shades of brown and red, all lightly streaked with white clouds. Where the hemispheres met was a white fringe of ice cap, edged with lakes where it didn't touch the sea.

Arkad spent some time peeling fruit for the vendor in exchange for a roasted sea crawler still in its shell, stuffed with fruit paste and ground seeds. The seeds made his mouth itch but he didn't mind. While he ate, he looked at the globe cart.

Ayaviz was there, right at the easternmost boundary between light and dark hemispheres, the spot worn down to bare metal by too many pointing claws and tentacles. Northward, the coast stretched a thousand kilometers, following the boundary between light and dark, cut by wide estuaries. The land was boggy and the sunlight weak, but some determined Pfifu farmers struggled to raise slow-growing plants that concentrated sea salt for harvesting, and there were a couple of Itooti fishing colonies by the rivers.

To the south, the land passed between forest and sea, then curved westward into the sunlit side, becoming a mountainous peninsula dotted with mines and more fishing villages. The peninsula ended at a wide strait, and beyond that was the main continent which sprawled across most of the dayside of Syavusa.

The dayside land had three lobes surrounding a central larger land mass. Two lobes on the eastern side were separated by a long curving rift, and the third, far to the northwest, was almost

separated from the main mass by a pair of shallow gulfs. Beyond
the largest ocean, over on the southwestern side of the world, a
smaller continent was half covered by ice.

Somewhere in that huge hemisphere was the *Rosetta*. If the
city made Arkad feel small, the thought of the whole planet made
him feel nonexistent.

He placed his hand on the warm metal hemisphere, covering half a continent with his fingers, and wondered what those
places were like. There were other worlds, other painted carts in
the heavens. If he wanted to see them, he couldn't hide himself
away here in Ayaviz.

He needed to talk to someone who had traveled a lot. He
didn't know any sailors—and lately some Pfifu toughs had been
making it clear that they regarded the docks as their private
preserve. That left tractor drivers; some of them roamed pretty
far across the surface of Syavusa, and they traded stories with
others. One of them might know something.

Arkad licked the inside of the shell clean and handed it back
to the vendor, then let himself down from the walkway onto the
roof of a repair shop and headed away from the sunlight.

The road trains usually assembled in the open plaza right
in front of the rail terminus. It was not far from Aviiva's tower.
Arkad didn't want the other humans to spot him, so he avoided
the plaza and headed for one of the bathing-houses nearby.

Inside the bathing-house, the air was chokingly thick with
steam and the eye-watering reek of cheap imitation plant essences.
The interior of the house was a single large pool, with a walkway
and lockers around the outer edge and a stage lit by reflected
sunlight in the center. At the moment a nearly life-size puppet of
a Vziim swayed and danced as it issued dire threats to a much
smaller Pfifu puppet. The movements of the puppets made a set
of complicated puns in Pfifu gesture language.

The audience were all submerged in the pool, with only
their tentacles above the surface, watching the performance and
sometimes making gestures that played off the dialog on stage.
Occasionally one of them would wave to the snack vendor on the
outer walkway, and she would drag her cart over and sell dried
fruit or cured fish. She simply tossed the requested snacks into
the water near the customer; there was a momentary maelstrom
of tentacles, and the food was gone.

Arkad made his way around the walkway to the vendor. "You tell me where Hupepuh is."

She pointed at one tentacle sticking out of the water, about a third of the way around the edge of the pool and close to the stage. Arkad couldn't reach far enough to poke it, and he didn't want to pay to enter the water, so he simply sat on the walkway with his back against a locker and waited.

He had come in about halfway through the puppet show, so the plot was a little hard to follow. A male Pfifu puppet formed a partnership with a female who apparently worked for the menacing Vziim. The partners opposed a lone female who seemed to be the heroine of the story, trying to turn others against her and making insulting remarks about her designs for advanced submarines.

But a wealthy partnership of older Pfifu eventually learned that the heroine had created the fastest and most efficient submarines, and hired her to construct one for them. She became their friend, though they also had dealings with her enemies, and seemed unaware of the feud.

The Vziim returned and flattered the older Pfifu by dances (which included a visual subtext which had the audience churning the water with their own gestures of amusement). The old Pfifu partners hired the Vziim's allies to create a new submarine for them, and the Vziim in turn bullied the poor Pfifu heroine into helping them in secret.

The puppeteer could not show the actual submarine, of course, but instead showed the various characters reacting to the design. From their poses Arkad gathered that it was supposed to be both beautiful and technically sweet. However, the heroine's enemies changed the design for egotistical reasons, and the heroine, in an elaborate tragic ending, blew up the batteries and destroyed both the sub and herself rather than allow it to be completed. The show ended with the older Pfifu partners taking on a new designer and telling him to create a submarine unlike any other.

Only when all the puppets had been brought out for a final display and the audience had waved vigorous approval did the show end and the bathers begin to emerge from the water. Hupepuh was one of the last, lingering to the end of the time he had paid for.

Arkad waylaid him as he opened his locker. As Hupepuh

pulled on his shoes, his transparent tentacle protectors, and a warm wrap for his body, Arkad made his pitch. "You tell me if you want to gain some wealth."

"No," said Hupepuh, and with two tentacles, the old Pfifu gestured, *"I am certain your promises are as insubstantial as wind-blown foam."*

"Some folk like me have come here, and they will pay a lot for a ride. If you tell me what I need to know, I will make sure they hire you."

Hupepuh aimed three tentacle tips at Arkad, studying him from multiple angles. *"Do not seek to cheat me, or I will thrash you like great waves breaking a rocky cliff,"* he gestured with his free tentacle. "You tell me where they wish to go."

Arkad spoke casually, not trying to seem secretive. Just business as usual. "They can tell you that. I need to know if you have heard of a space ship which came down on this world, some four eights and six more years past."

"I saw a ship crash once, out on the ice near the port," said Hupepuh, and gestured, *"It dove, rose on a wake of fire, then tumbled and fell. The fire slashed the ice like a blade, and then the ship exploded like sunrise in the perpetual night."*

"You tell me how long past that was," asked Arkad, feeling a little queasy. If the *Rosetta* had blown up, there was nothing to offer Jacob and Ree.

"It was when I still had a job at the gas mine. Eight and six more years in the past." He accompanied this with a sad gesture. *"I was strong and brave then, and my partners were quick and clever. We had plans as grand as the galaxy."*

Fourteen years was too recent. "You tell me if you know of more that were more in the past than that."

"I did not fill my brain with such things," the Pfifu driver said, and gestured, *"I should have gained an anchor of knowledge, but instead I let myself drift with the currents of idle pleasure until my partners were lost to me."*

The conversation was turning a bit too maudlin for Arkad. "You tell me who might know that thing."

"The AaaAa know all," said Hupepuh, and gestured, *"Their brains are as vast and rich as oceans."*

"You tell me if you drive a train south soon. I can get you good pay to let me and three of my folk ride."

"I wait for a load to come by rail. It should come in two or three eights of hours. Then I head out," Hupepuh said. *"I swim endlessly against the current of toil just to stay off the deadly reef."*

"Four like me will pay to ride with you."

"Tell me how much you pay," he said, while gesturing, *"In the treacherous waters I see a rich bed of sea plants."*

Arkad held up his most valuable possession: a centimeter of thick silver wire. "Seven eights like this."

"More," Hupepuh said. *"If I am to brave strong currents I need a strong line; pay me eight eights and two more eights of that."*

"Eight eights," said Arkad. There was a long silence and then he said, "Eight eights and four."

Hupepuh waited for a few seconds and then gestured, *"I must snatch up any swimming prey, even if it is not as fat as I would wish."*

"All of us must," Arkad agreed, then went out of the bathing theater. He decided to check for any messages from the visiting humans.

The red stone slab stood balanced on end in the middle of the street behind the terminal. It was a good five meters high and three meters wide, and more than a meter thick—which was why nobody had ever moved it out of the street. The slab looked as if it had once been part of some building, though nobody remembered what it had been or who had built it. The stone was from someplace far off to the west, and had been cut into an elongated hexagon shape and polished glassy smooth. Time had broken away the corners and covered the smooth surface with a patina of scratches, and on the bottom half, it was coated with layers upon layers of graffiti.

Arkad recognized the lines and crosshatches of Vziim ideo-grams, the swirls and curves of Pfifu script, and the colored dots of Itooti writing. Here and there he could see writing he didn't recognize. Some long-ago alien visitor had used a cutting device to inscribe a meter-long symbol with lots of branches, crossed by shorter lines of varying lengths; the lines were only a millimeter wide but at least ten centimeters deep. Another had marked the stone on the darker side with a glowing spiral of tiny polygons that somehow shone through all the layers of paint and charcoal on top of them.

But nowhere did he see any of the characters he had learned

from WOL. He felt both relief and disappointment. Had the other humans decided not to take him with them after all? Or had something happened to them? Maybe he should go check on them.

About fifty meters past the slab he saw movement out of the corner of his eye. A familiar-looking pale cloaked figure was keeping pace with him, staying at the edge of the street. He slowed, and turned into a side passage. He made a couple of turns and then stopped to wait. She appeared a moment later.

"Why are you following me?" he asked her.

She was silent for several seconds before replying, then said, "Jacob asked me to watch the stone and report if I saw you."

Arkad reached up and pushed back the hood of her cloak. She didn't blink, Arkad realized. Her all-black eyes remained open all the time. He wondered briefly if she closed them when she slept, and then he wondered if she just stayed awake all the time the way Pfifu did.

"I was just checking. Would you like me to show you around the city?" he asked on a sudden impulse.

"Yes," she said.

So he led her on a meandering path westward across town, generally heading for the harbor. Along the way he tried to think of things that an offworlder might find interesting. "That is the place where the Vziim burn their dead," he announced as they passed one of the few open plazas in the city. "They keep the bodies until they are dry and then make a big fire of corpses. It angers the Psthao-psthao because they cannot steal them. That tower over there is controlled by a syndicate of Pfifu; they took it from the Vziim who built it by force of arms and the others didn't intervene. Those cables overhead used to carry cargoes all over the city but gangs of Itooti began robbing the cable cars and so it was abandoned. That shaft leads to the deepest levels."

"Where do you live?" she asked him.

He shrugged. "Everywhere," he said. "I like to sleep by the South Shaft because it's warm. If it rains I have to go down to the lower levels but I don't like that. Sometimes I trade work for a place to sleep. When I can't do that, I stay with one of my friends."

He pointed across the street they were following. "That building shaped like a big sea creature over there is a school where Pfifu learn arts and tech. There's a rival school in Veva's tower, and sometimes they play elaborate pranks on each other. Last year a group secretly put power jacks under the building and raised it up ten meters."

"Who are your friends?" Baichi asked him.

"There's Zvev, she's a Vziim. She says her mother and aunts were once powerful matriarchs who had three towers, but some of her relatives murdered them and took over. She's working on a plan to reclaim her rightful property. Tiatatoo is an Itooti. I've known him since he was born. Fuee is a Pfifu; Zvev found him. He doesn't talk about his family."

"What do you remember about your family?"

"My mother died," he said. "Hey, come on up here. You'll like this." He climbed up a rope, entered a tower five levels up, and the two of them used the hand-cranked elevator to go up to the roof, ten floors higher. He emerged onto the open roof and looked up at the spire across the street, which loomed twice as tall. There was a crane on top of it, operated by a Pfifu in a transparent bubble.

Arkad used two fingers in his mouth to make a piercing whistle, then gestured with his arms. "Sometimes when he's not busy, old Pippeef will give people a ride."

They were in luck: the two-meter steel ring at the end of the quadruple cable swung down to the roof where they stood, and Arkad caught it. The massive ring dragged him halfway across the roof before he could halt it. "Come on!" He seated himself inside the ring and wrapped his arms and legs around it.

Baichi joined him, squeezing in beside him back to back and taking the ring in one hand.

"Hold on as tight as you can!" said Arkad. A moment later the hoist lifted them up and swung out over the city as Pippeef rotated the crane. The steel ring in which they sat flew out, pivoting from side to side; as it did so, they saw sky and then buildings below and then sky again.

Arkad loved the mix of feelings riding the ring gave him. There was fear, of course, but it was also exhilarating, as if he had wings like an Itooti and could fly over Ayaviz. Young Pfifu enjoyed riding the ring, too, but Vziim loathed it. He risked a glance over his shoulder at Baichi and saw that she was sitting still with her cloak flapping about her, perfectly composed as if she was in a chair on the ground.

But she was smiling. Arkad grinned at her and let out a whoop. She answered with a loud shriek of her own, and then the two of them screamed together as Pippeef brought the crane to a halt and then reversed it, so that for a moment the end of the hoist whipped out almost horizontally before beginning the big swing back. It snapped out again in the other direction when the crane stopped, and then the two of them hung on through a steadily diminishing series of swings until the ring was moving slowly enough that they could jump off and roll to a halt on the roof.

Arkad lay sprawled on the roof, laughing, then got up and had to rewrap his blanket around himself. After sitting on the cold ring and being swung through chilly air, he needed the warmth. Baichi watched him, showing no expression as usual.

"You are healthy," she said at last. "How do you get food?"

"I do jobs for people, I pick up scraps, I find stuff I can trade. Sometimes I catch animals."

"How do you know what is safe to eat?"

"I try new things and find out if they make me sick. Most foods are all right if you cook them enough. My book helps me remember what is safe."

"And there are no diseases you can catch here," she said.

"There are some. My mother and I both got sick with something, and she died. I don't know if it was a disease or something we ate. When the wind comes from the south, I get yellow circles on my skin. They itch like mad and then flake off. Pfifu get it, too, sometimes."

"I know a cure for that," she said. "Come back to the room."

He followed her back to Aviiva's tower, curious about how she would treat the yellow patches. He could dimly remember having a tube of ointment for cuts and scrapes during the year after his mother's death; he had used it up while learning how to get around the city on his own.

They used the upstairs cable to sneak into the tower, and she led him to the room the humans shared. Jacob and Ree were surprised to see him, but Baichi cut off their greetings by handing Arkad a brush and a cake of something white that smelled like plants. "Wash," she said.

Arkad did so, peeling off his blanket without a trace of self-consciousness. Baichi even heated some water for him, which was a wonderful sensation when he rinsed with it. Jacob watched the whole proceeding with amusement, but Ree seemed a little shocked for some reason.

She did pick up Arkad's blanket and gave it a sniff, then winced. "There's absolutely no point in getting him all cleaned up and then letting him put *this* on again. And those horrible layers of garbage he's been wrapping around his feet are even worse. We have to find some clothing for the boy."

"I can't give that up," said Arkad. "It has all my things in it."

"New clothes will have to wait," said Jacob. "We still don't know where we'll be going."

Ree wasn't willing to give up completely. "Well, even if he can't give up that nasty blanket, we've *got* to do something about that stuff on his feet!"

"Mmm. His feet are too big to use any of your shoes, and way too small for mine. I think I can put something together though." Jacob took a pair of very thick socks from his own bag and had Arkad put them on. Then he found a sheet of heavy smart foam, apparently part of a spare sleeping pad, and traced the outline of the boy's feet as he stood on it. He cut out the two soles and then glued them to the bottoms of the socks.

"There! That should hold. The glue and the cloth are both Machine Civ stuff, so we'll just have to replace the soles as they wear out. How do they feel?"

Arkad walked around, savoring the sensation of having feet which weren't numb from cold. The plastic foam felt absurdly soft. "They're wonderful!"

"Great. Maybe I can open up a cobbler's shop and settle down here, eh? Will you stay for lunch or dinner or whatever you want to call it?"

The offer of food was too much for Arkad to pass up. Jacob gave him some limp starchy disks with shredded meat inside them. The meat made his mouth burn, and for a second he was afraid he might be having an allergic reaction, but the hot sensation passed.

Jacob passed him a second disk wrapped around meat. "All right then. You won't tell us where the ship is. We still need to be able to make plans. Would you mind *suggesting* a direction we should go that might lead us generally toward it?"

"You will need a vehicle."

Ree looked unhappy at that, but Jacob only chuckled. "Unfortunately, I didn't bring along an ATV in my pocket. How do your more budget-conscious travelers get around on this planet?"

"I think we will need to buy space on a road train."

"What are those?" Ree asked.

"I don't know what else to call them. There's one or two big tractors, usually slaved together so they only need a single driver. They pull six or eight wagons. You can buy space inside, or just sit on top. They run up and down the coast road, and sometimes the whole train gets loaded on a ship to cross the ocean."

"How far are we going to be riding?" asked Ree.

He did some quick converting of Pfifu units to human ones. "About two hundred kilometers. Ten hours. It costs about five kilos of copper for one person. More if you have a lot of cargo."

"We can afford that," said Ree, after consulting her wrist computer.

"I'll find out when there's a train going in the right direction," he told them, even though he knew they would use Hupepuh's train. "Can you be ready to leave in a hurry?"

"Of course we can," said Jacob. He was still watching Arkad with narrowed eyes, but his mouth was half smiling.

"Then I will go right now to arrange things. Can I have some metal? A meter of silver wire would be enough, or maybe twenty-five kilos of copper."

There was a pause when nobody said anything, and then Jacob spoke. "Ree? If we're going to trust this young man there's no reason not to give him what he asks for."

Ree tapped a device on her left wrist, and for a moment her eyes unfocused and glinted green as it beamed images directly to her retinas. She made a few gestures with her free hand, then tapped the device again. "Here," she said, digging into one of the packs piled in the corner of the room and pulling out a roll of thick silver wire. She measured seventy-five centimeters of wire and snipped it off, then handed the length to Arkad. "I checked the exchange rates posted at the spaceport. This should be about right."

"I will come back soon," said Arkad. And then, feeling very awkward, he said, "Please don't follow me."

"I won't follow you," said Baichi before either of the adults could answer.

"Good luck, kid. Don't spend it all in one place," said Jacob as Arkad left the room.

Arkad had never before carried so much wealth at once. The silver wire wrapped around his upper arm felt heavy. He found a position atop a nearby building and watched the rail line, hoping to see the cargo Hupepuh was waiting for.

After fifteen minutes, Tiatatoo dove at him from behind, scoring an unblocked tail slap on the crown of Arkad's head. He banked around in a curve and perched neatly just out of reach on an antenna.

"Foppish Arkad looks grand in his new foot covers," he said. "With the help of skilled tailors and expensive materials, he may at some distant time be nearly as handsome as an ordinary Itooti male."

"Sadly, unfortunate Tiatatoo will never manage to be an ordinary Itooti male."

"Perceptive Arkad admits that glorious Tiatatoo is truly extraordinary!" gloated the Itooti. He glanced around suddenly, as if fearful. "Extraordinary Tiatatoo wishes to ask powerful Arkad's help."

"Busy Arkad wonders what vital task demanding Tiatatoo needs performed."

"Lovelorn Tiatatoo wants accurate Arkad to help eliminate two dangerous rivals. Persistent Tattat and vengeful Utto conspire to keep handsome Tiatatoo away from beloved Atett. Two or three well-aimed rocks may persuade cowardly Utto and fragile Tattat to seek female companionship elsewhere."

"Surely fearless Tiatatoo can defeat two inferior rivals without alien help."

"Cunning Tiatatoo does not want to risk the blissful love of fertile Atett on the random chance of close combat. Nor does fragile-boned Tiatatoo wish to suffer incapacitating injury which would interfere with prolonged and repeated copulation."

"Strong-armed Arkad will help talkative Tiatatoo. Can devious Tiatatoo tell resigned Arkad where his two hated rivals can be found?"

"Ingenious Tiatatoo has planned a clever ambush. Faithful Arkad and bold Tiatatoo will wait near the charming home of industrious Atett, and strike at the two blunt-tongued interlopers as they attempt offensive courtship."

"Dependable Arkad will meet ruthless Tiatatoo at the comfortable house," he agreed.

Tiatatoo jabbed Arkad's bare shoulder with his tongue, hard enough to draw blood. "Virile Tiatatoo will remember loyal Arkad forever for this vital aid." With that, he flipped backward off the antenna, extending his wings to convert his fall into a dive, then swooped away.

Arkad stretched himself, then climbed down to ground level. He wanted to have a full arsenal of things to throw, and the best place to find ammunition was by the pottery kilns, where Pfifu craftsmen discarded their failures. The kilns were over on the west side of town, so that the breeze would carry the smoke from the furnaces out to sea.

He had just reached the ground when he heard the squeal of brakes from the rail terminal as a train pulled in. Tiatatoo would have to wait, he decided. He hustled over to the stretch of road next to the tracks, where tractors were already pulling up. Arkad spotted Hupepuh's vehicle, several places back in line.

No time to lose! Arkad hurried over and swung himself up to the cab of the tractor. "I have wire," he said. "You tell me if you can give four like me a ride south."

"I will do it if you can get back here soon. When I have my freight I will leave, and I will not wait."

Arkad sprinted back across the plaza to Aviiva's tower. He rode the elevator up and knocked on the door of the room where the other humans were staying. Jacob answered this time.

"I was starting to wonder what happened to you," he said.

"I have got us transport," said Arkad. "A road train leaving town soon. We have to go now."

"And this is going to take us to the *Rosetta*?" Jacob asked.

Arkad hesitated, then decided to be truthful. "Not exactly. It will take us to someone who can tell me where it is."

Jacob raised an eyebrow. "I thought you knew."

"I will take you to it," Arkad answered. "I promise."

Jacob regarded him for a second, then smiled. "Okay then. I hope you're a man of your word. How soon does this train leave?"

"Right now, from the road by the rail terminal. It's not far."

"Any hoops we have to jump through before boarding, or do we just show up?"

"Just get on board. We don't have time to waste."

"Good. Ree? Baichi? Time to pack up."

They began stuffing clothing and gear into bags. Arkad was amazed at how many *things* the three of them had: each had a large backpack and at least one shoulder bag. Baichi, small and slender as she was, carried as big a load as Jacob. They had multiple sets of clothing, at least ten kilos of food each, bedrolls, a small stove, monofilament cable, power supplies, extra shoes, a water purifier, medical supplies, and tools.

One thing caught Arkad's attention in particular: his new companions had a lot more metal for trade than he had realized. Ree had several spools of silver wire, and both she and Jacob also carried heavy bundles of iridium strips, neatly scored to break easily into one-gram squares. They could practically *buy* a road train if they needed to. Yet they seemed to think they were poor.

When they were all packed, Baichi and Arkad led the way downstairs. Jacob sauntered along at the rear of the group with a faint half smile on his face.

Three road trains were making up in the plaza. Arkad saw Hupepuh standing atop his tractor, gesturing angrily at the crews using small tracked movers to push the wagons into position behind it and hitch them up. *"You move like a high cliff collapsing! Valuable freight will be smashed and lost, and you will labor until you are old to repay the owners."*

Arkad showed the three of them to a freight wagon. It was the typical mix of locally built and offworld tech: a simple steel frame with a bed of sheet steel and a canopy of waterproof cloth, but the suspension was made of whiskerlike struts of smart carbon fibers and the wheel bearings were diamond-surfaced. He helped lift the bags up to Baichi, who stacked them neatly next to a big tank of compressed helium. "I have to go pay the driver," he told Ree. "You might as well get comfortable because it's going to be a long ride."

"Don't worry about me," she told him. "I'm just glad to be on our way."

He swung down and helped secure the canopy, then walked over to Hupepuh's tractor and waved to get his attention. By now all four freight wagons were hitched and the old Pfifu had a couple of tentacles inside the engine compartment, inspecting it before starting.

"I have the wire," Arkad called up to him.

"You give it to me now," said Hupepuh, and with one free tentacle, added, *"Do not churn up more silt and make this water even murkier."*

Arkad climbed up, handed him sixty centimeters of wire, and stayed to watch.

First, Hupepuh fired up the butanol burners. Once the boiler had a chance to heat up, he opened a valve and let water flow through the pipes. He kept one tentacle tip close to the pressure valve, and when it reached the proper level, Hupepuh turned the valve to let the steam flow into the turbine driving the generator. As soon as the noise of the turbine rose to the right pitch, he fed power to the motors and the tractor began to lumber forward, the wagons rolling along behind. Hupepuh touched one tentacle tip to the telescope attached to the dashboard to make sure the way ahead was clear. Without visual aids, a Pfifu could barely see more than a few dozen meters.

Arkad dropped to the ground and let the road train go by until the freight wagon he had put the others into passed him. With easy skill born of many previous free rides, Arkad swung himself aboard.

The tractor and its four wagons rolled through the crowded streets south of the plaza. Hupepuh never let his machine stop completely, but it was maddeningly slow. As they approached the Ring, some merchants spotted the passengers and came over to offer fresh fruit and hot cooked meat.

But among the throng Arkad spotted a familiar four-eyed face. It was Zvev, and she gestured to him using a private sign.

"I need to talk to someone," Arkad told Jacob, and dropped down from the wagon to the street before he could answer. He pushed between a couple of vendors to Zvev.

As soon as he was within reach, she lunged at him; her powerful body hit him like a battering ram. He bounced off the side of the freight wagon and fell to the ground, and then Zvev was on top of him, her four thick arms pinning him down.

"Tiatatoo is hurt," she said. "He fought two and they beat him. You tell me why you did not help him."

"I could not wait. We leave town now."

She released him and reared up, but her claws were still ready and very sharp. "They broke his wing," she said.

The news made Arkad feel cold. No female Itooti would accept a male who could not fly. "You tell me how bad it is."

"It is bad. He will not fly for a long time, if at all."

"I did not know."

Zvev had recovered her composure a little; she folded back her arms so that her claws were no longer pointed at him, but the weight of her long body still rested on his legs. She bent down until her face was just above his, and her four little eyes spaced evenly around her mouth looked into his own.

"Your new friends are rich," she said. "They can do more for you than your old friends can. You are wise to go with them. I would do the same thing."

"You tell Tiatatoo I am sad to hear he is hurt. You tell him I wish I could have been there. You give him this." Arkad reached into his blanket and took out the fifteen centimeters of wire he had saved on the deal with Hupepuh. "You help him buy food and stay warm so his wing can heal."

She slithered off him and let him stand up. "You are not as wise as I thought. You should not waste your wealth on those you will see no more."

"You take care of him. And I wish you good luck," he told her.

"When I am old and rich, I will think of you once or twice," she said, and then slid away through the crowd.

Arkad watched her go, then looked after the road train, which had crossed the Ring and was picking up speed on the bridge out of town. He hesitated for just a second, then he turned and sprinted after the train.

CHAPTER 4

Beyond the hills south of Ayaviz, the forest began; a strange, two-dimensional forest. The trees ran in a line, just east of the road. They were a species found nowhere but on Syavusa: very tall, with straight trunks and branches sticking out in matched pairs at right angles, spaced closer as they went up the trunk. The leaves were long dark ribbons hanging from the branches.

Though tall, the forest was very shallow. Behind the first rank of trees was a second row of taller trees, and behind that was a scrubby growth of low ones, catching the scraps of light that passed between the trunks, waiting for a taller one to fall. Behind that last row the ground stretched back in permanent shadow, covered with years of accumulated snow which got thicker until it met the ice cap.

Arkad opened one corner of the freight wagon canopy and watched the landscape pass. Baichi did the same. Ree unrolled her sleeping bag and tried to rest, and Jacob produced a device like a tube with a right-angle bend in it, stuffed the large end of it with shredded plant matter, held the small end in his mouth, and set the shreds on fire.

The sight sent a thrill down Arkad's spine. It was a pipe! He had read about them in half a dozen stories but had never actually seen one. None of the species in Ayaviz ever inhaled smoke, although the Pfifu did enjoy absorbing aromatics and psychoactives through their skins. He wondered if Jacob would blow smoke rings, but he didn't.

Jacob sat and puffed the pipe until the stuff inside it stopped burning, then looked intently at Arkad. "All right, now I want some answers. Where are we going?"

"We are going about a hundred kilometers south," said Arkad. "There's a camp of AaaAa there, and they can help me figure out where the ship is."

"Ah-ahs?"

"AaaAa," said Baichi, making Arkad start in surprise. "An intelligent species originating in the Sagittarius Arm and widely distributed over all the portions of the galaxy we know about. They are nucleic acid-based life, oxygen-breathing, with an internal skeleton. AaaAa are known to settle in small enclaves on worlds inhabited by other species. Selected individuals travel between enclaves every few decades to maintain cultural and genetic continuity."

"They sound like interesting people," said Jacob. "But if they know where the *Rosetta* is, why do we need you?"

"The AaaAa don't know," said Arkad. "But I think they can help me figure it out."

"And you don't know? Arkad, I don't mean to sound suspicious, but I don't like being lied to. Do you know where the *Rosetta* is, yes or no?"

Arkad swallowed, and then said, "I don't know where it is. But I think I can figure it out! I have a book." He touched the pouch around his neck holding WOL and other treasures. "It has pictures of me and my mother from when I was little. Some of them are in different places, not around here. I think the AaaAa can tell me where the pictures were taken, and from that we can trace the route my mother and I took."

Jacob was silent for a moment. "That's . . . rather clever, actually. But why didn't you just tell us?"

"I don't know." The boy shrugged, not meeting anyone's eyes. "I just thought . . ."

Jacob didn't say anything, and the moment drew out agonizingly.

"I mean," Arkad began again, but still couldn't think of a way to end his sentence.

Jacob finally took pity on him. "Let's just keep it simple: *never lie to me again.* Understand?"

"I understand," said Arkad.

"Jacob, don't frighten the boy," said Ree. "He made a mistake, and now he's sorry."

"Mmm," said Jacob, and said nothing more.

Outside, the landscape moved past at a steady twenty kilometers per hour. As the road train traveled, the forest to the left gradually got younger. At first the trees were massive, full-grown specimens thirty or forty meters tall with trunks two meters across rising from thick undergrowth. A few kilometers down the road and the trees were only twenty meters high and a meter thick. Twelve kilometers from Ayaviz, they rode past spindly little saplings no taller than Arkad and no thicker than his wrist. Between the little trees were blackened pits where enormous tree stumps had been burned. And then, very abruptly, the new planting ended and they were passing old trees again.

"What do these AaaAa do, anyway?" Ree asked him. "How do they live out here?"

"They harvest the trees," said Arkad, pointing at the forest line. "And in the lands where the trees grow, there are plants, or things like plants. They grow underground and feed on things that rot. The AaaAa know where they grow, and tend them."

"You mean fungi?"

"I think so."

"How do you know about them?"

"They are valuable. The . . . *fungi* . . . are medicines for a couple of species offworld somewhere. When a ship comes in from those systems, traders come out to bargain with the AaaAa. As soon as they set a price, the AaaAa begin the harvest. They pull long strings out of the ground, with bunches of little round pods on them. They keep the strings to plant again, and trade the pods. They don't harvest until the pods are worth their weight in rhodium."

Once Zvev had managed to wangle a job for herself, Arkad, and a Pfifu named Fuee helping a young and hungry Vziim trader. They loaded and unloaded his trade goods, and filled sacks with the valuable fungus pods. The work had paid well—Arkad had earned enough to buy himself a new blanket—but Zvev had poisoned future relations with the trader by trying to pilfer some pods for herself. The trader had found out, confiscated the stolen fungi, and kicked the three of them out of his power-wagon twenty kilometers from the city.

Ree still looked puzzled. "How are a bunch of mushroom and timber growers going to help you find the *Rosetta*?"

"Oh, they do much more than that! The AaaAa preserve and share knowledge. They remember everything and keep no secrets. People come from all over Syavusa—and from other worlds, too!—to stay in their camps and learn from them. And the students teach each other, too. That was how I learned Itooti when I was little."

"So we're going to a school."

"Sort of like a school, only there's no buildings. Just the AaaAa camp, and those move along the forest line. The one we're going to is a couple of hundred kilometers from here."

The conversation kind of died down after that. Jacob got absorbed in a smart-paper map of Syavusa, Ree watched some entertainment beamed into her eyes from the device on her wrist, and Baichi wordlessly watched the forest roll past. Arkad thought of climbing along the top of the wagons to the tractor to spend some time watching Hupepuh drive the road train. But the maudlin old Pfifu was kind of boring.

He moved to the back end of the wagon and found a spot between the helium tanks and the canopy where he could have some privacy. Only then did he take WOL out of his pouch and turn it on. He called up his book's file of pictures, as he had done at least two thousand times before. Every time he did so, he held his breath, fearing that this time the little machine wouldn't be able to find them.

WOL jumped directly to the list of images Arkad looked at most often: a collection of pictures of the boy and his mother. A few were simple flat images taken by WOL itself. Most were more elaborate three-dimensional pictures, from some more sophisticated device.

Usually Arkad looked at the pictures just to remind himself of his mother, but now he paid more attention to the backgrounds, and to his own changing size and face. He was trying to work out where they were taken and in what order. The ones taken by WOL had dates, but the three-dimensional images only told when they had been transferred to WOL's memory, which had happened all at once, before the flat pictures were taken.

Arkad was smallest in three-dimensional images taken indoors, in some place with pale gray walls and tiny, cluttered rooms. He suspected that was the *Rosetta* itself, but wasn't sure. In those pictures he progressed from a tiny baby to a toddler walking on his own. Some of the images had other adults in them: his mother had identified the white-haired man as his grandfather Jules, and the big man who always seemed to be smiling was Yavuz. His father.

If he concentrated, he could remember a little about his grandfather: the scratchy feel of his beard, the sweaty smell of his clothing. But no matter how hard he tried, Arkad could remember nothing of his father. There were no pictures of the two of them together, either.

Nor could he remember what led his mother to leave the *Rosetta*, her little son on her back or trotting alongside. She had never spoken of it. If only she had told him more!

During the course of their journey, Arkad's image changed from that of a toddler to the small boy who had been awestruck by their arrival at Ayaviz. The trip had taken a very long time; his mother hadn't been traveling with any specific goal, just wandering across the planet in search of someplace the two of them could settle. Now Arkad had to put the images in reverse order. He worked silently as the wagon bumped along, and eventually created a sequence of five that showed useful background detail. In reverse order they were:

Arkad, skinny and suntanned, standing on a cliff, with sky behind him and a pair of Itooti whirling in the background.

Arkad, smaller and chubbier, in a stone-walled room, wrestling with a young Vziim.

Arkad, smaller still, and his mother standing in front of an immense ground vehicle, with tall mountains in the background.

Arkad, a naked toddler with dimpled knees, asleep in a small boat on a river, with tall rock walls on either side.

A very young Arkad standing on a vast flat plain of some dark substance.

He looked over the images a few times, trying to recall any fragments which might help. The cliff picture did bring up a definite memory: he could remember being unhappy that the wind didn't pick him up the way it lifted the Itooti. But he couldn't remember anything about playing with Vziim, or traveling in the mountains aboard a vehicle.

The river image brought back a smell: the stink of the water.

He knew it was somehow connected with the Psthao-psthao, which worried him.

He closed WOL and put the book away, then wedged himself against the helium tanks and let himself relax. The ride was smooth at the moment, and he dropped into a dream almost at once. In the dream he found an entire archive of pictures he'd never seen before, and he knew they would show him wonderful things. But he couldn't make WOL show them to him.

Eight hours later Arkad peeked around the canopy and called to the others. "There!"

To the left of the road was a line of recent stumps and crushed underbrush. Beyond the stumps a boggy meadow stretched nearly a kilometer, covered with fast-growing little trumpet-shaped plants taking advantage of the warmth and sunlight. At the south edge of the meadow, about half a kilometer ahead, Arkad could see a cluster of dark triangles and some large shapes moving around.

"What are those things? Draft animals?" asked Ree.

"Those are AaaAa. Haven't you seen one before?"

Jacob was silent, staring across the meadow at the beings they were going to visit. Finally he chuckled. "Cute little beggars, aren't they?"

Even from half a kilometer away, the AaaAa were impressive. A fully grown adult stood more than eight meters tall, on two legs so thick Arkad could not have put his arms around them. Their bodies were huge ovals covered in shaggy fur, with three manipulating trunks on the front which hung down to the ground. Each AaaAa had a single eye atop its body on a short stalk, which swiveled around constantly.

The camp of the AaaAa was centered on a single tall pole, a good thirty meters high, driven firmly into the boggy soil. Ropes stretched from the pole, each one supporting the triangular tent of an AaaAa. There were a dozen tents in all, radiating out from the pole in a semicircle facing the sun. South of the AaaAa camp was a scatter of other tents and even some temporary cottages where other beings stayed while they studied.

Hupepuh brought the train to a halt near the camp of visitors, but did nothing to help his passengers disembark. They had paid for a ride, not a stevedore. He walked around his train, tightening up some loose canopies and inspecting the wheels, then clambered down the rocky slope to the seashore so that he could splash some seawater over himself before starting up the turbine again and rumbling off down the road.

Jacob selected a dry(ish) spot at the southern edge of the AaaAa camp to pitch a single tent and set up the little stove. Arkad did his best to help, in part because he was fascinated by all the gear these humans had.

When there was a small fire of brush burning in the stove, Jacob asked, "Well, here we are. What now?"

Arkad looked over at the main camp. A dozen AaaAa stood in a group off to one side, evidently having some kind of meeting. It looked to Arkad like they were trading or negotiating—each AaaAa shifted between partners after exchanging just a few words. "Wait until they finish, I think," he told Jacob.

"How long will that take?" asked Ree.

Arkad just shrugged, which actually got a smile out of Jacob.

While they waited, Arkad took the opportunity to explore the camp. He stayed away from the AaaAa, as one of them could crush him with an inattentive step.

The belt of tents and shelters on the south side of the camp was the most interesting. Arkad saw Pfifu tents made in the shape of comical fish or giant fruit, topped with spinning wind turbines and streamers. In front of one made to resemble a heroic Pfifu in a spacesuit, a small knot of assorted beings watched an elderly Pfifu deliver a lecture on the conservation of energy.

Not far away a domed shelter made of carefully fitted stones betrayed its Vziim origin, and he could see some slapdash tents which had to be Itooti. But there were offworlders in the camp as well, and those drew Arkad's attention.

He saw a trio of Roon, tall and mournful-looking in their hooded robes, and a single massive Tkekta with elaborate gold and platinum decorations on its shell, being polished meticulously by a squad of small servitor beings Arkad didn't recognize. A pair of Ka sat by a campfire taking turns doing problems on a computer, and whichever one wasn't using the device retracted all its limbs to become a featureless sphere.

From a burrow under a boulder came the carrion scent of Psthao-psthao, which made Arkad hurry past, trying not to run.

Between two tents Arkad glimpsed a flash of paper-white skin and a neutral gray cloak. It was Baichi. Where was she going?

He decided to find out. She was moving quickly, with evident purpose, so he kept to the concealment of the tents, staying hidden as much as he could.

At the end of a row of Vziim-built shelters of timber and stone, there was a clear space, where a single black sphere a meter across stood on three legs no thicker than Arkad's little finger. The equator of the black sphere was a line of grainy laser light.

A Machine! He felt a twinge of alarm. The folk tales and legends of Ayaviz were full of accounts of dealings with the Machines that went catastrophically wrong for the hapless organic protagonists. A careless wish, a misinterpreted prediction, a poorly phrased question—all could bring disaster. Why was Baichi deliberately courting danger?

He watched as Baichi approached it. She stood for a moment about a meter away from the sphere, neither of them speaking. Then she raised one hand, palm facing the Machine. A sharp black spine emerged from the surface of the sphere and extended until its needle tip touched Baichi's palm and punched right through. The tip emerged from the back of her hand a centimeter, but she didn't flinch. A single drop of red blood formed on the tip of the spine and hung there. The girl and the Machine remained motionless for about half a minute, then the spine retracted and she lowered her hand.

And then, without any words or gestures of farewell, she simply turned and walked away from it, back toward Jacob's campsite.

Arkad watched her go, then ducked back around behind some tents to stay out of the Machine's sight before crossing into the main AaaAa camp. The big beings were still involved in their discussion, so Arkad found a spot safely far away from them and watched for a time. When that got boring, he followed Baichi's path back to their tent. Jacob was dozing on a blanket with his hat pulled down over his face. He pushed up the brim and looked at the boy. "Well?"

"They're still talking."

"Wake me when it's over."

It took about an hour. With no warning or ceremony, the AaaAa simply ended their discussion and drifted apart. Some of them headed out to the forest shadow to gather snow, others withdrew to the tents. One of them came toward the four of them and stopped, its eye fixed on Arkad.

"I will ask it if we can stay," said Arkad. He switched to the speech of the AaaAa. "AaaAAA-AAAaa-AaaaaA-AaAaaA..." he began. The speech of the AaaAa relied on changes in volume and duration, and speaking it for any length of time was very hard on a human larynx.

It looked at them for a moment, its limbs still. Finally it spoke, making a simple tone by blowing through its middle trunk and varying the volume. "One AaaAa. One human. One memory. Two humans. Adulthood. Infancy. One AaaAa. One welcome. Four humans."

"It welcomes us," said Arkad to Jacob before turning back to the AaaAa. "I'm going to tell it we're here to learn."

"Not technically a lie," said Jacob.

Their conversation went on until Arkad was hoarse, partly because his command of the language wasn't nearly as good as he had boasted. Arkad and his mother had stayed with the AaaAa for an extended visit—he couldn't remember how long exactly, but it must have been at least a quarter of a year—but even a five-year-old's sponge of a brain couldn't learn a language that quickly. As a result, more than half of the conversation consisted of halting attempts by Arkad to explain what he meant, interspersed with patient guesses and brief vocabulary lessons from the AaaAa.

After about half an hour, he managed to establish that this AaaAa remembered Arkad from the time he and his mother had lived among the huge beings.

He gulped some water. "Its name is AaAaAA."

"I hope to God it didn't take you thirty-five minutes to find that out. I'll be dead of old age if you have to ask it anything complicated. Did you ask it about your pictures?"

"It's busy for the next twenty hours. It has to work for a while and then teach, but it promises to help me when all that is done."

"Great. Looks like we're going to be here for a while."

"We ought to eat and rest," said Ree. "I'll warm up some food packs, and Arkad can share the tent with me."

"Told you we should have brought a spare," said Jacob.

"I can sleep out here," said Arkad quickly.

"No, you can't," said Ree. "How long has it been since you've slept indoors? You deserve it."

"Never mind. I've slept in worse places than this"—Jacob

waved his pipe around at the field—"and Baichi doesn't sleep at all, so there's plenty of room for the two of you."

The food packs were filling but dull, and when Arkad finished eating, he went behind a boulder to empty his bowels. When he returned, Jacob handed him a packet of damp flimsy sheets with a sharp smell. "Know what these are for?"

It took Arkad a moment to figure it out. The sheets were considerably more comfortable than scraping himself with leaves or pieces of stone.

"Don't forget to clean your hands, too."

It seemed a monumental extravagance to waste one cleaning his hands, but Arkad was happy to do so. The grime embedded around his nails and the lines of his palm was impossible to get out, but for once his hands could be called clean. He waved a little awkwardly to both Jacob and Baichi, then crawled into the tent.

Ree was already inside, wrapped in a shiny sleeping bag. Arkad watched her for a moment. He could vaguely remember watching his mother sleep. He remembered cuddling up next to her and feeling warm and safe. It had been a very long time since he had felt that way.

Would Ree mind if Arkad slept next to her? Arkad didn't know what was proper. In his stories there wasn't much about how people slept. In the end Arkad wrapped his blanket around himself and took a place on the ground just next to Ree. If they happened to bunch up together, well, he was just trying to share some heat.

Her shiny bag didn't let much warmth escape, but a little bit was better than none at all, and Arkad dropped off quickly.

For the next twenty hours, Arkad was able to indulge in something very rare in his life: leisure time. He didn't have to hustle for food, or guard a sleeping place, or avoid potential threats. His next meal was waiting in one of the backpacks, he could crawl into the tent and sleep whenever he chose, and if anything tried to give him trouble, Jacob had a device he called a "dangerous laser tool."

Ree spent her time playing an elaborate game with her own computer. Baichi sat for long periods on a huge granite boulder at the ocean's edge. Jacob was restless and took long walks around the camp. He spent a couple of hours chatting with the Tkekta, doing a fair imitation of its chittering speech.

"Fascinating fellow," he told Arkad afterward. "He's a political philosopher, studying different forms of social organization. I think he's trying to come up with a set of universal principles for optimizing all forms of government, no matter what species."

"What kind of government does your home world have?" asked Arkad.

"My home *planet* was invaded by aliens and is ruled by conquerors and quislings. The *habitat* where I live is supposedly a direct democracy but in practice it's an *ad hoc* meritocratic oligarchy."

"Were you on Earth when the Elmisthorn took over?"

Jacob put his hands in his pockets and walked toward the road. "I was just a kid then, barely out of my teens. For some reason they shipped me out to join the multinational force based on Rhea. That's a moon in the outer Solar System. Our job was to protect the gas mining operations. Fat lot of good we did anyone: the Elmies bypassed us and went straight for Earth. Took them eighty-seven days to conquer the planet."

They crossed the road to the slope leading down the sea, and Jacob continued. "On Rhea, my unit spent six months rationing calories and arguing about when to surrender, and then a ship managed to sneak in past the blockade and take some of us out of the system. We got out just before the Elmisthorn hit the base on Rhea with relativistic projectiles. Made a big shiny new crater."

"My mother said the *Rosetta* was one of the last ships to escape Earth," said Arkad. "She said she didn't think they would make it past the Elmisthorn fleet."

Jacob looked puzzled. "That's what I don't understand. All that was fifty years ago. Unless you're a hell of a lot older than you look, there's about thirty-five years missing."

"I know I was born on this planet," said Arkad. "I remember my mother said so."

"But was *she* born here?"

"No," Arkad answered slowly. "No, she talked about when she was a girl on Earth."

"Hmm. Okay, assume she was a young adult fifty years ago when the *Rosetta* left Earth. The ship was on the run from the Elmisthorn, bouncing around this part of the galaxy, for about two years. Then nothing. Now without some serious medical help, your mother can't have had you in her late sixties or early seventies. Rejuvenation drugs can do a lot—Lord knows I wouldn't be running around an alien planet right now without them—but they can't extend women's fertility that long."

He sat down on a large rock about twenty meters above the surf. "So what was your mother doing for forty or fifty years? Were they in cold sleep for some reason?"

"I don't know."

Jacob eyed him for a moment. "Well, if you don't know, you don't know. When we find *Rosetta*, the ship's log will probably explain it all. Want something to eat?"

Arkad followed Jacob back to camp and ate another meal, and then when the twenty hours were done, all four humans walked over to AaAaAA's tent in the center of the encampment.

"Four humans, one shelter, one entry," said AaAaAA when they arrived. It opened the tent flap and let them in. Inside the air was almost as chilly as outside, but at least there was shelter from the wind and a layer of springy foam and waterproof cloth between them and the ground. The front part of the tent, where it was tall enough for a grown AaaAa to stand, was open space. Beyond was a kind of nest made of inflatable cushions, and in the narrow pointed end of the tent was a miscellaneous pile of food and goods. The sickly bitter-sweet scent of the AaaAa was strong inside the tent.

The fabric of the tent glowed on the inside, about as bright as the dim sunlight outside. A sheet of smart cloth was stuck to the tent fabric at eye level for an AaaAa. It currently displayed a series of lines crossed by strokes of varying lengths, which Arkad recognized as AaaAa script, but he didn't know how to read it.

Arkad and AaAaAA resumed their conversation from twenty hours earlier as if there had been no interruption. "It says it is willing to share wisdom," Arkad said to Jacob.

"It?"

"The AaaAa are each both male and female."

"Simplifies things, I bet. Okay, show it your pictures and let's see if we can find that ship."

Displaying pictures from WOL in a way that AaAaAA could see turned out to be difficult. Arkad's book couldn't talk to the smart-cloth displays stuck to the tent, so finally AaAaAA just reached down with one trunk and lifted the boy onto its shaggy domed back, so that he could hold the book close to its single eye.

They went through the pictures over and over. At first AaAaAA just looked, then it began to make brief comments, and finally it delivered its opinions about where they might have been taken. When it seemed satisfied, it lowered Arkad to the floor again.

"And?" said Jacob.

"I know where the *Rosetta* is. It's somewhere in the Black Land in the middle of the noon country."

"East of the Sun and west of the Moon. Only there's no moon here, is there? Are those actual places? Can you show me on the map?"

First Arkad had a long drink of water to soothe his chafed throat. Then the four of them sat down on the floor of the tent around Jacob's map and Arkad showed them the pictures from WOL while he traced the route that AaAaAA had described. "These cliffs are on the peninsula south of here. AaAaAA thinks it's one of the towns near the western end. My mother and I probably crossed over from the main continent there. The Vziim could be from one of their towns in the mountains, past these swamps and the forest. Probably near one of these passes. This land cruiser is the kind of vehicle they use on the plains beyond the mountains. There's a huge canyon with a river in it that cuts through part of the desert west of there, and AaAaAA is sure that's where the picture in the boat came from. And here, right in the center of the dayside of Syavusa, is the Black Land. That's the oldest picture, and that's probably where my mother and I started."

"What if you just passed through there on your way from someplace on the other side?" asked Ree.

"The Black Land is the hottest and driest place on the planet," said Arkad. "Nobody goes through it."

"Explain the name," said Jacob. "Are we talking about a land that's actually colored black, or is this some kind of metaphor?"

"No, it's really black. I can even remember it. The ground is covered with a kind of carpet as dark as soot. I think it's some kind of plant that grows there."

"That's good. I thought maybe it was where the Lord of Evil lived. That's kind of traditional when you're going on a quest."

"We are on a quest?" asked Arkad.

"Of course we are! We've got an unlikely crew of misfits, a treasure map, and a long way to go. What more do we need?"

Jacob laughed, then zoomed in on the map to show the location of the AaaAa camp. "Our first order of business is to figure out where to go next. This peninsula you visited—can we catch a boat there to get across the strait?"

"I think so," said Arkad. "I know the Itooti there have fishing boats."

"Never mind that," said Ree. "How are we going to get to that peninsula? It's at least five hundred kilometers from here. And it looks like that far again to the end."

"There's a fuel station on the road south of us," said Arkad, pointing at the map. "We can try to get a ride on another road train there."

Jacob touched the map at the site of the camp and the fuel station, then translated the measured distance from standard Machine Civilization units to kilometers. "Huh. About a hundred klicks."

"We're going to walk a hundred kilometers?" asked Ree.

"To begin with," said Jacob.

Arkad stood and turned back to AaAaAA. "Four humans. One AaAaAA. Assistance. Information. Twenty-seven thanks."

It didn't reply, and after a moment they left the tent and went back to their own campsite.

They ate a big dinner and slept a long time before setting out. When Arkad woke inside the tent, Ree was already sitting up, and had adjusted the fabric to let in enough light to see by.

"Sleep well?" she asked him, and then lowered her voice. "Before we start packing, there's something I have to tell you. A little friendly warning. About Baichi. You may have noticed she's a little . . . odd?"

Arkad shrugged. "I haven't seen that many humans."

"Well, she's not *entirely* human. The Machines made her. Some kind of experiment, I don't know the details. I think they were trying to make an improved version, but . . . the Machines don't think the way we do. Anyway, don't expect her to act like a normal girl. She's a very nice person, don't misunderstand me, but she's not quite . . . *real*. Remember that."

Ree unsealed the tent and went out. Arkad thought a while before following.

They packed up the gear, and this time Jacob distributed everything into four packs. He handed one to Arkad. "Time to take up the load, young man. We'll cover more ground if Ree and I aren't as heavily loaded."

Arkad hefted the pack. "I can carry more if you can't," he said.

Jacob laughed at that. "I'm not that infirm! Tell you what—if I get tired, you can just carry me and my pack. How about that?"

"I don't know," said Arkad seriously. "You look pretty fat."

He expected Jacob to laugh, but instead the man's expression turned serious.

"I didn't mean—" Arkad began, but then he realized Jacob was looking past him. He turned to see AaAaAA approaching. The huge being stopped and began speaking without preamble. Arkad realized it was telling a story, and he translated for the others.

The past. Many years. One mother. One youth. Size. Age. Departure. One mother. Advice. Work. Peace. Truth.

One youth. One desire. Cunning. Idleness. Fraud. Trickery.

One road. One meeting. One traveler. Size. Age. Equality. Friendship.

One journey. Fatigue. Hunger. One garden. One hundred sweet vines.

One vine-tender. One greeting. One offer. Exchange. Transport. Water. Two stomachs. Satiation.

One youth. Two buckets. Transport. Water.

One other traveler. One suggestion. Eating. Idleness. Two buckets. Two holes.

One vine-tender. Two buckets. Two leaks. Repairs.

One youth. One other traveler. Twenty sweet vines. Satiation.

One vine-tender. Two buckets. Two patches.

Two youths. One departure. Haste. Idleness. Congratulations. Cunning.

One day. One road. One trader. Two baskets. Abundance. Merchandise.

One other traveler. One suggestion. Numbers. Strength. Threat. Violence. Theft. Baskets. Merchandise.

One youth. One memory. One mother. Advice. Peace. Reluctance. Consent.

One youth. One other traveler. One trader. One threat.

One trader. Fear. Two baskets. The ground.

One youth. One other traveler. Two baskets. Merchandise. Congratulations. Strength. Cunning.

One day. One road. One other traveler. One suggestion. Mating. Children. Double-siblings. Friendship. Two lifetimes. Flattery. One youth. Desire. Mating.

One youth. One discovery. One other traveler. Pregnancy. Scent. Disguise. Children. Double-siblings. Impossibility.

One youth. One other traveler. Accusation. Dishonesty.

One other traveler. One statement. One vine-tender. Fraud. One trader. Robbery. One youth. Expectation. Honesty. Foolishness.

When the story was done, AaAaAA turned and lumbered away again without waiting for a response. Arkad borrowed Jacob's water bottle and took another long drink.

"Well, that didn't make any sense at all," said Ree. "What did it mean by that?"

"It's a fable—you know, like Aesop," said Arkad, handing the water bottle back to Jacob.

"Who?" asked Ree.

"A Greek guy," said Jacob. "Never mind. I'm not sure I got the point of that story."

"Don't you see?" Arkad was surprised. It was an old story; he'd seen Pfifu puppet-show adaptations and heard Itooti poems on the same theme. "The youth was willing to rob and cheat other people, but then got all unhappy when the other traveler tricked it. The other traveler was already pregnant so their children wouldn't be double-siblings after all."

The other three just looked at him blankly.

"It's a warning about choosing bad people as your friends," he said.

"Maybe your AaAaAA friend doesn't like our looks," said Jacob. Arkad wondered what he meant by that, but didn't say anything.

They drank water before refilling the filter bottles, adjusted their packs one final time, and then set out on the road to the south, with the sea on their right. They soon separated into two pairs: Baichi and Arkad moving ahead briskly, while Jacob and Ree kept a more easy pace and fell behind.

Arkad was determined not to let Baichi show him up. She might be quick and strong, but so was he, and he had lived for years by hard work and swiftness at running. He resolved that anything she could do, he could match. Despite the chilly breeze off the ice cap to the east, he was soon sweating. A couple of times he glanced over at her, to see if she was also breathing heavily, but her blank white skin showed no trace of flush or sheen of sweat.

Twice in the first couple of hours, road trains rumbled past them, but despite all of Arkad's waving and shouting, neither of them stopped.

"Going to be a fun walk," Jacob shouted after the second one passed.

"We'll have better luck at the fuel station," Arkad shouted back.

The four of them stopped to rest every two hours, and made camp when the map showed they were halfway to the fuel station. Ree made a soup by boiling some food bars in water from a nearby stream until they disintegrated. Arkad volunteered to show Baichi some edible plants that grew among the rocks by the ocean.

"See the brown fibers that cover the rocks on the sunlit side? That's the mother plant. They make round seeds about as big as the tip of your finger. They're hollow so they can float, and let the surf spread them around. Here, try one," he said, picking one out of a cluster on one rock.

She put the little ball in her mouth and bit, then smiled. "They pop!" she said.

"You can dry them out in the sun and they get all crunchy, too," he told her.

Watching her move around on the wet rocks with perfect balance, Arkad thought of what Ree had told him. *Was* Baichi really human? Being graceful didn't prove anything. He had seen Pfifu standing on metal pipes in heavy rain with equal ease. Nothing unreal about them.

The two youngsters used Baichi's cloak to carry a mound of the pop-seeds back to camp, where they shared them around. Ree tried a couple but was doubtful. Jacob found them enjoyable and added some to his soup.

When the meal was finished, Arkad found a place to sleep at the edge of the forest. He thought he should let Jacob have a turn in the tent—and he had a faint vague hope that maybe Baichi would sleep near him. Possibly even huddle together to keep warm. Just imagining the possibility was enough to give Arkad an erection, and he was glad nobody was nearby to notice. He had never worried about anyone noticing before; Itooti were always showing off when they were aroused and Pfifu didn't really have any visible signs. But now he felt as secretive about it as a Vziim.

He need not have worried. Even after walking fifty kilometers, Baichi didn't sleep at all. She sat again on the rocks by the sea, her face to the unmoving sun. Arkad wrapped himself in a borrowed blanket, covered his head against the wind, and slept alone.

CHAPTER 5

WHEN ARKAD WOKE THE WEATHER HAD TURNED NASTY, WITH shifting, gusty winds and a mix of rain and sleet from heavy clouds. Jacob looked at the slush accumulating on the ground and made a face. "How far is it to that fuel station?" he asked Arkad.

"Another fifty kilometers."

"Gah." He cast an eye at the sky. "Well, those clouds are moving pretty fast. Either it'll get better or it'll get worse. No sense in sitting here anyway." He passed Arkad a poncho and then set to work packing up the tent.

The road turned muddy and the wind always seemed to be blowing into Arkad's face. He was obscurely pleased to see Baichi struggling to keep her own cloak from billowing open. It was the first time he had ever seen her having difficulty with anything.

The sleet turned to light snow for an hour, then shifted back to rain and finally stopped as the wind died down. The sun peeked through the clouds and then shone steadily, lighting the undersides of the clouds overhead in shades of gold. Even with the break in the weather it took them nearly twelve hours to reach the fuel station.

During their third rest, while Baichi had wandered off on her own and Jacob was standing twenty or thirty meters downwind to smoke his pipe, Ree sat next to Arkad and bent close.

"Arkad, I want to make sure I understand where we're going." She tapped her wrist device and it projected an orbital map of Syavusa into Arkad's eyes. "We're here, right?" She zoomed in on a spot south of Ayaviz, where the coastline still ran generally north-south.

"That's right."

"And this is the route you think you and your mother followed?" She moved a blinking gold triangle along the road south, then westward along the peninsula, then across the strait to the main continent, and then overland to the dark splotch at the center of the day lands.

"Yes, I think so. I don't know exactly where we sailed from to cross the strait, and I don't know which pass we took through the mountains."

"But you're pretty sure about where you must have left the Black Land."

"Oh, yes. I remember a big canyon, and AaAaAA said it has to be this one here," he said, pointing to the air.

"Good. It's good to know where we're going," she said. "Well, I guess we'd better push on. Are you ready?"

He got to his feet and shouldered his pack again. The novelty of walking in shoes had worn off, and he was tired and stiff all over. But he didn't want to show how tired he was, so when they resumed walking, he made sure to stay ahead of Jacob and Ree.

Arkad was nearly exhausted when the fuel station finally came into sight ahead beyond a low hill. He called out to the two older members of the party to let them know, but was interrupted by a cry of pain.

Ree had fallen, and was nursing her left leg. "I put my foot down on a rock and it shifted and my foot bent sideways. I think it might be broken."

"A break seems unlikely," said Jacob, "but you could have a sprain. Can you walk at all?" He helped her up.

Each step she took made her cry out. "I'm so sorry," she said. "I feel so stupid."

"It's okay," Jacob told her. He took Ree's pack and had Arkad and Baichi support her on either side. The four of them moved along at a slow hobbling pace, and it took them half an hour to cover the last kilometer to the fuel station.

It looked like a fort, with massive concrete walls enclosing a space large enough for road trains to turn around in, and a single wide gate. Behind the walls Arkad could see a big wind turbine atop a low tower.

A couple of Pfifu came out of the station as the four humans approached. One hurried forward in the odd spinning gait Pfifu used when running: she whirled her body along with only one foot at a time on the ground and her tentacles spread wide for balance. The second one remained near the massive gate, holding a complicated-looking device of copper tubing and glass bulbs filled with liquid. Arkad recognized it as a poison sprayer, and had no wish to find out if the poison in it would affect humans.

"We need help here," Arkad called to them in pidgin. "One of us is hurt."

The whirling one stopped and waved her tentacles at the one with the poison sprayer. *"Put down the projector of painful death and go like windblown spray to fetch the powerful little tractor."*

The one back at the door hesitated, then went back inside. A moment later it emerged driving a small machine so odd-looking it had to be offworld tech: it appeared to be nothing but a pair of wide solid wheels in tandem, joined by a single flimsy strut connecting the wheel hubs. An obviously handmade seat was clamped to the strut on the right-hand side, and the Pfifu sat there, working a little control panel. With so much weight on one side, it looked as if it would topple over any moment, but even as it bumped across the unpaved road, the tractor remained absolutely vertical. Arkad noticed that the wheel treads even adapted to the surface of the road.

The Pfifu operator pulled up in front of the four of them and dropped down out of the seat. "Tell me which one is hurt," he said, adding with gestures, *"Is it four separate creatures, or one eight-legged monstrosity? And how can one tell if something so crippled-looking is actually hurt?"*

They got Ree into the tractor seat, and then the three humans and two Pfifu walked alongside as they went back to the station. The tractor operator detached the control panel and used it as a remote to drive with.

As they walked, Arkad made introductions in pidgin. "My name is Arkad. This is Jacob, this is Baichi, and this is Ree. We are *humans*."

"I am Puufi and this is Pfipafo," said the female Pfifu. To her partner she signed, *"A storm has brought strange flotsam to this shore."*

He answered the same way, *"Trash may bob around the ocean for years before the surf finally casts it up."*

They passed through the gate, and Arkad saw that there was no wall on the seaward side of the compound. Sheltered from the wind and open to the sun, the enclosure was a couple of degrees warmer than outside.

The main building was a squat tower, topped by the wind turbine. Tanks of butanol stood at one side of the enclosure, as far from the building as possible, shaded by a photoelectric panel.

Pfipafo stopped the little tractor at the door of the main building. It was typical fortresslike Vziim architecture: a cylinder built of slabs of synthetic stone with a deep cellar. But the Pfifu station operators, stuck between forest and sea with nothing to do for long periods, had encrusted the massive walls with a colorful fantasia sculpted from silicone sealant, gravel, and bits of trash.

On the sunlit side of the building, they had created a miniature forest with vines made of sealant and old hoses coiling up the walls, and brilliant flowers cut from scrap plastic. Among the blossoms, attractive miniature Pfifu cavorted, and their gestures were rude puns.

The shadow side boasted fantastic caverns and pits haunted by horrible monsters, all enveloped in carefully directed cascades of real ice formed by condensation from the heat exchanger on the roof. Tiny Vziim lurked in the caverns and peeped out from the ice. Arkad suspected there were tensions within the operation.

Arkad and Baichi helped Ree inside. The ground floor was a repair shop, where Puufi and Pfipafo were building what looked like a giant mechanical Itooti. Up a spiral ramp was a single common room for road train drivers and passengers, with windows looking to the east and translucent panels of stone on the west to let in light without glare. Arkad saw a ladder leading up and guessed that the top floor was for the two Pfifu.

Jacob spread out a sleeping bag for Ree by the radiator and then got her boots off as gently as he could. She whimpered as he took off the left one and then peeled off her sock.

"It's not turning purple, so I'm pretty sure you didn't break anything. It does look a little puffy though."

"Jacob," she said through clenched teeth, "it's going to be days before I can walk again. Weeks, maybe."

"Lucky we've got a place to stay."

"And it's going to be even longer before I can hike any long distances. You should leave me here."

"Here? You don't even speak the language."

"I can write in Roon symbols. There's bound to be someone who can read them."

"Are you sure about that? We're pretty far from the spaceport. Are a bunch of truckers and mechanics going to understand interstellar trade signs?"

"Even if they don't, I'm sure they can understand pointing and holding up metal. I can get back to the city and wait for you."

Arkad felt a rush of fear. "You can't stay here on your own if you're hurt," he said, louder than he intended to. Both adults looked at him curiously. "The Psthao-psthao will take you."

"Who?" asked Jacob.

Baichi's quiet, calm voice cut off Arkad before he could answer. "Psthao-psthao are a DNA-based, oxygen-breathing species with interstellar capability, home world unknown. At least twenty enclaves of Psthao-psthao are located on planets we have information about. They do not appear to build space habitats or bases on lifeless worlds, but settle on planets with compatible biospheres. Psthao-psthao have segmented bodies with multiple limb pairs and are capable of tool use. They are nocturnal and reclusive; little more is known about their biology or culture. They occasionally exchange rare bioproducts and organic chemicals for manufactured items."

Jacob made a shushing gesture at her. "Arkad, why do you think they'll take her?"

"It happened to my mother. She was sick and then she disappeared. They took her. I *heard* them."

"I'll be all right," said Ree. "They can't get out here."

"They have tunnels everywhere!" said Arkad, close to panic.

"Okay," said Jacob. "Calm down. Ree, I don't know what's going on with these critters, but Arkad sounds pretty scared of them and it's obvious we don't know as much about this world as we'd like. Better safe than sorry. We'll sleep, have some food, maybe put some ice on your foot if it swells up. All of us just walked a hundred kilometers; we can use a day or so of rest."

"Jacob, I can't walk on it. Some ice and a nap isn't going to help. You three go ahead. No creepy nocturnal things are going to get me. It doesn't get dark here, remember?"

"I will stay with you," said Arkad.

"Ree, I'm starting to wonder if your confidence comes from

too much pain medication. There's no way we can leave an injured person alone on a world where she can't even speak any of the languages. And if we leave Arkad with you, then there's no point in Baichi and me going ahead. If you really can't walk, then we'll all go back to the city and regroup."

Arkad didn't say anything. He couldn't go back to Ayaviz. Not after abandoning Tiatatoo.

Ree gave an irritated sigh. "All right, let's see what it's like in the morning—but if I can't walk, you three should go ahead without me."

Jacob helped make her comfortable, and made sure she ate a food bar and drank some tea. Then he went out for a smoke. Baichi vanished. Arkad decided to stay with Ree. He had managed to frighten himself so much that he half-expected a band of Psthao-psthao to come scuttling up the ramp and drag her away.

She lay with closed eyes for a while, but then opened them again and beckoned Arkad over. "I can't get to sleep just yet. Tell me what's ahead. What kind of places are we going to have to pass through to find the *Rosetta*?"

"I only remember a few things," he admitted.

"Was it a hard trip?"

"I think so. Once we got to Ayaviz I remember my mother said she never wanted to do that again."

"But the two of you made it, and you must have been just a baby," said Ree. "It can't be that dangerous."

"My mother did tell me she had to hide us from bandits a couple of times, and she was afraid of animals carrying me off when we were in the jungle."

Ree nodded, as much to herself as to Arkad. "I think I'm feeling sleepy now. Would you mind leaving me? It's hard to sleep with you fidgeting by me. You can stand guard downstairs if you want. Tell the others I want to be alone."

Reluctantly, Arkad went down the ramp to the workshop area. Puufi and Pfipafo were hard at work on their machine. He didn't interrupt them, though he did catch a friendly gesture from Puufi as he passed. *"Let your friend float in warm seas,"* she signed.

Baichi was nowhere to be seen, but Jacob sat outside with his back against a smooth sun-warmed patch of wall and his hat pulled down over his eyes, puffing his pipe. He looked up as Arkad approached.

"Is she asleep?"

"I think so. She asked me to go away."

"Maybe that's a good sign."

Arkad squatted next to Jacob and they sat for a while without saying anything. A trio of Pfifu driving a tractor with no wagons had come in from the south and were taking turns bathing in the surf while refilling their butanol tank. If they noticed the two humans, they gave no sign.

"Is she going to be all right?" Arkad asked.

"No way to tell. If we had a modern medical suite, there'd be no problem: shoot her ankle full of nanobots to scaffold the tissue while she heals, pain blockers, drugs to speed up regeneration and prevent scarring—even if she had a broken bone she'd be on her feet in a few days. Here, all we can do is wait."

"Pfifu medicines wouldn't help."

"Nope. Invertebrates aren't much good at fixing bones. But don't count Ree out. She's tougher than she looks."

"Do you think so?"

"Let me tell you about Ree. She was born on Earth, did you know that? One of the first generation born after the Elmisthorn took over. In fact, she's one of the 'New Humans' they created to replace us obsolete old homo saps."

Arkad risked a question. "Like Baichi?"

Jacob raised an eyebrow at him, but then nodded. "Sort of. The big difference is that the Machines created Baichi and her siblings in a... *well-intentioned* attempt to help us do a better job of fighting the Elmisthorn. Didn't work out, but never mind about that. The point is, they were trying to help. Ree—and an increasing proportion of children born on Earth every year—is designed to fit into the Elmisthorn empire."

"The Family of Species," said Arkad.

"They can call it Happy Funland if they want, but it's still an empire. All the species in their 'Family' are modified to make them better servants of the Elmisthorn. Now it's humanity's turn."

"How is Ree different from old humans?"

"Oh, let me see. She's got a better immune system than mine, her hand-eye coordination's fantastic, she doesn't need drugs to keep her bone density in space, and her arteries won't get clogged. There's probably some other stuff I'm forgetting."

"That doesn't sound bad," said Arkad.

"Well, it's not all good. The Elmos decided that human sex and reproduction are a problem. They don't want humans falling in love with each other or having kids without permission. Cuts down on loyalty to their glorious Family if you've got one of your own. So all the New Humans are neuter unless they get a big shot of hormones and other stuff. There's also some neurological tweaks: the New Humans are capable of intense focus on a task, and they're supposed to be instinctively obedient to Elmisthorn. I guess that didn't work out so well in Ree's case."

"Why do you say that?"

"Because when she was just a kid, she started sneaking out of the dormitory at night and made contact with a Resistance cell! This was in northern Australia, too—not a good place for a kid to be walking around at night. Anyway, Ree got in touch with the Resistance in Darwin, started feeding them some information about what the Elmos were doing at the research station in Shoal Bay. Most of it was pretty minor stuff, the kind of intel a kid your age could gather, and she was under close supervision a lot of the time. Still, her info did help the Resistance pull off a couple of robberies, steal some gear. They learned they could rely on her."

Arkad tried to imagine Ree as a girl his age, sneaking around helping the humans fight their alien rulers. "Did they win?"

Jacob sighed. "No. Maybe the Elmos got suspicious, or maybe the Resistance in Darwin got careless. Whatever the reason, the Elmisthorn and their human quislings came down hard on the Resistance there. Started rolling up the whole network. Ree knew she'd be killed, if only so the Elmo scientists could pick apart her brain and find out where they went wrong. The Resistance people got her across the Timor Sea, and then through the islands to the space elevator at Suliki, on Sumatra. Do these place names mean anything to you?"

"No, but they sound like music." He rolled the words around in his mind: Darwin, Suliki, Australia, Sumatra.

"Ah, well. They were able to get her up the elevator hidden in a cargo shipment. I think that route's been compromised since then, but Ree got out. At the orbital terminal, she managed to avoid the Family security services somehow, and got onto a Roon merchant ship. Not even the Elmisthorn would dare interfere with those guys. Six months later she reached the human colony on Invictus, near Roon space."

"Invictus is a planet?"

"Yeah. In a couple of centuries it may even be habitable. The Roon gave it to a bunch of human refugees on the condition that the humans do the work of terraforming it and give one continent to the Roon when the job's done. It's the biggest human community off Earth nowadays. The Combined Free Human Forces are based there. What's left of them, anyway. Mostly a bunch of self-appointed commanders.

"Ree settled there and worked with the intelligence division for a while, helping them build networks inside the Family of Species. She said she had to stop because it was just too damned heartbreaking. They'd send in agents, recruit people, and then have to watch as the Elmos found out and shut them down, again and again. After a while she couldn't handle the guilt."

"How did she wind up looking for the *Rosetta*?"

"Oh, that's all my fault," said Jacob, and chuckled. "I'm the one who's been trying to track it down for a couple of decades. Ree heard about me, somehow, and told me she could help pay for the expedition. I assume the money's really coming from her old bosses on Invictus, but she won't admit it."

The light dimmed as a squall out at sea covered the sun's disk. Without the warmth of the sunlight the air was chilly, so Jacob got to his feet and tapped his pipe against the wall to knock the ashes out. "We should all get some sleep," he said. "It's been a long day. So to speak," he added. "This planet messes me up; I'm constantly jet-lagged. My body's ready to collapse but my brain refuses to admit it's time to sleep."

"Where's Baichi?" asked Arkad.

Jacob shrugged. "She can take care of herself. I don't worry about her."

Arkad and Jacob went inside, but Jacob insisted on having a look at the flying machine their Pfifu hosts were building, and engaged Pfipafo in an enthusiastic but ultimately futile attempt at conversation. Arkad was too tired to act as interpreter, so he went on up the ramp to the guest quarters.

As he neared the top of the ramp, he heard someone speaking in a low voice. It sounded like Ree's voice, but she was using a language Arkad didn't recognize. A lifetime of habit kicked in and Arkad continued moving silently, keeping his head down until he was crouched just below the edge of the floor.

He couldn't tell what she was saying, but she sounded unhappy, and there were pauses, as if she was listening to replies that Arkad couldn't hear. Finally Ree ended the conversation and then said, "Fuckers!" in a loud whisper.

Arkad slipped down the ramp a few meters, then came walking up without trying to be quiet. Just as he reached the top he heard a faint thump, and when he looked over at Ree, she was lying still with her eyes closed. He unrolled the foam pad which had two foot-shaped holes cut in one corner, and curled up on it to sleep.

When Ree woke several hours later, her ankle was much improved. "You were right, Jacob," she said as he and Arkad brought her some tea. "I just twisted it. I think I can go on."

Jacob looked at her foot, gently flexing the ankle and feeling the tendons. "No swelling at all that I can see. Does it hurt?"

"It's a little bit tender, but not enough to keep me from walking," she said. "I'll wrap it in a bandage just to be on the safe side. When do you want to start?"

"Now you can't wait to get going! Relax, we can spend—well, we can't spend the night, but you know what I mean. Spend twenty hours or so."

Ree looked unhappy at that. "It's such a waste of time... and money, too. Every food bar we eat sitting here is one we may need later."

"You could try some of the local cuisine. It's cheap enough. Arkad seems to know what's safe to eat, and what's good."

She reluctantly agreed, so Arkad went down to the workshop to bargain with Puufi and Pfipafo for some of the bottom crawlers they harvested out at sea. He made a fire of scraps outside and used his skewer to cook four of them for breakfast, then presented them to Ree and Jacob.

"Kind of tough," said Ree after chewing the first one.

"They're better if you can steam them for a long time."

Jacob pulled his off the skewer, tried a bite, then rummaged in his bag for a small glass bottle of cloudy red liquid. "I made this myself; my version of Tabasco sauce. Not as good as the real thing, but we have to make do." He added some drops to his grilled bottom crawler and nodded in satisfaction. "A little lemon would be good, too, but I don't have any."

Arkad tried a drop of the red sauce and found it made his

mouth burn. It should have been unpleasant, but he discovered he liked it.

Jacob grinned at him. "When we get you to Hinan, you're going to love trying all the different foods there. Curry! Tortillas! Ice cream!"

"You're going to teach the boy all kinds of bad Old Human habits, Jacob," said Ree. "He'll start eating sugar and caffeine and alcohol."

Jacob grew solemn. "Now you're making me think of all the things I won't be able to offer him. Nobody got asparagus off Earth, or olives, or cinnamon. He'll never have tuna, or salmon, or wine from old vines. The only beef he'll ever taste will be vat-grown."

"I grew up on Earth and I never had beef, either," said Ree. "Cattle are wasteful."

"So what?" asked Jacob, suddenly angry. "Why does everything have to be *efficient*? What's the point of being *efficient* if you can't have things you like? The Elmisthorn have turned Earth into a giant forced labor camp, and the free human colonies are almost as bad. If you're not working yourself to death for the Family of Species, you're sacrificing everything for the fight against them. Do you know there was a time when humans actually decided for themselves what they wanted to do? What things they wanted to have? To eat and drink? To entertain themselves with? There were huge commercial organizations which catered to their whims. People used to complain about 'consumerism.' Well, we sure got rid of that. On Earth and in the refuges, you get what you're *allowed* to have and that's it. I can't say I think it's an improvement."

He got up and went noisily down the ramp.

Arkad took the last of the grilled bottom crawlers and went looking for Baichi. He couldn't find her on the seashore, or anywhere within the fuel station enclosure. Then he looked up.

She was sitting quite still at the base of the wind turbine on the roof. He wondered if she had been there since their arrival. What did she think about?

The elaborate decorations on the walls made it easy to climb up. The roof was surfaced with self-sealing plastic, and was gently rounded to shed rain and snow. The support pylon for the wind turbine was in the exact center, and the heat exchanger for the heating system was on the west side, coated with frost despite the bright sunlight.

Arkad stopped a meter from Baichi and held out the cooked crawler. "I brought you some breakfast," he said.

She didn't answer, and he felt a jab of irritation. Would it kill her to be polite? He tossed it to her, and her hand flashed up to catch it.

"Try it," he said.

She ate it in four bites.

He sat down next to her and tried to think of something to say, but then decided not to bother. If she wanted to just sit there in silence, so could he.

After about five minutes Baichi said, "Thank you for the seafood."

"You're welcome," said Arkad. "Why are you hiding out up here?"

"I prefer to be alone."

"Don't you get bored?"

"I can put my mind into a resting state," she said. "I do that often. Even while walking."

"How can you walk and sleep at the same time?"

"I am part Machine. Either Jacob or Ree has told you that by now."

"It was Ree."

"She is afraid of me."

"I'm not afraid of you," said Arkad. "I think you're nice."

She looked at him then, her face still expressionless and her eyes all black. "That is a mistake," she said. "I am not nice."

He wanted to reassure her, but he was still just irritated enough that instead he said, "Well, you're definitely rude. Also, you're grouchy and unfriendly all the time. So I guess you're right: you aren't very nice."

"I am not rude. I thanked you for the tough and burned-tasting ocean vermin you threw at me."

He grinned at her. "Now you're being even grouchier than usual."

"You don't—" she stopped in midsentence and her head snapped up and to the right. "What is that?" she pointed.

Arkad shaded his eyes from the sun and looked. A black ball about the size of his head was hovering a few meters away.

Wings on either side of the ball fluttered invisibly fast, making a faint buzz.

"I don't know," he said. "I've never seen anything like it before." He got to his feet and broke an icicle off of the heat exchanger, getting it ready to throw.

The black thing bobbed back and forth for a second, then moved closer. Arkad threw the icicle, using the same technique he had practiced endlessly for throwing bones or lengths of pipe, sending it tumbling end over end as it flew. It hit the hovering ball dead center and shattered.

His target hung there for another couple of seconds, as if to make it clear that the impact hadn't damaged it, and then the buzz of the fluttering wings rose in volume and pitch to an earsplitting howl; the ball changed shape to a streamlined arrowhead, and it shot away, heading inland.

Arkad looked at Baichi, who was still staring after the disappearing whatever-it-was. "Do you think your Machine friend sent that?"

"It is not my friend," she said. The slight hint of playfulness he thought he had heard before was utterly gone, and her voice was flat and dead-sounding. "I don't want to talk to you any more right now."

Then she turned and took a running jump off the edge of the roof. Arkad hurried to see if she was all right, but she was already halfway to the gate. She was gone before he could draw breath to call after her.

Jacob and Ree were both alarmed at the news.

"Could be Elmos," said Jacob.

"Or something else," Ree pointed out. "I think Arkad's right—it sounds like Machine tech."

"But there aren't any Machines here," said Jacob. "We're outside Machine space."

"There was one at the AaaAa camp," said Arkad. "I saw it." He decided not to mention that Baichi had been talking to it—or whatever it was they had been doing—not just yet.

"Still, that's a hundred kilometers away. Why would a Machine be snooping around here?"

"The most unusual thing at this fuel station is us," said Ree. "The only four humans on this planet."

Jacob suddenly laughed aloud. "Yep, and I even know why

they'd be interested. They probably think we're working for the Elmisthorn ourselves! Humans being part of the big abusive Family of Species, after all." He thought for a moment and then nodded to himself. "All right, then: we've got to get out of here, the sooner the better. We're getting on the next vehicle going south, no matter how much it costs."

The next vehicle turned up about five hours later—a beat-up old freight wagon powered by a steam turbine, with a very smoky fire of wood and trash burning in the boiler. It was driven by a mob of a couple of dozen Itooti, who had loaded the cargo bed with composite boat hulls and rolls of myoplastic cable from off-world. The control cab had been rebuilt as a sort of deckhouse, with three or four females down in the former Pfifu operator's seat working the throttle and brakes, and a splendidly striped male standing on the roof steering with a big tiller to give him mechanical advantage.

It lumbered through the gate and the female engineer flapped over to the entrance to the repair shop. It didn't take a mechanical genius to see what the problem was: the pipe from the boiler to the turbine was shooting out jets of steam in three or four places.

Arkad took the opportunity to climb up to the top of the control cab to speak with the gorgeous pilot. In his experience, male Itooti were more prone to spontaneous gestures of generosity, while the females paid closer attention to costs.

"Your impressive vehicle appears to be large and comfortable," said Arkad.

The male Itooti emptied a bottle of fruit juice and rubbed his forelimbs before answering. "This massive freight wagon requires much sustained effort to operate."

"What pleasant town is your ultimate destination?"

"Remote Ziiviz is the distant place we are going to—if clever Attatuttait can repair the lazy engine."

"A skilled female will surely be able to fix a simple engine. Your great wagon has ample space for some extra passengers."

"This overloaded wagon struggles to negotiate the impassable road."

"The massive load is so large a few extra kilograms would make no perceptible difference."

"The flightless Pfifu have a wise saying: 'you can pile stones onto a boat and one of them will sink it.'"

"Humble Arkad is impressed by your broad education. A well-informed male Itooti such as yourself is wasted at the dull task of steering a heavy freight wagon."

"Bizarre-looking Arkad's perceptive statement cannot be disputed."

"A large human with strong arms could take over the tiresome task of operating the heavy tiller," Arkad suggested.

"An inexperienced alien might steer the expensive freight wagon into the treacherous ocean, or crash the fragile machine into a massive tree."

"Not if the obedient alien had a skilled male Itooti to provide constant supervision."

"Generous Tuttetut will allow helpful Arkad to assist with steering the slow freight wagon."

"Grateful Arkad asks if kind Tuttetut will also allow three other compact humans to ride on the capacious vehicle."

"Charitable Tuttetut will permit them to stay in some small space where they will not interfere with the complex operations of the hard-working crew."

"Happy Arkad will tell his grateful companions." He jumped down from the control cab and hurried over to where Jacob waited.

"Well? How much does he want?"

"One of us has to help with the steering."

Jacob smiled and raised his eyebrows. "At this point, I'm starting to think you could talk your way off this planet without any help from us. Well done. When do we leave?"

Arkad shrugged. "When the engine is fixed."

The repairs took about three hours. The actual mechanical work only required about forty-five minutes, but Attatuttait—who was both chief engineer and majority shareholder of the vehicle—kept breaking off to go up to the roof of the cab to argue with Tuttetut. Their conflict was eventually resolved when the two of them disappeared off to the roof of the repair station together for half an hour, to loud hoots of approval from the other Itooti. While they were occupied, one of Attatuttait's sisters finished replacing the leaky steam line with quiet efficiency.

Jacob and Arkad helped Ree board the wagon, then got the bags piled around her. Baichi appeared at the last moment without anyone noticing where she had come from. As Attatuttait got steam up, Arkad climbed up to the tiller position, where Tuttetut perched on his shoulders and gave him instruction coupled with insults and tail slaps.

For a human, even a skinny boy like Arkad, the tiller was easy to manage. If anything, it was *too* responsive—he had to keep it lined up very precisely to keep the wagon from veering wildly. Tuttetut didn't help matters by jumping from one shoulder to the other, grabbing Arkad's ears to get his attention, and occasionally leaping down to the deck to wrench the tiller himself.

With a full head of steam, the freight wagon could manage nearly forty kilometers per hour on the unpaved road, though it was painfully obvious that this vehicle didn't have any advanced alien-built suspension, just steel springs. Arkad braced his feet on the low rail around the top of the cab, with his back against a boat hull. Jacob and Ree stayed in the cargo bed, more or less wedged in place with the backpacks. Baichi kept moving around, scanning the sky for the mysterious flying ball, and not even seeming to notice how the wagon lurched and bumped.

The other twenty or so passengers alternated riding atop the cargo and flying alongside or overhead, trading jibes with Tuttetut and Attatuttait about the wagon's slowness.

After Arkad had been steering for four hours, Jacob cautiously climbed up to the cab roof. "Want to switch? I've driven lots of ground vehicles in my time. I can even ride a unicycle."

Arkad gratefully let Jacob take his place, and then scrambled as quickly as he dared to the back of the wagon to empty his bladder. Jacob seemed to get along with Tuttetut better than Arkad had, perhaps because he couldn't understand a word of what the Itooti was saying.

Ree was lying among the backpacks, staring at the passing landscape with distaste, so Arkad left her alone. He saw Baichi walking forward atop the narrow rim of the cargo bed, completely oblivious to the lurching and bumping of the vehicle. She ignored his wave.

Well, two could play at that game. He climbed up to the top of one of the boat hulls, where a dozen of the Itooti passengers were sunning themselves. They were a mix of young males and females, and evidently didn't know he could understand their speech.

"One of the great clumsy hairless beings approaches our crowded space," said one of the females.

"A handsome young human would not bother to display any bright colors to a peevish female of any species," Arkad replied loudly, so the others could hear.

"Your flightless species has two distinct sexes?" she snapped back. "Incredulous Toatitas doubts that with such dull skin you can tell male humans from hypothetical females. Perhaps unappealing humans release airborne spores."

"Keen-eyed Arkad can see subtle differences which dull-witted Itooti cannot perceive." He lay down on the sun-warmed composite of the boat hull and felt his back tingle.

The first female gave a dismissive wing flap, but one of the young males demanded, "Can boastful Arkad demonstrate his hypothetical keen vision? Tell which lumbering humans are male and female, and describe how short-sighted Arkad can tell them apart!"

"Unobservant Itooti cannot see that male humans have abundant hair on the front of their well-shaped heads, while female humans do not."

"Dishonest Arkad has no such alleged hair," said the young male.

Arkad sat up and pointed to the wispy caterpillar on his upper lip and the scattered growth on his chin. "Oblivious Itooti cannot see lush hairs as thick as giant cables!"

"All-seeing Aitettit can barely see those nonexistent hairs, and doubts that any half-blind human could see them from even a short distance."

"Perceptive humans can observe other important differences. Male humans are usually larger than female ones. Even unobservant Aitettit can see that powerful Arkad and venerable Jacob are taller than pale Baichi and convalescent Ree."

"Honest Aitettit would need a precise measuring device to detect any significant difference in excessive height between talkative Arkad and silent Baichi. Besides, if two members of your weird-looking party are female, why isn't young Arkad courting them? Is skinny Arkad afraid of his larger male leader?"

"Ignorant Aitettit does not understand subtle human courtship," said Arkad. "Patient humans do not simply display brilliant colors and then fly off with the first lustful female who responds."

"Skeptical Aitettit wonders if shy Arkad has even tried doing that."

"Dubious Arkad wonders why irresistible Aitettit is not surrounded by his adoring harem of plump females."

"Listening to you two young males talking of sweet courtship is like hearing two massive AaaAa argue about which is the more graceful flyer," the female put in.

Aitettit caught the breeze in his wings and circled around her. "Admire virile Aitettit's glorious spots of hot flame from a respectful distance, aged Toatitas, for these strong wings will never enfold your bony carcass!"

"It is impossible to admire what cannot be seen," she replied, and turned away again, although Arkad noticed she was quieter than she had been.

"Subtle humans do not display bright colors," Arkad continued. "Young males show their great strength and invincible courage, but above all other things, their sincere devotion." He based this on what he had read, but even as he said it, he wondered if the limited selection of novels stored in WOL gave a complete picture.

"Demonstrate your unmatched prowess, then," demanded Aitettit. "Show how to subtly seduce a nubile female."

"One key difference between our divergent species is that modest humans do not perform their private courtship in front of a hooting audience," said Arkad.

"A truly glorious male makes the hills echo with his boasts," said Aitettit. "Only a frail weakling with colorless wings approaches desirable females in secret."

"A foolish little Itooti knows nothing about exotic humans," said Arkad, and slid down the side of the boat hull to the bed of the wagon.

Baichi was working her way back to the rear along the right-hand side of the wagon, completing her circuit. Her head was raised and turned to the left, so that she could scan the sky in that direction, while she walked slowly but without hesitation along the top of the low wall of the cargo bed as the wagon swayed and bumped down the rocky, unpaved road.

As if she was the only person with good balance! Arkad had been running on high cables and narrow beams as long as he had lived in Ayaviz. He jumped lightly up to the top of the wagon side, just at the right rear corner of the vehicle, and stood there, waiting for her.

She stopped a meter or so away from him. "You are in my way," she said, still watching the sky.

"And?"

"I want you to move."

Slowly, with arms outstretched to maintain his balance, Arkad moved his hips from side to side. "Like this?"

That made her look at him. "I want you to get out of my way."

He didn't say anything, but slowly turned around as he kept wiggling his hips. *"Bak bir beyaz ordek..."* he chanted, remembering a silly song his mother had sometimes sung to him. *"Vik viki vik vik vik."*

Did that get a smile out of her? He wasn't sure and he never found out because just then the wagon's left front wheel hit a bigger-than-average rock and the jolt caught Arkad by surprise. He fell off, landing heavily on a patch of sod and then tumbling down the steep slope beyond to end at a boulder.

It took him a minute to catch his breath, and then he very slowly got to his feet and took inventory. His blanket was muddy and wet and stained yellow from crushed plants. His right arm was scraped from elbow to shoulder, and he could feel growing lumps on his head, hip, and knees. The pouch around his neck holding WOL and his firestarter was intact, and his cooking skewer was still tucked into one of the shoes Jacob had made for him.

The wagon continued on its way. Arkad plodded after, trying to rewrap his blanket as he walked, and felt considerable relief when he saw it slow to a stop a few hundred meters away. Baichi jumped down to the road, as annoyingly graceful as always, and walked toward him.

"Are you injured?" she asked.

"Why should you care?" he answered. He was angry and embarrassed and felt a surge of resentment toward her. Always showing off what she could do—as if she had anything to do with it! No super-intelligent Machines had "improved" him. Everything he could do he had learned by falling down and getting hurt and trying again.

She halted, and he walked past her without stopping. More than anything in the world at that moment, he didn't want her to see the tears accumulating in his eyes. He rubbed them away angrily with the back of his hand.

"Are you injured?" she repeated, catching up with him.

"I'm *all right!*" he shouted, and then made himself run toward the wagon, ignoring the warning twinges from his bruised knees.

He could see Jacob watching him from the top of the control

cab. The older man looked, shook his head with a wry smile, and turned back to the tiller.

Arkad got up into the bed of the wagon and found a spot at the left corner between the two rolls of cable, where nobody could sit next to him. He sat miserably, dabbing at his scraped arm and ignoring Baichi as she went past. She was still walking on the edge of the cargo bed, and he thought about trying to trip her the next time she came around.

CHAPTER 6

HE GOT CLEANED UP, WITH SOME HELP FROM REE, UNPACKED A dry blanket to wrap himself in, and dozed for a few hours before relieving Jacob at the tiller. They traded off twice more as the wagon forged steadily along.

The road hugged the coast, rising and dipping as the terrain became more hilly. At streams the wagon had to slow and churn up the mud as it struggled across, usually accompanied by another loud argument between Tuttetut atop the cab and Attatuttait down in the engine compartment. The road gradually curved from south to southwest, turning toward the sun. A line of mountain peaks poked above the southern horizon. Off to the east, behind the wagon, they were completely snow-capped, while ahead to the west only the shadowed faces were white. Instead of the dense mats of intertwined brown and green fibers that covered the slope down to the sea, the ground sprouted sharp golden spines as long as Arkad's hand, with occasional clumps of big dark knobby spheres as tall as Jacob.

After they had been traveling for eight hours, the road—and the seacoast—led straight west, so that when Arkad was steering he had to cover his eyes with a hand to block the glare. The wagon began to pass signs of civilization: thick-walled Vziim mining camps in the foothills, or small Itooti enclaves on the seacoast. The rocky dirt road turned to packed gravel, making the ride considerably smoother. Tuttetut called down to Attatuttait and the sound of the steam turbine went up in pitch as the wagon sped up to nearly fifty kilometers an hour.

The space between the mountains and the sea shrank as they continued westward. The seashore became a high cliff, cut at intervals by deep gorges where small rivers came down from the mountains. Sturdy-looking arched stone bridges crossed the gorges, and at places where there was no way to detour around the bridge, enterprising Vziim females had erected fortified toll gates. Armed male Vziim demanded two hundred grams of tungsten to allow the wagon to pass.

At one toll stop Jacob wandered forward from where he had been sitting in the cargo bay. "How does this work?" he asked, gesturing at the armed Vziim blocking the bridge.

"They built the bridge—well, probably their aunts and sisters did it—so they can charge people to use it."

"Sure, but who enforces that?"

"They do. They've got flame-projectors and spears. If we cross without paying, they can set the wagon on fire."

"What keeps them from doing that anyway, and taking all our stuff?"

Arkad shrugged. "Then people from the other towns along the peninsula would come and pump poison gas into the Vziim burrows, or hire mercenaries to fight them."

"I'm just surprised nobody has tried to create a state bigger than a village. Even that city where we met you didn't have a real government."

"Nobody trusts anyone else," said Arkad. "If one Vziim clan got too powerful, the other clans would scheme to bring them down. Pfifu might be able to set up some kind of giant contract operation, but it would fall apart as soon as the contract expired. And Itooti don't live very long, so they don't think of making things that will last a long time."

"You'd think some civilization with a bit more cohesion would have come along and taken over the whole planet by now."

"The old machines wouldn't like that."

"Ah. Yes, I can see how they might be a problem," said Jacob, his gaze straying to an immense broken girder rising thirty meters from the carpet of golden spines above the seashore. "So the ticks and fleas can fight each other because they live on a big scary dog."

They had to stop at three toll bridges before reaching Ziiviz, the wagon's destination. According to Jacob's map it was only fifty kilometers from the end of the peninsula. The town was actually two distinct villages: an Itooti settlement built on the walls of a gorge where it met the sea, and a Vziim enclave upstream. Between them, where the gravel road crossed the gorge, a partnership of Pfifu operated a small refueling station and repaired mining machinery and boat engines with impartial skill.

Tuttetut took over the tiller and steered the wagon along the edge of the gorge to the end of the trail. A steel crane stood right at the point of the cliff where the gorge met the sea. Arkad looked down into the gorge as they passed and saw a series of small dams and powerhouses tapping the fall of the little river.

The Itooti village was clustered in a narrow stretch of cliff on the eastern side of the canyon, between the edge of the shadow cast by the western bank and the place where the cliff turned into a heap of loose rocks battered by the surf. On the cliffside where the sunlight shone, a vertical jungle of vines and clinging shrubs grew. The Itooti had filled it with a jumble of structures braided into the vines or supported by stakes and cables, all linked by ladders and rope bridges. A couple of more solid-looking structures stood on stilts. Down at the waterline were some haphazard-looking piers where fishing boats tied up, and a much more solid stone mole where bigger ships could take on cargo from the mines. The base of the cliff was a big refuse pile, where the very old and the very young picked through scraps.

The humans were too tired from the ride to help unload the boat hulls excepting, of course, Baichi. They left the task to the mob of Itooti fluttering up from the gorge. The sight of four strange beings disembarking from the wagon drew a lot of attention. Young Itooti males began swooping down to take a look at them, and the more daring ones shouted insults.

"Foul-tasting scavengers are often found creeping about the unsanitary refuse," said one. Another called out, "The shocking absence of colorful wings not only makes graceful flight impossible, it is also aesthetically displeasing!"

"Flying creatures conserve essential weight by lacking functional brains," Arkad called back.

An older female with a meter of copper wire coiled around her tail circled the four of them, then perched atop one of the solar panels that dotted the cliff top. "A new arrival demonstrates good manners and peaceful intent through polite introductions and detailed explanations."

"Tired and hungry travelers always need appetizing food and warm shelter before attending to any important business in a new town," Arkad answered.

"Foreign travelers can usually find adequate lodgings at comfortable fuel stations along major roads," she pointed out.

Jacob came over to where Arkad stood and raised his eyebrows. Arkad summarized the conversation for him. "Ask her where we can get passage across the strait," said Jacob.

"Important voyagers naturally seek a swift ship to carry them across the stormy strait," said Arkad.

The female let her wings droop. "No prudent captain dares sail the perilous strait right now."

"Surely bold Itooti mariners have no fear of the predictable weather."

"The fickle weather is never a serious problem. The alarming thing which keeps the unhappy sailors in port is the ominous presence of vicious pirates off the rocky cape."

"Pirates?" Jacob demanded when Arkad finished translating for him. "You mean real Zodiac and AK-47 pirates? Why doesn't anyone shut them down?"

"Sometimes, when they get too bad, the big shippers in Ayaviz put soldiers on their ships or hire privateers to fight them. Some of the pirates work as privateers part of the time, to thin out the competition."

"Enterprising fellows. So how bad are they? If we can find a boat and try to cross, will they sink us, hold us for ransom, rob and release, or what?"

"It depends on who the pirates are," said Arkad. "I've heard that Itooti just take what they can and then let the ship go on. Vziim take prisoners for ransom, and often make deals to leave some ships alone in exchange for protection money. Pfifu take everything and toss the crew into the sea."

"Ouch. Although I guess it's not so harsh if you're amphibious, or can fly."

"Vziim can't swim."

"Ah. So if we see tentacles, it's bad news."

Arkad turned back to the Itooti female. "Are there any brave captains who are not afraid of cowardly pirates?"

"No sensible ship owner would risk her valuable vessel on such a foolish voyage. For now, we hungry Itooti must fish close to the perilous shore, hunt scarce game in the rocky hills, or beg the unsympathetic Vziim for aid."

"Great," said Jacob once this was translated. "How long are we going to be stuck here?"

"She says the pirates have been in these waters for a twentieth of a year already."

"Tenacious bastards, then. You'd think word would get out and ships would start to avoid the area."

"She thinks the pirates are allied with the village of Tetaat, at the tip of the peninsula. She says the people there are trying to get control of all the trade across the strait."

Jacob looked thoughtful. "Maybe we should try our luck there," he said.

"It's another fifty kilometers, and there's at least one more toll along the way. And"—Arkad glanced from the female to Jacob—"I'm not sure they'd let us."

"Hmm. Yes, I see what you mean." Jacob looked at the female, then out to sea. "Okay, I guess we'll sleep here, have a good meal, then figure out our next move. Can you find us a room?"

"Rain-spattered travelers need warm and dry rooms in which to sleep," Arkad told the female.

"Large beings are too heavy for a snug cliffside house! Only the stalwart home of greedy Attatootot could hold such bulky creatures." She pointed with one wing (in a slightly rude gesture) at the biggest and most substantial structure in the village below the cliff: a house with four triangular floors standing on three thick stilts. It hardly looked like Itooti construction at all. The windowless walls of thick, close-fitted planks suggested Vziim work.

The others waited on the cliff top while Arkad climbed down to see if Attatootot was willing to rent them a room until they could find passage. He had to knock rather firmly on the door, which was as thick and solid as the walls, before anyone answered. It opened just a handsbreadth, and a haggard-looking older female Itooti looked out.

"Wealthy travelers wish to rent a comfortable room for a brief time," he said without preamble, before she could shut the door.

"The patient visitor may wait while hard-working Tati fetches her proud sister Attatootot," she said, and disappeared into the dim interior. Arkad hung beside the door, since there was only a ladder, not even a little porch to stand on.

Eventually a bigger and older female, with jeweled bands around her torso and a very suspicious expression arrived. "What weird vagabonds seek to impose on my orderly household?"

"Four rich alien travelers wish to rent a small space in your humble dwelling," he answered.

"My keen eyes see only one freakish alien."

"My dignified companions wait atop the steep cliff. If your little house cannot accommodate paying visitors, we will take our lucrative business elsewhere."

She peered more closely at him, and as her head emerged from the door, he could see some bare patches where she had painted her skin to look like healthy fur. "Wise Attatootot remembers hearing of bizarre creatures like your grubby self from her ancient grandmother. What dubious errand brings these mysterious aliens to my placid town?"

"My impatient colleagues and I have no great desire to stay in this remote village. We seek swift transport across the wide sea, and until that becomes available, a quiet place to stay. Do any of your friendly neighbors have available space for us?"

"For two meters of thick silver wire, the four overlarge beings can stay until I need the useful space. That reasonable amount will not include exotic meals or wasteful fuel."

Arkad did some figuring and then agreed. He helped his companions haul their luggage down the cliff, and the four of them went into the house. Jacob nearly had to crawl in order to keep from bumping his head on the ceiling.

Their quarters were on the lowest floor, in what looked like a vacant storage room. A stout cargo hoist was folded against one wall next to a pair of heavy shutters, tightly fastened with metal bolts. Their hostess would not hear of opening them for some light and air. "Cautious Attatootot does not want her secure house open to all idle gawkers and lustful males," she said, and then went out.

Their room had a level wood floor, a stove made of tough ceramic with a hand-riveted metal flue, and barely enough room for the four of them and their bags. Jacob built a fire in the stove and they boiled some dried fish to make soup. After eating, Arkad had WOL read to him. He wanted to seem grown-up, so he selected the hardest story he could think of.

The book's voice changed, becoming deep and husky-sounding, with an English accent. *"Among other public buildings in a certain town, which for many reasons it will be prudent to refrain from mentioning, and to which I will assign no fictitious name, there is one anciently common to most towns, great or small: to wit, a workhouse; and in this workhouse was born; on a day and date which I need not trouble myself to repeat, inasmuch as it can be of no possible consequence to the reader, in this stage of the business at all events; the item of mortality whose name is prefixed to the head of this chapter."*

"What's that all about?" asked Ree.

"It's a story about a boy who grows up and—"

"Oliver Twist, right?" Jacob put in.

"Yes. You've heard of it?"

"Heard of it? I've read it half a dozen times, once when I was too young to get most of what was going on and again when I was older. Not to mention watching the black and white movie with Alec Guinness—*and* I can sing most of the songs from the musical, which makes me a one-man cultural resource. Crank it up so we all can hear."

"Must we?" asked Ree. "It's all ancient history, and I can't make sense of what it's saying."

"Since when is something barely four hundred years old 'ancient'?"

"I want to sleep," she said.

Jacob gave an irritated snort, but agreed. Arkad switched to visual-only, read a couple of chapters, and then slept along with the others.

He woke before Jacob and Ree, and crawled cautiously out of the house. He emptied his bladder into the air, then climbed up the web of vines to the top of the cliff, hoping to find Baichi. But she was nowhere to be found, so he walked around the solar panels and wind turbines.

Some young Itooti were swooping among the turbines, daring each other to fly between the turning blades, or seeing who could hover in one place the longest on the steady breeze. Arkad felt a surge of memory. He had been here before, or someplace very much like it.

A young male dove at Arkad, trying to tail-slap him on the

head, but Arkad ducked out of the way. He recognized the male as Aitettit, his verbal sparring partner from the wagon trip. "Envious Arkad wonders where potent Aitettit's adoring harem of nubile females has gone," he teased.

"Flame-spotted Aitettit cannot confine his delightful attentions to just a small group of plump females. Also, virile Aitettit has been busy with other important tasks lately. How many colorless human females has lusty Arkad impregnated recently?"

Embarrassed, Arkad hurried to change the subject. "Four impatient humans seek a safe way to cross the narrow strait," he said.

Aitettit circled his head and came to rest on Arkad's shoulder. "Savvy Aitettit knows a valuable secret," he said softly.

"Serious Arkad is not interested in foolish rumors."

"Well-informed Aitettit knows more than mere gossip. Handsome Aitettit has a trustworthy half-brother with a swift boat. For an entirely reasonable quantity of shiny metal, honest Aitettit can arrange safe passage for four stranded humans."

"Skeptical Arkad wonders if humorous Aitettit is attempting to play an annoying trick on the easily angered humans."

"Sincere Aitettit assures paranoid Arkad that his friendly offer is perfectly genuine."

"Intrigued Arkad wonders where this evasive boat is."

"Follow agile Aitettit!" The Itooti leaped from Arkad's shoulder, caught the wind and hovered for a moment, then banked away to the left and dove into the gorge. Arkad ran to the cargo hoist where the road ended at the cliff point, and slid down the cable as fast as he dared.

The bottom of the cliff was a jumble of boulders, but at some point long ago someone (Vziim, to judge by the style of the work) had constructed a massive stone and concrete mole extending past the cliff to create a sheltered anchorage for larger vessels. Over the years sand and gravel from the river had accumulated on the inner side of the mole, and now that pebbly stretch was a convenient place for Itooti to beach their smaller boats.

Itooti loved sailboats, and with their intuitive understanding of airflow and lift, they could squeeze impressive performance out of even crude material and simple-looking designs. They liked outriggers and catamarans, and especially loved to build boats with hydrofoils. The more they could make sailing like flying, the better.

There were four boats on the strand. Two were big utilitarian fishing catamarans, with paired hulls of carbon fiber, broad decks with refrigerated bins for fish, and paired tall masts set at an angle, so that from fore or aft they made giant V shapes. Those two used smart-cloth sails and had elaborate rigging to shift and control them.

The third boat was a powerboat, unusual for Itooti, with a long narrow central hull and two outriggers housing powerful hydrojet motors. It looked like a racer, but the massive winch attached to the afterdeck suggested it was used most often as a tug.

The fourth boat was a lovely little sailing hydrofoil, with three sets of vanes: two forward and one stretched out behind. The sail itself was a tall rigid airfoil mounted at the center of mass. Lines leading down to the cockpit could adjust the orientation of the rigid wing-sail or control the pitch, and a set of rods controlled the angle of the hydrofoils to keep her level. The whole thing was made of graphene and fractal crystals and probably weighed less than Arkad.

"Truthful Aitettit challenges amazed Arkad to find a swifter seaworthy boat anywhere on the mountainous peninsula," said his companion, indicating the sailing hydrofoil with a nod of his head.

"Impressed Arkad admits the elegant boat appears very swift, but prudent Arkad wonders if the frail boat can evade the deadly weapons of fierce pirates."

"The agile boat can turn and dodge with marvelous quickness."

"Tall Arkad wonders how many sturdy humans can fit into such a compact boat."

Aitettit flew around Arkad a couple of times, sizing him up, then landed on the boat and stuck his head into the hatch. "The capacious hull has sufficient room for four supple humans—and the level deck has much more useful space. Surely no spirited humans would wish to spend a long voyage uncomfortably packed inside a tiny cabin!"

Arkad thought of going back up the cliff to tell Jacob and Ree about it, but then he thought that presenting them with a solution to their problem, all arranged and settled, would be much more impressive.

"Cost-conscious Arkad wonders how much valuable metal greedy Aitettit wants for brief passage."

The young male circled him a couple of times and finally came to land on Arkad's shoulder. He bent close to speak quietly. "Hopeful Aitettit will arrange a significant discount if kind Arkad will perform a trivial favor."

"Wary Arkad wonders what kind of onerous task deceptive Aitettit is thinking of."

"Sincere Aitettit assures suspicious Arkad that the simple task involves no perceptible difficulty or significant risk."

"What is this perilous job, then?"

Aitettit looked around with almost comical stealth, and then leaned so close the tip of his mouth was actually inside Arkad's ear. "Lovelorn Aitettit wants helpful Arkad to carry a vital message. The old female, selfish Attatootot, refuses to allow any of her lovely daughters to be courted by handsome males. Like a scheming Vziim matriarch she seals up her unhappy family in a dour fortress, compelling her sad relations to devote all their scarce time to hard work and tedious study. Her loveless sisters and downtrodden daughters make avaricious Attatootot the richest female Itooti on the whole prosperous peninsula, if not vast Syavusa itself. But helpful Arkad and the other impatient humans are renting comfortable space from greedy Attatootot. Resourceful Arkad can deliver an important message within the fortified house."

"Sympathetic Arkad feels sorry for the oppressed relatives of overbearing Attatootot, but doesn't know with whom secretive Aitettit wants to communicate."

"Desirable Utitaat!" said Aitettit, then looked around again to see if anyone had heard. "Lovely Utitaat is the most beautiful daughter of bossy Attatootot, and is as kind and generous and good-natured as her grasping mother is cruel, selfish, and spiteful."

"What is the brief message?"

Aitettit spread his wings and began a long, passionate recitation. He had obviously been working on his poem for a long time, and it was quite good, but after a minute Arkad stopped him. "Fallible Arkad cannot remember so much. Talented Aitettit should write down his romantic verse."

"Sterile writing cannot convey the underlying passion!" Aitettit protested, but in the end he agreed. For the next hour Arkad hung around the harbor, watching some females patching one of the catamaran hulls with sheets of smart cloth and molecular glue. Eventually Aitettit returned with some ribbons decorated with colored dots, the most formal style of Itooti writing. "Stealthy Arkad must give this private message to lovely Utitaat in person. Under no circumstances is careless Arkad to entrust these vital ribbons to any untrustworthy other person."

"Dutiful Arkad will deliver the important message. Now honest Aitettit must arrange a swift boat to cross the dangerous strait."

So Arkad accompanied Aitettit up the gorge to a house hanging only a few meters above the riverbank, where Aitettit's half-brother Otateetat lived. He heard a male Itooti voice from inside, reciting poetry, and the two youngsters went right in.

Otateetat stood in the center of the room, his great scarlet-striped wings extended as far as he could manage indoors. Three young females listened admiringly. The big male looked up as they entered, darting his tongue threateningly.

"It is irritating to be interrupted during passionate foreplay," he said. "Especially by shiftless young relatives and bizarre alien beings."

"A strong male need not hurry to mate, as he has no fear that a greater rival will arrive and drive him off," said Arkad.

"A magnificent male fears no rival," Otateetat agreed, "but all cultured species agree it is rude to interrupt another's pleasurable reproduction."

"Wealthy travelers seek affordable passage aboard a swift courier," said Arkad.

One of the females stirred restlessly, and Otateetat lashed his tail with impatience. "Advanced couriers carry important cargoes like essential mail and vital components. Deformed wanderers sometimes travel aboard slow bulk transports or wallowing sea barges. A wise being leaves when his unwanted presence interferes with more pleasant activities."

Arkad and Aitettit withdrew. Behind them, Arkad could hear Otateetat resume his chant inside the house. "A deadly hunter's jagged teeth can tear the tender skin from a brave male's muscular leg. Bold and strong males ignore even severe injury in the hot frenzy of maritime battle. A powerful tail blow on the narrow base of a sharp dart lodged in the terrible monster's armored eye drives the irresistible point into the vital nerve plexus there. The dying hunter screams in agony and thrashes about. Indomitable

Otateetat clings to the writhing beast's bloody head until cold death claims the mighty animal."

When the older male's narrative gave way to rustling and soft hooting, Arkad climbed back down to the riverbank and threw sticks for Aitettit to catch in midair. Eventually Otateetat crawled out of the door flap and stretched his wings.

"Tactless Arkad wanted to ask handsome Otateetat some bothersome thing," he said.

"Four busy humans must cross the narrow strait quickly," he answered without any preamble. "The four humans will give idle Otateetat thirty grams of dense platinum for the brief trip."

Otateetat glanced at Aitettit, who was hovering nervously next to Arkad.

"Truthful Aitettit told the desperate humans that brave Otateetat is willing to cross the calm strait," Aitettit told his half-brother.

Otateetat darted his tongue at Aitettit, then said, "Forty."

"Done," said Arkad. It was the quickest price negotiation he had ever experienced, and for a moment he didn't know what to do.

"Candid Otateetat cannot guarantee the physical safety of the daring humans."

"Knowledgeable Arkad understands." After a moment of silence, he thanked Otateetat and went off to deliver his message. Behind him he could hear the two Itooti half-brothers plunge immediately into an argument.

Finding Utitaat turned out to be much more difficult than Arkad had expected. Even though Attatootot's house had only four floors, it boasted a positively Vziim-like profusion of locked doors, with inquisitive Itooti females demanding to know why Arkad wanted to pass through each one. He didn't want to broadcast that he had a secret message to deliver, so instead, he claimed to be admiring the construction of the house, and made sure to get the name of each female he talked to.

After two hours of this, he had still not penetrated past the second floor, and the attitude of the inhabitants shifted from indulgence and curiosity to grudging toleration and finally to outright impatience. So he gave up and returned downstairs.

He found Jacob sitting in front of the house on the riverbank, with his legs dangling over the white water surging from the last set of hydroelectric turbines, smoking his pipe. He moved aside to let Arkad sit beside him. "Good morning, or whatever it is. What have you been up to?"

"I found us a boat!"

Jacob put a finger to his lips, then knocked out his pipe. "Let's talk inside."

Arkad was a little surprised to see that Baichi was there already. Ree was huddled next to the stove.

"Now, what's this about a boat?"

"There's an Itooti named Otateetat who has a fast sail-foil. He's willing to take us across the strait for forty grams of platinum."

Ree winced at the price but said nothing.

"What about the pirate situation?"

"He's willing to risk it."

"*He* can fly," Ree pointed out. "We can't."

"What kind of hardware are these pirates likely to be packing? Muzzle-loading cannon? AK-47s? Some Machine Civ tech that decays your protons all at once?"

Arkad thought about the gangs he knew back in Ayaviz. "Pfifu can't see things far away very well, so they seldom use guns or beams. When fighting close up, they like to swing blades on long handles or barbed chains, or use projectors to spray boiling acid or poison."

"When those guys go bad they get *nasty*," said Jacob. "Others?"

"Itooti have good aim but are too small to carry guns. They do use explosive darts or rockets, and they might have big rockets to shoot at ships. They never risk fighting hand-to-hand with bigger creatures."

"Okay, so don't get under them. Anybody else?"

"Vziim don't see well, either, so they use shotguns and flame-projectors. When they fight they wear steel claws, sometimes electrified. Against ships, I think they would try to grapple and board."

"They all sound terrible," said Ree.

"Actually, I was going to say they don't," said Jacob. "Most of the weapons Arkad describe are all up close and personal threats. No rifles, no lasers, nothing that could get us from long range—except for rockets, I suppose. How common are those?"

Arkad shrugged. "You'd have to have Pfifu to make them and Itooti to aim them."

"Well, if that boat's as fast as you say it is, we hardly have to

worry. And if the bad guys do get close, we've got some coun-
termeasures," said Jacob. He patted the laser tool, then looked
at Baichi and raised his eyebrows slightly. She said nothing, but
shook her head almost imperceptibly. Jacob shrugged. "I'm willing to try it. How about the rest of you?"

"Of course!" said Arkad.

"I figured as much. Ree?"

Ree had a look of intense concentration on her face. After
a moment, she nodded to herself and then looked up at Jacob.
"All right. It wouldn't do to give up now."

"Baichi?" Jacob asked in a quieter voice.

"I am not a weapon."

"That's not what I'm asking. Are you willing to go along?"

"I am willing to go. But I will not betray my vow if we are
attacked. I am not a weapon. I will not harm anyone, not even
to protect you."

"Of course not," he said. "I wouldn't expect anything else."

She looked right at him then with her all-black eyes. "Yes,
you do. You think I will abandon my vow to save others. You
think you understand me. You are wrong."

After a brief silence, Jacob said, "Well I'm still willing to
risk it. If nobody objects... Ree, do we have enough platinum?"

"Yes—but I think we're going to have to start doing more
camping and foraging, or something. We can't keep spending
at this rate."

"If I'm reading the map right, once we cross the strait it
shouldn't be hard to reach the mountain passes, and then it's a
straight shot across the plains to the Black Land."

"Remember that we have to come back, Jacob. *All* of us,"
said Ree.

He raised his eyebrows at that, but otherwise ignored it.
"Okay, then. Arkad: go find this Otateetat person and let him
know we can be ready any time he is. No point in wasting any
more time here than we need to. Oh—this boat have a name?"

"Itooti don't give names to things like vehicles. Only people
and places."

In the end they didn't even go aboard the boat for another
eight hours, and it took another three before Otateetat was ready
to venture out of the harbor. Arkad was used to Itooti organization methods, in which one began the task at once and started

preparing afterwards. They got their gear aboard the sail-foil, and only then did Otateetat decide to replace one of the control rods for the hydrofoil vanes. Ree seethed at the delay, Baichi vanished, and Jacob found a quiet place to read and smoke. "Just like back in the Army," he said.

Arkad was delighted to help get the sail-foil seaworthy. He wound up carrying the old rod all the way up the cliff and along the trail to the fuel station and repair shop at the bridge. He and one of Otateetat's young romantic partners from earlier handled the negotiations with the Pfifu at the station. The key issue was that Otateetat wanted the Pfifu to do the work on credit, and so his paramour was accusing them of faulty workmanship on an earlier job as a way to get bargaining leverage. The Pfifu made counteraccusations and threats, and the whole negotiation seemed about to spark an interspecies war when the female Itooti finally agreed to put down half the price in advance and pay the rest with interest later. Within minutes the Pfifu produced the new rod and they were on their way back down the gorge.

"Cunning Titett certainly bent that gullible fool to her implacable will, didn't she?" the young female asked Arkad as they walked down the trail. He smiled to himself and politely agreed.

Halfway back he suddenly stopped, feeling as if someone had just smacked him in the face with a board. Aitettit's message! He had forgotten all about it and now the boat was almost ready to sail.

"Do you know attractive Utitaat?" he asked Titett, trying to sound casual.

She darted her tongue and seemed irritated by the question. "Stuck-up Utitaat and her snobbish family don't associate with me," she said. "Reclusive Attatootot and her slavish daughters seldom socialize with their tolerant neighbors."

"Could observant Titett point out shy Utitaat to curious Arkad? Or show where hard-to-find Utitaat might be? But not in an obvious way."

"There," said Titett. "Unsociable Utitaat and some of her hardworking sisters are at the irradiating hut, wearisomely packing valuable fish." She pointed to a structure at the top of the cliff, near the hoist and the wind turbines.

Arkad climbed up the side of the gorge and paused at the top to catch his breath before hurrying to the irradiating hut.

The building was little more than a shack, with rocks and dirt heaped up on three sides and a roof made of sheet metal. Inside the shack were a couple of machines—a simple metal apparatus with levers and pistons, and a complicated-looking device with heavy magnetic coils surrounding a long glass tube.

Four Itooti females were hard at work at the shack. One unloaded frozen (or at least still chilly) fish from a pallet by the hoist, the second slipped them into plastic bags and vacuum-sealed them using the piston machine, the third put stacks of sealed bags under the glass tube device and flipped the power switch (which made the tube glow purple while the wires made exciting sparks), and the fourth gathered up the finished product and stacked the irradiated seafood on a wheeled cart ready to drag up the trail to the road.

He approached the female loading the cart and said, "Dutiful Arkad seeks unknown Utitaat." She gave him a suspicious look, then aimed one wing at the female operating the vacuum-sealing device. Arkad thanked her and went into the shack.

"Discreet Arkad has a vital message for reclusive Utitaat," he said, and held out the ribbons. At this, the female Itooti at the irradiator gave a screech and leaped across the shed, snatching at them. The one at the vacuum sealer also grabbed the ribbons, and the two of them engaged in a wing-flapping tug-of-war, bouncing off the ceiling and crashing into Arkad.

"Stupid Arkad gave the important message to the wrong female!" one of them shrieked, while the other screamed, "Sneaky Utitaat should not be getting secret messages!"

Arkad plunged into the melee, trying to separate the two. One of them finally managed to tear the ribbons out of the other's grip, and flew off through the open entrance. The loser in the struggle fell to the ground and gave a howl of anger and frustration.

"What is your real name?" he asked her.

"Furious Utitaat can't believe idiotic Arkad has to ask that stupid question! What was that stolen message about, and what mysterious person was it from?"

"Love-struck Aitettit wrote the troublesome message," said Arkad. "Helpful Arkad believes the lost message was desperate Aitettit's sincere declaration of his love for unattainable Utitaat."

"And spiteful Iitii will take the lovely message straight to disapproving Attatootot. Pitiable Utitaat will never be allowed out of the dark house again!"

He looked around. The other two females had gone—either joining Iitii as tattletales or simply wanting to be elsewhere when trouble hit. "Go to yearning Aitettit now," he suggested.

"Wealthy mother will disinherit poor Utitaat," she said.

"Why does put-upon Utitaat stay in her bossy mother's house?" Arkad asked, genuinely curious.

The question seemed to have a real effect on her. "Why indeed?" she said, fluttering up to Arkad's shoulder. "Unhappy Utitaat must work hard on her own, or for her rich mother. Either way, pitiable Utitaat labors without end. Now defiant Utitaat has little chance of any valuable inheritance. Why stay indeed?" She spread her wings and jumped, catching the wind and rising, then banking to veer off toward the harbor. A male climbed to meet her, and as the two of them rose above the cliff shadow, Arkad could see the flame-colored spots on Aitettit's wings.

He was halfway down the cliff when half a dozen of Utitaat's sisters and aunts came boiling up out of Attatootot's house, led by Attatootot herself. When he saw they were vectoring toward him, Arkad began climbing faster, dropping from climbing rope to walkway hard enough that the support cables made an alarming cracking noise.

They caught up with him when he was ten meters above the ground. "Vile sneak! Wingless traitor!" Attatootot yelled, landing on Arkad's shoulders and clutching his hair. "Deceptive Arkad must tell angry Attatootot where her rebellious daughter has gone with that irresponsible young male!"

"Ow! Let go! Innocent Arkad does not know!" He batted at her, and she took off but scratched at his flailing arms. A couple of other females dive-bombed him, slapping him with their tails.

Arkad ran along the walkway and used one hand to grab a thickish vine, while fending off the angry females with the other. He swung himself off the walkway and more or less slid down the vine, using his shod feet to slow his descent.

"Gullible Utitaat has gone off with that lustful young male," Attatootot shrieked. "My foolish daughter will wind up living in some crude hovel, raising ungrateful children while disloyal Aitettit flies off in search of some plump younger female, and meddling Arkad deserves some of the rightful blame!" She caught the wind and rose again, then shouted orders to the rest of her flock. "Fly east and west along the rocky coast! Find your disobedient sister and her worthless lover!"

By now Arkad was on the ground, sprinting across the beach toward the sail-foil. The three others were already on board. "Go, go!" Arkad yelled, swatting at one of Utitaat's sisters who was still trying to rake his face with her claws.

With everyone else aboard, Arkad pushed Otateetat's sail-foil off the pebbly beach and scrambled onto the T-shaped deck. His last attacker made a half-hearted dive at Arkad before veering off to join the search parties.

Arkad's respect for Otateetat's skill went up considerably once they passed beyond the little harbor. The sail-foil was tricky to manage. Otateetat had to keep the wing-sail properly angled to the constantly shifting wind, and adjust the vanes to keep the craft level. As the boat picked up speed, the vanes on the windward side were no longer generating lift but rather pulled *down* into the water to keep the whole thing from tipping over. Wind pulled one way, water resisted, and the battle of forces sped the boat along at more than forty kilometers per hour.

There were tiny cabins above the hydrofoil vanes at either end of the top of the T, and a cargo hold at the bottom of the T over the third set. Otateetat sailed the boat from a cockpit just forward of the cargo hold, using cables to direct and shape the tall wing-shaped sail, and rods to adjust the hydrofoil vanes. For balance, Otateetat insisted that passengers be divided by mass, and Arkad was startled to discover that Baichi's slim form weighed more than Jacob did. The result was that Ree and Jacob took the portside cabin, and Arkad and Baichi the starboard.

For the moment, the weather was good—gusts of cold wind from the east alternating with warmer breezes from the north. The cold air made streamers of mist along the surface of the ocean, and kicked up choppy waves so that the ride was as bumpy as the power wagon on the worst stretches of unpaved road. None of the four humans were seasick; Ree and Baichi were immune to it by design, Jacob had years of experience in free fall and boats of all kinds, and Arkad had spent much of his life in bouncing Itooti houses or walking on swaying ropes above the streets of Ayaviz.

The strait was nearly a thousand kilometers across, from the tip of the peninsula to the nearest cape of the main continent. The first six hours of the voyage were relatively calm, but then the sunlight was blocked by a line of dark clouds ahead.

"The great northwest current flows through those deep waters," Otateetat called from the cockpit. "It brings salty water from sunlit seas, and where the warm stream meets this cold wind at our shaded backs, a perpetual line of savage squalls lashes the gray water."

Arkad looked back to shout a reply, and saw a dark plume against the blue haze beyond. "One powered ship follows us," he called to Otateetat, pointing east-northeast.

The Itooti pilot looked back, his barbed tongue poked out a couple of times, and then he turned onto a new tack, angling the boat south by southwest to get maximum power from the wind on the wing-sail. Only a few minutes later the sail-foil passed through the first gray curtain of rain, and fine drops on the steady wind felt like needles on Arkad's skin. He slid down into the little starboard cabin and closed the cover.

With the lid down, Arkad and Baichi had only a couple of cubic meters to share. The space was too narrow for them to sit up. It would probably be more efficient if he lay with his head by her feet and vice versa, but Arkad chose the other alignment, and found himself quite comfortably pressed against her from feet to cheek.

"Do you breathe?" he asked after a moment. They were so close he spoke in a whisper.

"When I need to," she said. "There is enough oxygen in this space for us both."

"Oh. I wasn't really thinking about that. It's just weird how still you are."

She took a deep breath and let it out. "Is that better?"

"You said you're part Machine," he said, and then thought for a moment to phrase the next thing he said very carefully. "How big a part? I mean..." He gave up and just spoke plainly: "Are you a human with some Machine parts added, or are you a Machine that just looks human?"

"Both," she said softly. "I'm a blend of living cells and molecular-scale machinery. There is no part of me which isn't both."

"Okay," he said. "You're very pretty," he added. It was true, but he cringed inside after he said it. It sounded so dumb. He wished he could sound like the people in stories. He tried to recall some of the impressive-sounding things he had read. "I mean... your every feature is chiseled and exquisite."

She made a sound he had never heard from her before, and after a second he realized she was giggling. "Chiseled and exquisite," she said in a pompous voice. "Like a statue?"

He gave her arm a squeeze. "You're too squishy to be a statue." He left his hand where it was, holding her arm gently, and she didn't pull it away. He was just about to kiss her when the boat exploded.

CHAPTER 7

THE BLAST SLAMMED BOTH OF THEM HEADFIRST INTO THE NOSE of the little compartment. The cabin flipped forward, standing Arkad and Baichi on their heads, and seawater gushed in through the cracked hatch cover. Arkad struggled to get his head out of the water.

"Swim!" Baichi shouted, bracing her legs against the top of the compartment. Arkad had just enough time to take a breath before the top and bottom halves of the cabin snapped apart and the sea surged in.

Arkad swam blindly, trying to find the surface and air. One direction was marginally brighter than the others, but it seemed to take ages for him to reach it. He was on the verge of panic as his head finally broke the surface. He took in a lungful of air, then spluttered and choked as a wave caught him in the face. He paddled desperately to keep his head above water in the churning waves and rain.

A chunk of floating debris bumped him and he clutched at it desperately. With one hand, he undid the sodden blanket that weighed him down and kicked free of it. He coughed and got a full breath of air, then looked around.

As he rose to the crest of a wave, he could see the wreck of the sail-foil, about ten yards away. The stern was entirely gone, but the wing-shaped sail floated flat on the water. With the little cabin he had shared with Baichi torn apart, the other cabin was under the water, hanging from the floating sail.

Ree and Jacob were still in there, Arkad realized. Clutching the piece of debris, he swam toward the wreck. He looked around but couldn't see Baichi anywhere. Another wave lifted him, and he saw a boat beyond the wreck of the sail-foil. It was a Pfifu vessel, a narrow hull holding a smoky boiler and a steam turbine engine, with open underwater decks along the sides. Tentacled swimmers shot out from the boat as it approached.

They might just want the wreck, thought Arkad. Maybe if the humans could get away, the Pfifu would ignore them. He took a deep breath and dove, feeling his way along the carbon-fiber strut hanging from the mast, down to the cabin holding Jacob and Ree. He knocked on it, and felt a stab of relief when there was an answering thump from inside.

He couldn't stay down any longer. Arkad let himself float back up to the surface and got another lungful of air. The Pfifu boat was closer now, and swimmers were fanning out to collect the flotsam.

Arkad dove again, and kicked down to the cabin. He banged on it, harder. Did they even know they were under water? They must; otherwise they would open the hatch. It must not be leaking much.

Then Arkad felt strong tentacles grab his torso from behind. He struggled and kicked, trying to pull out of the Pfifu's grasp. He found one tentacle tip and pinched, digging deep into the soft flesh with his fingernails. But the Pfifu only tightened its grip and Arkad was getting desperate for air. He tried to pull himself to the surface along the carbon-fiber strut, but the Pfifu dragged him down. He felt the trapped air bubbling from his mouth and then blacked out.

Someone was pushing down hard on his chest, and someone else was blowing air into his mouth. He coughed, gasped, and then his rescuers rolled him onto his side as he threw up. Arkad inhaled again, and for a moment just savored the sensation of being able to breathe. Then he opened his eyes.

It was dark. The only light was the oval outline of a hatch overhead. He could see Jacob and Ree kneeling over him. Jacob was shirtless, but Ree was dressed in her coverall, still immaculate, and only her wet hair showed that she had been in the ocean at all.

"Can you hear me? Can you understand what I'm saying?" asked Jacob.

Arkad nodded. "Yes," he croaked.

"Are you hurt?"

His scraped arm was in agony where it touched the deck underneath him, and his whole body felt like a single bruise. "No," he managed. He pushed himself to a sitting position and spent a minute just breathing. "Where are we?" he finally asked.

"A boat," said Jacob. "The pirates got us. I'm glad to say you were wrong about the Pfifu. They pulled us out of the water before they looted the wreck."

It was too hard to think, so Arkad just nodded. "Baichi?"

"Haven't seen her."

"The ocean is a bad place for her," said Ree. "Her body is very dense. I don't think she can swim."

"Now, now," said Jacob. "She might have been able to grab hold of something. No reason to give up hope just yet."

"What about Otateetat?"

"Dead or flown away," said Jacob.

The three of them were cold and wet, with new bruises and scrapes from the wreck. Fortunately, the boat's engine compartment was just aft of the hold they were locked in, so that wall was warm to the touch. Arkad huddled against the warm bulkhead with Jacob and Ree close on either side, until he stopped shivering and only his hair was damp.

He dozed and lost track of time in the darkness, but when the hum of the turbine against the wall at his back dropped, Arkad came awake at once and nudged his companions. "We're slowing down."

The fore-and-aft pitching of the boat stopped, and instead, it began rocking from side to side with the swell. After a few minutes, the hatch above opened; the light was dazzling. Two Pfifu swung down into the hold, one with a spear tipped with a fan-shaped blade, and the other holding an acid sprayer. "You three come up now," said the one with the spear in pidgin. With his two free tentacles, he gestured, *"A rich catch for a grand feast,"* but the exaggerated sweep of his movements made Arkad think he was being sarcastic. Pfifu up on deck tossed down ropes and hauled up the human prisoners.

It was still raining, but the air was noticeably warmer and shafts of sunlight occasionally pierced the shifting clouds overhead.

Ocean stretched away in every direction, but a single vast steel pipe, easily a hundred meters across, rose thirty meters from the surface of the water to end in a jagged crown of torn metal. The pipe was rusty and crusted with the shells of reef creatures and marine parasites, in distinct bands by species depending on how far above the waterline they could survive. A great tangle of boats and barges were moored downcurrent, held by an enormous loop of iron chain that ran all the way around the pipe.

The Pfifu had built houses and workshops atop and underneath the mass of hulls, but by far the biggest was a structure shaped like a giant predatory fish, with brightly painted fins and four eyes lit from within. The door, of course, was set inside the gaping toothy mouth. Four Pfifu, including the one with the acid generator, led the human captives toward it.

The interior of the fish building was a single large hall, lit by stained glass panels on the sunward side. The vaulted ceiling was decorated with painstakingly carved wooden reliefs of heroic Pfifu capturing ships, spearing sea monsters, and constructing impressive machinery. All of it looked new, and Arkad could smell fresh paint and sawdust.

The three of them and their guards stood waiting for a time. Finally three more Pfifu accompanied by an Itooti came in through a door at the far end. One of them gestured to the guards. "*A favorable breeze brings the catch this way.*"

The guards prodded their captives with spear butts and they approached the newcomers. Arkad could see that everyone seemed to defer to one Pfifu, an old male with big, milky, burn patches covering nearly half his skin.

"You tell me what you can give," said the old one in pidgin. He made no gestures.

"Is that the boss?" Jacob whispered to Arkad.

"I think so."

"Tell him we're visitors from offworld and have powerful friends who'll come looking for us if anything happens."

Arkad translated for the Pfifu.

"You tell me if they will pay for you," the old one answered. With one tentacle he gestured to the guards, "*This poor catch may be useful as bait for something more filling.*"

"Tell him yes," said Jacob. "We're explorers from offplanet; the Combined Free Human Forces will pay big bucks to get us back."

Arkad translated into pidgin, then whispered to Jacob, "Is that true?"

"Of course not. If the boys at CFHQ somehow found out I'd been killed they'd probably celebrate because I won't be bugging them anymore."

The half-burned old Pfifu conferred with a couple of his pirate colleagues. Arkad couldn't hear them but he could make out scraps of their conversation from their tentacle gestures.

"The speech of strangers is like a wind driving us toward rocks."

"...no reason not to spread our nets."

"Not much meat on them..." (Arkad suspected that was meant entirely literally.)

"We don't know what is holding the other end of this line."

"You never find the biggest catch in safe waters."

Finally the old Pfifu spoke aloud to the captives. "You tell me where to find those who will pay for you." He added with his tentacles, *"Is there anything beyond the fog?"*

"There is one like us in the big town," said Arkad, improvising on the spot. "His name is Sun Wukong, and he is at the spire of Aviiva. He has great wealth and will pay as much as you ask for us."

"Trap them again and give them some food. Soon we learn if they are bait for plates of iridium, or merely for ocean fish."

Without further ado, the guards led the three humans to an empty cargo container sitting on the deck of a rusty barge near the edge of the raft of ships. They shoved the three inside, then tossed in a fish the size of Jacob's leg, fresh-caught and still thrashing, before locking the door.

One corner of the cargo container's roof had a neat circular vent cut in it, with a steel bar welded across the center to keep them from using it as an exit. Directly under the vent, there was another hole in the floor to serve as a drain.

The walls, floor, and ceiling were covered with the curves and swirling lines of Pfifu writing: an intricate and elaborate pattern of the vilest insults in their language. There didn't seem to be any particular target for the vituperation. Apparently it had been done simply for its own sake.

Before doing anything else, they killed and ate the fish. Jacob grabbed it by the tail and bashed its head against the steel wall, then Arkad used his teeth and fingers to tear open the skin along the belly. He warned Jacob and Ree which parts were safe. "The blood is good, and the entrails. The meat has to dry out and age awhile before you can eat it."

"Could we ask them for our food bars?" asked Ree.

"Don't like sushi?" Jacob asked her. "Though I guess this is more like lutefisk."

"I don't know what that is and I'm glad I can't look it up."

"It's an old Norwegian dish. See, you take dried whitefish and—"

"Jacob, if you make me vomit you're going to have to clean it up."

"Never mind, then." He winked at Arkad, then looked more serious. "If the Pirate King's got a radio, it'll be just a couple of hours before he figures out you were lying. At most, we've got however long it takes to send a messenger there and back." Jacob looked around the echoing empty cargo unit. "Inventory: I have a pair of pants. You have a pair of shoes. Ree has a survival suit and underwear. Did they leave anything in your pockets, Ree?"

"No," she said. "And they searched inside my suit, too."

"This hold has...I don't even know what that thing is."

"I think it's part of a pump," said Arkad. Even working together neither of them could move it.

"And most of a dead fish. That's all. Anybody have any superweapon plans?"

"If we could get out maybe we..." Ree began, then stopped.

"Okay, how about this?" said Jacob. "When they come back, as soon as we get out of the hatch, I'll rush the one with the sprayer. You two scatter, try to find a boat and get away."

"No," said Arkad. He had once seen a Vziim take a shot from an acid generator during a fight over who would control one of the harbor cranes in Ayaviz. Even with a Vziim's thick oily fur and tough skin, the boiling acid had burned an area bigger than Arkad's outstretched fingers, clear through the skin and deep into the muscle below. That Vziim had used a cart to get around ever afterward.

"Any chance you could squeeze through that vent?" Jacob pointed at the ceiling. Arkad and Jacob tried to pry off the bar blocking the center of the vent hole, but it was attached too solidly. While they were trying, they heard a noise from the door of the cargo unit, and were dazzled by bright daylight as it swung open.

"That was quick," said Jacob.

"Boss wants to talk to you more," said the Pfifu at the door, holding his spear ready. Two more were behind him with sprayers.

Instead of taking them to the fish-shaped building, the guards led the three captives to a space nearby where stout girders held a couple of the barges apart, making a sheltered little pool for Pfifu to soak. The guards ushered them right to the edge of the water, and the burned old Pfifu surfaced in front of them.

"You tell me what our friend Wukong said," Arkad asked, trying to sustain the lie.

"No word back yet," said the old one. "I want to know why you three are here." He gestured, *"You dive in deep, cold waters."*

"Should we tell him about the *Rosetta*?" Arkad asked Jacob and Ree after translating.

"I don't see why not," said Ree.

"She's got a point," Jacob added.

"We seek a space ship on this world," Arkad explained in pidgin. "An old ship full of the wealth of our folk."

"You tell me where it is," said the old Pfifu.

"It is far from here, in the hot dry noon lands."

"You tell me what wealth is in the ship." He added in a gesture, *"A well-crafted lie will at least entertain me."*

Arkad turned to Jacob. "What *is* on the *Rosetta*?" he asked. "You never answered when I asked."

"Operational security. But Captain Morgan here doesn't look like he's working for the Elmisthorn, and nobody else seems to give a damn anyway. Tell him the *Rosetta* holds a big chunk of humanity's cultural and historical heritage. Artworks and historical artifacts from half the cultures on Earth."

Turning that into pidgin wasn't easy. "The ship is full of things my folk have made. Some are good to look at, and some are old and were part of big things that went on."

"That is not wealth," said the Pfifu, and gestured, *"Useless things have no value. Beauty without utility is a sterile egg."*

When Arkad translated that for Jacob, the older man sat down on the edge of the pool and leaned forward. "You tell this... Pfilistine that he's wrong, for two reasons. Ready? First: historical artifacts *are* useful. They provide a link to the past and help preserve our identity. The Elmisthorn won't be able to turn humans into obedient little slaves as long as we can keep that connection to who we were."

"Slow down," said Arkad to Jacob, and then began laboriously translating. "My friend says you are wrong," he said in pidgin to the Pfifu pirate chief. "He says you are wrong two ways. The first way you are wrong is that old things have much use. They help us know of past time, and who we are, and that helps keep us free."

"You tell me how your folk lost your world then!" snapped the old Pfifu, gesturing angrily, *"Pride and wisdom and love of beauty mean nothing when a predator has you in its jaws."*

"Second," Jacob went on, "it *is* possible for something to have value purely for its aesthetic merits, because otherwise there is no point to making things aesthetically pleasing at all, and everything around here has obviously been made with attention to—"

"Stop, stop!" said Arkad. "I don't know half of what you're saying even in English."

"Sorry, I shifted into lecture mode there for a second. Okay, tell him beauty has value of its own, because no one would make beautiful things if it didn't. Simple enough?"

Arkad translated, and the pirate chief—obviously enjoying the argument—replied promptly, "But things look good if they work well." He gestured, *"Our ability to feel beauty and ugliness comes from our ability to judge whether a partner is healthy or a tool is well made."*

When Jacob heard this from Arkad, he started to launch into a reply, then stopped himself. "Hang on. Should I be just agreeing with him?"

"Oh, no!" said Arkad, almost feeling shocked. "Pfifu love arguments, especially when you use complicated logic. You're doing a great job."

Over the next couple of hours, Jacob and the pirate chief came to an agreement on the beginnings of a theory of aesthetics, but remained completely irreconcilable on the importance of history.

Finally, Arkad had to call a stop, as he had to repeat both sides of the conversation and was losing his voice. The pirate chief ordered some fresh water for him and permitted his captives a short break, but half an hour later he hauled himself out of the sea and took a seat on the deck next to where Arkad and Jacob were resting. Ree groaned when she saw him approach, and even Jacob sighed a little.

"You tell me why you think old things help keep your folk free," the Pfifu began without preamble. *"A warrior does not burden himself with loot until the battle is won."*

"Okay," said Jacob after hearing Arkad's translation. "Tell him this: the Elmisthorn want to cut off humanity from our own history and culture, and make humans part of their own civilization. By reminding humans of what we've accomplished, and our own identity, we can oppose that."

Arkad cleared his scratchy throat and told the pirate, "Those who took our world want my folk to know of their ways and not our own. The old things from the ship can tell our folk of our old ways."

"Is this some kind of sophisticated torture?" Ree asked. "Forcing us to sit out in the broiling sun and listen to a boring argument?"

"I don't know. I'm starting to like this guy. How many pirate captains have a theory of beauty?" said Jacob.

The next few hours were a nightmare for Arkad. Pfifu did not sleep, so the old pirate chief kept coming back every time he thought of some new argument, and Arkad had to translate increasingly complicated ideas back and forth between English and pidgin. Sheer fatigue made Arkad start falling asleep in the middle of translating, so that his responses got less and less coherent—which of course meant he had to spend even more time straightening out misunderstandings.

He was trying to express to the Pfifu what Jacob meant by "a sense of group identity" when he saw something at the edge of the deck behind the old Pfifu. It was a hand—a delicate-looking human hand, chalk-white and glistening wet in the sunlight. A pale head appeared behind it, rising just high enough to reveal Baichi's all-black eyes, and then both head and hand disappeared.

Arkad tried to sound casual when he asked Jacob, "Did you see that?"

"See what?"

"Never mind." Maybe he had dreamed it. He finished explaining Jacob's position to the pirate leader, and then fought to stay awake while the old Pfifu began his own long-winded reply.

"I know that your folk are not like mine, and that you like to be in a group more than my kind do. But I do not grasp how a thing can make a group more strong. It seems to me that the folk have a bond to the thing, not to the group." His tentacles added, *"Fish can form a school and swim together, but what fish will follow a floating scrap of plastic?"*

"He says he doesn't understand how old things can make people feel more loyal to a group," Arkad said to Jacob.

"It's obvious: the artifact can serve as a potent symbol. That's why it's so important that we keep the *Rosetta* out of the grabby mouths of the Elmisthorn. Otherwise they'll be able to co-opt the symbolic power of human history."

As Arkad struggled to turn that into pidgin, he heard loud hoots and the sound of loud chimes from the upcurrent edge of the raft, near the giant anchor pipe. He saw a billow of smoke rising from that direction, and smelled butanol fumes and burning plastic.

"Trap them," the old pirate ordered, before whirling off in the direction of the smoke. One of the guards poked the humans with her spear butt and pointed to the cargo container.

"We should run for it now," said Arkad quietly, as the three of them got to their feet.

"Yep," said Jacob casually. "NOW!" He made a grab for the acid generator, pinning the two tentacles the Pfifu was using to hold it under his right arm and swinging both of them around to face the one with the spear.

Arkad bolted, running along the deck in the downcurrent direction, away from the smoke, toward where all the smaller boats were tied up. He risked a look back at Jacob.

The spear carrier swung the fan-shaped head of her weapon at Jacob, who blocked it with the acid generator. A feed line cracked with the blow, and foul-smelling sulfur dioxide hissed into the air. Both Jacob and the Pfifu he was grappling with immediately let go of the weapon, and all three combatants danced back warily as the acid generator bounced and spun on the deck, still hissing. Jacob took the opportunity to hurl the now-disarmed Pfifu at the other one, and sprint away from them, following Arkad.

Ahead, Arkad could see several Pfifu hurrying to intercept him. When Pfifu wanted to move fast on land, they tilted their bodies and spun, whirling along with only one foot touching the ground and their tentacles held tight against their sides. They were fast enough, but not agile. He grabbed a post to swing himself into a sharp left turn, and jumped across the narrow gap between hulls to the next barge.

A gorgeous gold Itooti dove at Arkad, trailing a sharp grapple from his feet. Arkad ducked to avoid it, stumbled, and fell sprawling on the deck, sliding on the wet steel. He scrambled to his feet and risked another look around. Jacob was behind him, and half a dozen Pfifu were scrambling from hull to hull, coming at Arkad from both right and left. Ahead there was only one barge left, and then the ocean.

At that moment Arkad came to a decision: better to take his chances in the ocean rather than get acid-sprayed or slashed or strangled. He ran as hard as he could, straight ahead, leaping the gap to the last barge and sprinting across it to the edge. He could hear Jacob behind him; he had no idea where Ree was or what had happened to her.

The edge of the barge was just ahead. He jumped, stretching into a dive as he fell, and splashed into the sea. The water here, in the salty northwest current, was warm, and he stayed in place, treading water until Jacob hit the surface a few meters away.

Just then something grabbed his ankle and pulled him down. He struggled and kicked, but whatever it was, it was strong. It pulled him into cold dark water.

"Where the heck did you find a submarine?" Jacob demanded, once he could breathe again.

He was the last of them, and had been the most difficult for Baichi to catch. Arkad had to take the controls and hold them steady while she stood on his back, with only her shins inside the membrane canopy that held the sub's bubble of air, and groped for Jacob's kicking feet. She was very heavy.

"The Pfifu had three of them," she said. "I took the one that looked big enough for us and disabled the others. The difficult part was finding you. I tracked down some of our gear in one of the cargo holds. Ree's wrist computer sends out a tracer signal every five minutes, so I simply followed that."

Ree looked surprised at the news. "Better shut that off," said Jacob. "Don't want anyone else tracking us."

"We thought you drowned," said Arkad.

Baichi looked at him, expressionless as usual. "I don't breathe unless I want to."

"Nice little boat," said Jacob, looking around. The submersible was pretty bare-bones: a four-meter boat with electric water-jet motors, topped by a retractable canopy of smart membrane. The membrane let solid objects pass through, but not air and water. Arkad amused himself by sticking his hand through and pulling it back, entirely dry. Once he put his hand in sideways, then bent his fingers so that they were separated at the knuckles but still touching at the fingertips, and was rewarded with a spray of cold seawater.

The controls were simple and bore faded, flaking labels in the elaborate, curving Pfifu script. There were prominent warnings that the canopy could only be used at depths of less than ten meters. Judging from some of the droppings on the floor and graffiti, the sub had often carried Itooti. Arkad figured that a squadron of subs with flyers aboard could patrol a vast area without being spotted. No wonder the pirates had been able to dominate the straits.

"We'd better keep moving," said Jacob. "It won't take those Pfifu long to miss a sub. Set course west, Mr. Arkad, and full speed ahead."

"Aye aye," said Arkad. There were four throttles on the floor, spaced symmetrically around the pilot's stool. He had to pull up on the throttles to make the sub move, which grew tiresome very quickly. With Ree's help, Arkad improvised some more convenient controls using string and a pair of the tent rods.

The power cells for the water jets lasted just over twenty hours, long enough for Arkad to trade off piloting with Baichi and then relieve her when he woke again. Toward the end, Arkad could feel the thrust getting sluggish, and finally blew the ballast tanks to take them up. The flat-bottomed submersible rocked dreadfully on the surface, so they left the membrane canopy up and just stuck the oars right through it in order to row.

All four of them took turns at the oars, though by unspoken consent, Baichi's turns lasted longer than anyone else's. She didn't sweat and, in any event, could drink seawater if she had to. The others strained the ability of Jacob's water-purifying canteen to produce enough drinking water.

When he wasn't rowing, Arkad read. He was delighted to get WOL back, and celebrated by rereading one of his old favorites, about a scientist who went on a sea voyage. At one point he looked up at Jacob, who was taking a turn at the oars. "Can animals on Earth really talk?"

"What?"

"In a lot of my stories people talk to animals. But there are others where they can't, or where the animals only talk to each other. There's nothing about talking animals in my encyclopedia. Does that really happen?"

"Well," said Jacob, with pauses as he pulled at the oars. "When I was a kid...I saw plenty of people...who talked to their pets...but the animals...never talked back...so I'm afraid... the answer is no."

Arkad had suspected that was likely to be the truth, but it still made him feel a little sorry for people growing up on Earth, especially back in the days before star travel. They only had other humans to talk to. It meant, he realized, that they didn't know the difference between being intelligent and being human. For most of his own life, Arkad's face had been rubbed hard in the differences between his own ways and those of the species he lived among.

Compared to any Itooti, he was patient, calm, and persistent. Pfifu thought him unable to appreciate beauty, but constant and dependable. His Vziim friend Zvev had once told him to his face that he was too quick to forgive and lived too much in the present rather than planning for the future and remembering the past. She was always thinking of her family, both the long dead and those to come.

Looking at Jacob, Ree, and Baichi, Arkad could see that they shared many of his own traits. Without other beings to point those things out, how had people on Earth been able to separate their own personalities from human nature?

After watching Pfifu conduct long logical arguments to decide who was best qualified to lead, or Vziim scheming for rank, or Itooti trying to outdo each other in boasting, Arkad could see that the four of them let Jacob lead simply because he took charge and acted like a leader. Evidently that was just how humans did it.

When Jacob's shift at the oars ended, he rummaged in his remaining bag and tossed Arkad a shirt and a pair of pants. "Put these on. You'll probably have to roll up the sleeves and the legs. I think we can rig up some kind of belt."

Arkad put the clothes on; the shirt reached almost to his knees. He tried tucking it into the trousers the way Jacob did, but that made a huge uncomfortable wad of cloth, so in the end he just left it untucked. He was fascinated by the buttons. So many of his stories had mentioned buttons, and now Arkad had buttons of his own! Joseph showed him how they worked. The zipper on the trousers was also a source of endless enjoyment.

After a few minutes, something occurred to Arkad, and he nudged Jacob. "How do you shit in these?"

"You don't. You take 'em off."

"What if someone steals them while you're squatting?"

Jacob shrugged. "It's never happened to me before."

Arkad resolved privately to tie the trousers around his neck when he needed to empty his bowels, just in case.

They had been rowing for about sixteen hours when Ree pointed off to the southwest. "What's that?"

A dark spot on the horizon became a line stretching from south to west, with a golden streak and fleeting white dots where it met the blue-gray water.

"That," said Jacob, "is land. We made it."

Getting ashore was almost a disaster. It was Baichi's turn at the oars, and she rowed steadily toward the line of orange sand south and west of them. As the submersible got into shallow water, the surf began to toss it about violently.

"Do you need me to take over?" Arkad asked Baichi. "You've been rowing awhile."

She didn't answer, and her steady rowing tempo didn't change.

The ocean swell turned into surf, with foaming white crests as the tops of the waves outran their bases. At first it was exciting as the breakers slammed into the boat from behind and drove it faster toward the beach. But each wave made the thin transparent membrane of the canopy bulge inward ominously.

About a quarter mile out, the bottom of the boat began to scrape the bottom between waves. The first few were just grinding scrapes in the sand, but then the boat struck hard, knocking Arkad to his knees. The next moment, he was drenched as a wave hit the immobile boat and broke completely through the membrane.

"Grab the bags!" Jacob yelled. "We'll have to wade to shore!"

Getting to the beach was a struggle. The water where they had grounded was about waist-deep, so Arkad could hold one bag over his head and keep it out of the water. He had to pace himself, pushing forward when the water was dropping around him, then bracing himself for the slam of the next wave hitting him from behind. After the crest of the wave passed, he could float for a moment and let it pull him forward until his feet found the bottom again, and then wade four or five steps again. It took them a good fifteen minutes to reach dry land, and all of them—even Baichi—flopped down to rest on the rusty orange sand.

CHAPTER 8

"**S**O," SAID JACOB AFTER ABOUT TWENTY MINUTES. "WHERE ARE we?"

He dug through his bag and pulled out the map. He spread it on the sand and they all crowded around.

According to Jacob's map—and Arkad's vague memories—the thousand-kilometer strait separating the twilight lands from the main continent was bounded by two peninsulas. The one they had set out from, to the east, was mountainous and carved by glaciers into many bays and offshore islands, while the one to the west—where they were currently standing—was lower, broader, and on the northern side had a line of barrier islands stretching northwest from the tip, guarding a belt of coastal swamp.

"I think we're on one of these," said Jacob, indicating the line of long skinny barrier islands. "If we're lucky, it's inhabited or there's a connection to the mainland. If we're not lucky, we're marooned. What's our food situation?"

"There are only a few food bars, and about a kilo of soybean butter. We do have a whole bottle of vitamin supplements, though," said Ree. She looked over at Arkad. "How good are you at finding things to eat?"

"I know most things that are safe." He tapped the pouch holding his book. "My mother started a list, and I've been adding to it my whole life. It has all the foods that are safe, the ones that are really dangerous, and the ones that taste best."

Jacob squinted at the sun, which hung about a quarter of the

119

way up the sky to the west. "We're going to want shelter. Which way's more likely to lead somewhere?"

Arkad shrugged. Jacob looked northwest, then southeast, then said, "Well, we're going west anyway."

The beach sloped very gently up from the water's edge, and then the loose orange sand gave way to a dense carpet of thin brown plants which grew in horizontal coils, half underground and half above. The coils tangled in among each other to create a surface almost like a thick rug, very pleasant to walk on—which was fortunate because only a few meters back from the beach, the coil carpet was shaded out by tall spiky plants with sharp edges, like a thicket of swords.

They walked until hunger and fatigue made them stop again. Arkad waded in the surf, looking for some of the little flat-bodied burrowing creatures he had sometimes gathered on the seashore near Ayaviz with Fuee. The ones here were smaller, with longer bodies. He took a bite of one and it tasted about the same—sweet and kind of rusty.

It seemed as though years had passed since he had left his friends behind in Ayaviz, but when he thought about it, Arkad realized he had only slept a few dozen times since then. He wondered if Tiatatoo's wing was mending, and if Zvev had kept her promise to look after him.

Jacob built a fire of bones and wood cast up on the sand by the surf, and they cooked the sand burrowers by wrapping them in wet turf and letting them steam. "Not bad," Jacob pronounced. "Some tartar sauce would help, but one can't be picky." They each had three of the burrowers and went to sleep hungry.

When Arkad woke, it was dark and he couldn't move. Something was wrapped around him, squeezing with increasing force in waves moving from his head to his feet. His right arm was pinned at his side, and his left was folded across his chest with his left hand resting on his right shoulder. He tried to push out with his left arm and found that whatever was wrapped around him was stretchy and slick and slightly warm. It was hard to breathe.

It suddenly dawned on Arkad that he was being swallowed. He kicked and pushed with his arms and twisted his head around, trying to get more air. Above him he could see a light, and realized it must be the mouth of whatever was eating him.

With painful struggles he managed to get his left arm extended above his head and groped around. He could feel moving air and sand, and what must have been the lips of the thing eating him, around his wrist. Pulling with his left arm, kicking and flexing his body, he pulled his body back up the thing's throat and took a welcome breath of fresh air. Now he could get his elbow out and lever himself upward until his head emerged. He could see Ree and Jacob stretched out on the sand, sound asleep.

"Help!" he shouted.

Jacob looked up, spent what seemed like an eternity staring at Arkad in blank amazement, then scrambled to his feet while smacking Ree on the shoulder to wake her. He grabbed Arkad's arm and pulled while kicking at the thing trying to swallow him.

"Ow!" Arkad yelled as Jacob's booted foot got him hard in the side, with nothing but the muscular wall of the thing eating him to cushion the blow.

"Sorry." Jacob stopped kicking and pulled harder, until Arkad's arm felt as if it was about to pop out of its socket.

Behind Jacob, Arkad could see Ree looking around for something to use as a weapon.

"Never mind that, come help me pull!" called Jacob.

She crawled over and grabbed the edge of the thing's mouth, peeling it down off Arkad's chest. The creature itself was now actively trying to get rid of Arkad and get away. The waves of pressure had reversed direction, and the thing was wriggling backward, away from Jacob and Ree.

Now that he was halfway free, Arkad could look down and see what was devouring him. It was a simple tube, colored to match the ground below, with walls only a couple of centimeters thick. The tube was stretched over his lower half, and below his feet, it was only about as thick as his thigh. The long tube, or body, or trunk, or whatever it was, stretched away between the sword plants.

Ree moved down to Arkad's feet and stomped her foot on the thing just below the bulge which enclosed him, using her weight to squeeze him out.

He got his right hand free and began pushing the thing's mouth down past his hips. Once they were out he could kick and wriggle and finally free his legs as Jacob dragged him away from the creature. As soon as he was out, the tube withdrew rapidly into the thicket.

"Are you okay? What *was* that?" Jacob asked as soon as Arkad was free.

"I don't know. I've never heard of anything like that before."

"Well, I guess it's good to hear they're not common. I just wish someone could tell me about all the *other* dangerous things around here you don't know about."

"Where's Baichi?" Arkad asked, looking around. "Do you think—"

"No," said Jacob firmly. "Wherever she is, she hasn't been swallowed by something in her sleep. For one thing, she doesn't sleep. Still, I wish she was here, because right now I kind of feel like choosing a different place to camp. How long were we out, anyway?"

"Six hours," said Ree.

"Good enough, I guess. Let's pack up and start moving. If she's ahead of us, we'll meet her on the way back, and if she's behind us, she can catch up."

The bags were a lot lighter than they had been before being looted by the pirates, but the one on Arkad's back still felt heavy. Jacob carried two of them, and they set out southwest along the beach. The belt of coiled turf was too useful as a walkway, but all three now kept a careful watch on the thicket of blade-shaped plants in case more predators wanted to taste a human.

"That little encounter suggests we're pretty far from any civilization," said Jacob as they walked. "I don't imagine anyone would want things like that around if they could avoid it, ecological balance be damned."

"Jacob!" said Ree, sounding genuinely shocked.

"Relax. I'm not talking about driving the critters to extinction. Anyway...haven't you noticed something weird about this planet's ecosystem?"

"Not really," she said. Arkad shook his head.

"I think it's artificial. Lots of species from other worlds—I think I've seen those blade things elsewhere—and Arkad said there's food plants for all the intelligent species."

"They all brought plants and animals with them."

"There you go. Maybe we should scatter some seeds around. Got any rats in your bag, Ree? They go everywhere humans do."

"If you think it's an artificial ecosystem, why are there predators like that thing?" said Ree.

"Artificial doesn't mean the same thing as safe. At least, it doesn't have to. Whoever set it up apparently felt the need for some hunters or scavengers. What I can't understand is how it stays in equilibrium. You'd think it would take constant management. Ah, there's Baichi," said Jacob, pointing ahead at a familiar small figure in a dark hooded cloak. She stood absolutely still as they approached, even though it took them nearly ten minutes to reach her.

"Let me guess," Jacob called out as they approached. "You didn't find anything up ahead."

"I did find something," she said. "I found water. This island ends at a wide channel."

"Lovely," said Jacob. "We either turn back and look for a way to the mainland—which may not exist—or try to come up with some way to cross the water."

They camped by the channel, on the inland side of a large dune. The channel itself was a good two or three kilometers across, and it didn't take an expert to see that the water was perpetually rough. On the inland side was a broad lagoon, much calmer, and far off they could just make out a dark line of land on the horizon.

"I guess we have to build a boat," said Jacob.

"Out of what?" asked Ree. "Sand?"

"We've got a waterproof tent—I'm sure we can cobble together some kind of coracle. It just has to be big enough to carry two at a time; we can make multiple trips back and forth."

She looked at him as if making calculations in her head, and finally agreed.

They spent the next several hours gathering materials. The only things on the barrier island stiff enough to make any kind of structure were the sword plants, which meant that they had to find a way to keep the sharp edges of the plants from cutting the creepers they used to lash them together, or punching holes in the tent fabric. Just to complicate matters, the sharp edges were the strongest and stiffest part of the plants, so cutting them off left only the stringy flexible core.

When they stopped working to eat and sleep, Baichi did not wander off as usual, but took a place next to Arkad and sat in silence while he finished his steamed bottom crawlers.

At first he tried to wait her out, but his curiosity overwhelmed his patience. "Yes?" he said at last.

"Your storage device," she said, pointing at the pouch where Arkad kept WOL. "I want to examine it."

He took out the battered old reader and handed it to her. "Be careful with it."

She began tapping the touchscreen. "Why do you carry this around with you?"

"I like the stories. There's hundreds of them—at least, there used to be. I can't get to all of them anymore."

"I want to transfer them directly to my own memory," she said. After a slight pause she added, "May I do so?"

"Well...why don't I just read you something?"

"That will take much more time."

"I think you'll like it better. I mean, that's how you're supposed to learn them, right? By reading or listening. It wouldn't be the same if you just scanned the whole thing."

Another pause, and then she gave him another one of her rare smiles. "Yes. Please read me a story."

He took WOL back and pulled up his list of favorites. "This is a good one," he said, and then cleared his throat before beginning. "Chapter one: The River Bank. The Mole had been working very hard all the morning, spring-cleaning his little home...."

She sat beside him, looking out at the ocean as he read for half an hour. When he was done with the first chapter, he put WOL away and had a long drink from the purifier canteen.

"Why are you stopping?" she asked him.

"I'm tired and my throat's dry. I'll read you another chapter next time we stop to sleep."

"But that will be nearly thirty hours from now!" she said. Arkad smiled at the note of genuine disappointment in her voice. He could dimly recall feeling the same way when his mother stopped reading to him.

Jacob spoke up, surprising Arkad who had assumed he was asleep. "When I was a kid, my father tried reading me *Treasure Island* at bedtime, but I got so keyed up wondering how it was going to come out that I wouldn't sleep for another hour. Finally he switched to just after dinner, so that I'd have enough time to calm down again before bed."

"I am not keyed up," said Baichi. "I control my emotions. And I do not need to sleep."

"Maybe *The Wind in the Willows* is too exciting for you," said Arkad. "I could read you something quieter. How about *Goodnight Moon*?"

That brought a suppressed laugh from Jacob, and Baichi lightly punched Arkad in the shoulder. "You are both being very silly. Perhaps it is past your bedtime."

"You're the one who wanted me to stay up and read to you," said Arkad, stretching out on the sand. He could hear Jacob give another chuckle, and then there was nothing but the sound of the waves.

About twenty hours later Arkad was sitting at the water's edge, trying to weave the stiff, sharp-edged plants into some kind of framework, when a flash of light out on the water caught his eye. He scanned the expanse of smooth water and haze, then saw the flash again. Something out there was reflecting sunlight at him. And whatever the shiny thing was, it was moving.

His shouts and waving must have attracted someone's attention because he saw a dark spot where the flash had been, which grew until he could see it was a boat—a wide flat-bottomed boat ten meters long, almost a barge. More than a dozen assorted Pfifu and Vziim were aboard, and a pair of burly Vziim near the front of the boat were rowing it with long sweeps.

As the boat came closer to shore, Arkad noted with alarm that there were a lot of weapons on board. All the Vziim except the ones rowing had armored greaves on their arms and long steel claws over their fingers. The Pfifu had polearms or projectors.

A single female Vziim wearing elaborate segmented armor and gold-plated claws reared up out of the crowd and called over to Arkad. "You tell me what you are."

"We are four *humans* stuck on this land. We need a ride to shore. You tell me if you will give us a ride on your boat."

"This band of mine are bound for war," said the Vziim female. "We can not take on those who will not fight. If you will fight for me, you can get on my boat."

Arkad relayed that to Jacob, who grimaced. "They want us to join up or they'll leave us here? Wonderful. Ask if they can take a message and send someone for us."

"We go now to seek the foe," said the female when Arkad had translated Jacob's question. "If you fear too much to fight by my side, then I will not help you when the fight is done. You choose now."

"Vindictive bitch, isn't she?" Jacob commented. He turned to the other two. "What do you think, ladies? Apparently we have the choice of going with this weird little press-gang, or trying the improvised-raft scheme."

"You know I will not fight," said Baichi.

"I assume you're planning to desert as soon as we're on the mainland," said Ree.

"Of course. After all, an agreement made under duress is never binding," said Jacob. "Okay, Arkad, tell them we accept."

"We will fight for you if you take us to land," Arkad called to the Vziim. She said something to the males at the sweeps, and a few minutes later the boat's flat bottom grounded on the sand a dozen meters out. The four humans gathered their remaining baggage and waded out to the boat, where helpful hands and tentacles pulled them aboard.

They were shoved, in a more or less friendly way, to the center of the boat, where the armored female sat atop a pile of metal crates. "We take you to fight," she said. "If you fight well and win, you get loot and we let you go."

"Ask her who we're going to be fighting," Jacob whispered to Arkad.

"You tell me who we fight."

"We go to fight my vile kin and take back my home. All will get pay."

The rowers got the barge off the sand and turned around, and then set up a steady if somewhat leisurely pace across the lagoon.

As they got away from the channel, the water grew more and more calm, until the waves were nothing more than ripples, barely a hand's width high. The hazy air seemed to muffle sounds, until Arkad felt as though the boat was just sitting still and the sun and sky were nothing but projections on a roof a few meters above him.

The journey across the lagoon took about six hours. Only in the last hour could they see anything of the approaching shore. Long fingers of swampy land fringed by thick bands of floating weed alternated with wide estuaries which branched into smaller and smaller tributaries like the veins of some giant creature.

Beyond the swampy shore a dense forest of huge, feathery,

greenish-purple plants rose dozens of meters high. As the boat entered one of the estuaries, they began to see a few cleared areas, all on the eastern shore where nothing would block the direct sunlight. The houses seemed to be Pfifu construction—elaborately decorated structures shaped to catch the breeze off the water, all of them right on the shore or even built on pilings in the shallows. The clearings held neat rows of fruit vines, arranged on frames which rose at a precise angle back from the shore to maximize the sunlight reaching the plants.

"Okay," Jacob murmured to the other humans. "We're not going to make a run for it too soon. When we get to shore would be the obvious time for us to try it, so that's when they'll be watching us. I think we should wait a couple of hours, act like good little recruits, and then go over the wire."

Out of the corner of his eye, Arkad could see Awiza, the female leader, watching them, so he turned and picked his way through the crowd to stand in front of her. "You say we go to fight your kin. Tell me why we fight."

"My twin stole what our mom gave both of us."

"You tell us why you do not just build a new one of your own." That was the usual path for Vziim females who came out on the losing side of an inheritance dispute.

"You ask and ask so much! We have much time so I tell you the whole tale," she said. "Then you know why we need to hire you to fight for us, and then you keep quiet."

One of the male Vziim said something to her in their family's private language, and she answered him before looking back at Arkad.

"I am Awiza," she said in pidgin. "Long time past my mom Wavviz built a great dam of stone and dirt on a stream in the hills. She dug shafts and brought wise techs to set up great wheels to run mills which cut logs into boards, or spin plant stalks and hair to make yarn, or grind stone to dust to sift out ore. Her male kin ran the mills and sold the goods, while Wavviz built strong forts to guard the dam, and deep shafts hid well. We had fish traps and pens for our herds.

"She wed three, all strong and rich from old clans. Each male had to beat one of her kin in a fight to wed Wavviz—but it was just a show, not like in the old time. She had many young, and our clan grew great.

"Wavviz was wise, and as she got old, she did not tell us which one would get it all at her death. We all did hard work to show her how good an heir each of us was. I built a keep on top of the dam, to catch the wind and let us watch for foes. My twin dug locks so that boats can pass down the stream and pay us a toll. Our male sibs kept herds and bred more beasts. They held our land and kept the peace, and some went off to win a wife and sire young.

"Then Wavviz was dead. My bad twin Zveemaa found the key she had with my name on it. She stole the key and put her own name in place of mine and kept the dam and all Wavviz's wealth. I told our kin of her lie, but they did not hear me. With eight of my true male kin, I fought my twin to make her tell the truth.

"I had a plan to find the room where she slept and hide there to catch her, but Zveemaa is hard to trick. She had a thin cord at the door so she could tell if one had gone in. We fought and our kin fought. Two of my male kin and four of hers fell in her room, but she had more. I set off a flash and we fled.

"We went to my male kin Vemviizuvo who has a wife with a strong house by the sea. She let us stay for a time but did not give us any help to hire a band to fight, and soon she heard the lies of my twin and said we must go. When we left, I took as much iridium from her vault as I could, for she is on the side of my twin so I am not her friend.

"With my loot I got a small band, but not as big as I need to fight Zveemaa. So we go to these small towns to hire more troops. Now I have what I need so we go to take back my dam and kill my twin."

On the west side of the estuary, the rowers steered the boat up a side channel barely wider than the boat itself. The big feathery plants overhung it completely, so that it was like entering a tunnel. After about a hundred meters, they reached a place where the Vziim had constructed a two-meter palisade of rocks and dirt, faced with wicked-looking stakes. Beyond the wall Arkad could see tents and a plume of smoke.

"All off here!" Awiza shouted. Her brothers urged the Pfifu and Vziim in the boat onto the shore, and passed gear to them. Arkad and the other humans carried their own bags.

"Not yet," said Jacob. "Be ready when I give the word—and don't unpack."

Beyond the wall there were half a dozen large tents, all solidly fortified with walls of dirt and stone. Each tent had a ditch around it, and the ditches were connected in a carefully graded network to carry water through the camp and flush away waste. This, for Vziim, was a bare-bones temporary encampment.

The four humans found space in a tent where a trio of Pfifu were not happy to find themselves sharing with unknown aliens. They didn't say anything, but one gestured to the others, *"Let us hope these intrusive creatures quickly meet death in combat, before the loot is divided up."*

Jacob peered out through the gap between the solid wall of the tent and its fabric roof. "I take it the wall around the camp is for defense, not to keep us in, since there's no spikes on this side. If this was the army I served in, we'd be pulling duty right now, scrubbing latrines or whatever. It's kind of weird that they're just letting everybody hang around like it's some kind of low-budget resort."

"I think we should just go right now," said Ree. "The longer we wait—who knows what could happen?"

"I think you're right. I keep wanting to say we should wait until dark," said Jacob. "But that's not going to happen, is it? What an inconvenient planet. We need some kind of diversion. Any ideas?"

"Start a fire," said Baichi.

"We need a diversion, not a massacre," said Ree.

"I think I could start a fight," said Arkad. "There are at least a dozen Pfifu here."

"So?" asked Ree.

"Pfifu like to be alone. They form partnerships for a business or to raise a family, but they can't really understand the idea of belonging to anything bigger. So once you get more than maybe ten Pfifu together, some of them will be unhappy about how things are being run, or what they're trying to do. Usually they just leave, but if they can't, everyone gets more and more cross. I can try to stir them up."

"I'm not sure..." Jacob began, but Arkad didn't hear the rest because he had already dashed outside.

He left the tent and walked across the camp. Jacob was right: it was surprising how little was going on. In all the stories Arkad had read, armies getting ready for battle spent their time doing exercises, or polishing their weapons, or something military. But most of the company inside the dirt wall were idle. The only ones who seemed to be busy were Awiza and her brothers. They were constantly going back and forth between their respective tents, or sending out messengers, or checking on the half-buried weapon store which stood right next to Awiza's tent.

The other Vziim in the company were mostly sleeping, but the Pfifu—who didn't sleep anyway—were awake and bored. Arkad found half a dozen of them sitting on stools around a pair of braziers in the food tent, cooking fish on skewers. He stopped to talk with the smaller group—a pair who looked like partners.

"I wish to learn of your kind," he said in pidgin.

One of them poked a tentacle tip close to Arkad's face, focusing on his mouth. "Do that one more time," he said, while gesturing, *"This curious being has a hinge in its head!"*

Arkad pretended not to notice the tentacle signs. "I am not from here and have not seen your kind much. Tell me how you live."

"We are Pfifu. We are here to fight for pay," he replied, but added, *"It is all sticks held together with stretchy strings, with a thick opaque hide on top. No artist could imagine such a thing!"*

Across the brazier his companion took a lens from her belt pouch and held it in front of one tentacle to get a better look at Arkad. *"It reminds me of Itooti, but bigger and flightless. Do you think it might walk the same worlds where they soar?"*

He passed from that pair to the quartet around the other brazier. "I wish to learn of your kind," he repeated.

The larger group were less astonished at his appearance. "I heard of one like you in town once," said one. *"Long ago in the great iron-walled city at the edge of the ice, I heard of an angular flightless thing like this,"* she gestured.

Arkad chose the topic the old pirate chief had been arguing with Jacob about. "I have heard that some of your kind make things that look good. You tell me what you do to make a thing look good."

To Arkad's surprise, these Pfifu didn't rise to the bait. One of the four merely said, "If we knew that, we would not be here now," and with gestures added, *"Attempts to create beauty inevitably bring sorrow."*

"Those two there said the shape of a thing is what looks good," Arkad persisted.

"I doubt they know more than we. Those who do good work, do work. Those who do not do good work must fight or steal or beg." She added, *"Had I learned that when I was young, I could have enjoyed my life much more than I have. Now that I have the knowledge which could make my life happy, I no longer have the time or the good health to apply it."*

Frustrated, Arkad turned to one of the other three around the brazier. "You tell me if you think as those two do, that the shape of a thing is how it looks good."

Only one of them even bothered to aim a tentacle tip at him. "None of us care at all for such things now," he said, and gestured, *"By the time a stream reaches the sea, the water is calm and slow-moving."*

"If you care so much how to make a thing look good, go and do it," said the first one to Arkad, and gestured, *"This being is like a stone asking a statue what child-rearing is like."*

"I guess I waste my time here," said Arkad. As he turned to go, he noticed that the fins on one of the fish being broiled were starting to catch fire. "You cook your fish too long," he cautioned.

"I do not cook too long!" said the Pfifu, who had not spoken before. "These fish need to cook a lot or they taste too strong." With gestures he added, *"The metallic flavor of the carrion they scavenge must be masked by spices and the scent of smoke."*

"That is not true," said the female Arkad had first spoken with. "The fish needs just a light heat to cook it well." She gestured, *"Excessive heat gives the flesh an unpleasant gritty texture."*

"You are a fool to say so! If you do not cook the fish a long time the small things that live in its flesh will make you sick." He used all four tentacles to make an exaggerated satirical gesture: *"If you cook the fish too much, you lose the delightful sensation of parasitic vermin piercing your digestive sac."*

The pair at the other brazier approached. "You can kill the things in the flesh if you soak the fish in sour juice," one said. *"The acidity makes the meat more tender and imparts a wonderful flavor."*

"Strong juice will hide all taste," said the female, waving a skewer holding a half-eaten fish at one of the newcomers. *"One should choose the freshest, fattest fish, cook it lightly, and savor the natural flavors rather than burying them in smoke and marinade."*

"You do not know what is good," said the long-cooking

enthusiast. *"To rely on the innate flavor of the fish leaves no room for skill or craft. A scavenging Itooti could dine as well! Proper cookery reflects the knowledge and dexterity of the cook."*

All six of them were talking and gesturing at once, so Arkad didn't see which one accidentally launched a steaming fishhead from the tip of a skewer with a vehement remark. But he did see it hit the marinating devotee, who responded by hurling himself at the well-done advocate, and in a moment the melee was general.

Mercifully, the Pfifu didn't use their skewers as weapons. Instead they tried to grapple with one another, so the food tent quickly became a huge tangle of tentacles. Arkad had fought plenty of feral young Pfifu on the streets of Ayaviz, so he reacted by jumping back, staying out of reach, swinging a stool at anyone who got too close, and trying to get out of the tent.

Unfortunately for Arkad, the angry hoots and commotion inside had attracted the attention of some Pfifu outside, so the exit was blocked by more tentacled beings who plunged into the brawl with the vigor of people who had been storing up resentments for some time. One of the Vziim in armor tried to break it up, but quickly went down in a writhing mass since most of the accumulated Pfifu resentments involved bossy Vziim. As he tried to fight them off, his thrashing tail happened to hit one of the braziers, knocking it end over end and sending a shower of hot charcoal across the tent like an indoor fireworks display. A few of the coals landed on wood stools or cloth cushions, and soon Arkad's eyes began to sting as the smell of smoke grew stronger.

He gave up on trying to use the entrance, and scrambled up the wall to squeeze through the gap between the fabric roof and the dirt walls. A tentacle wrapped around his foot, and he heard an angry voice say, "You are a fool who can not taste good food!" Arkad kicked the tentacle hard with his free foot and wriggled free, then tumbled down the outside of the wall to the ground and took off at a run.

The other three were waiting behind their tent with the bags. "Any trouble?" asked Jacob.

"Not at all," Arkad replied. Someone back at the food tent was banging a gong. "Let's go right now."

The four of them scrambled up the earthwork, and Arkad risked a look back over the tents. A plume of black smoke rose from the food tent, and he could see a bucket brigade of Pfifu tossing water on the blaze while some of the Vziim tried to drag the burning sections of fabric away from the food and fuel inside the tent.

"You!" An armored Vziim atop the earthwork a few meters away reared up and brandished his steel claws. "You stay in camp."

"Awiza told us to go this way," said Arkad as he began to pick his way among the stakes on the outer slope.

"You tell a lie! You all stop now!"

"If they come after us, scatter," said Jacob. "Keep the sun on your right and keep going inland. The map shows a road there."

The Vziim atop the wall paused to blow a whistle, then dove down the wall in pursuit, his long body slipping easily between the stakes. Arkad knew that once he reached level ground no Vziim could ever catch him.

Then Baichi fell. Arkad saw her go over out of the corner of his eye, and he actually stopped to watch. At first he thought maybe she was doing it on purpose, but then she hit the bottom row of stakes and her bag flew from her grip to spill open on the ground below. Baichi sprawled limp between the stakes, her cloak snagged on the sharp tips, and made feeble twitching movements.

"Jacob! Ree!" he shouted, and abandoned his own bag to dash over to Baichi.

He tried to lift her and was shocked at how heavy she was. Jacob arrived a moment later with a shocked expression. "What *happened* to her?"

"I don't know! She's too heavy to pick up."

"I've got her," said Jacob. He managed to sling Baichi's slender form over his shoulder and then grunted with the effort as he got to his feet.

Just then, four powerful arms gripped Arkad from behind, and he felt the steel claw tips pressing into his skin. "You do not move," said the Vziim.

"Get away!" he yelled to Jacob, who managed to break into a lumbering trot carrying Baichi, and was soon hidden by the giant feather plants.

"I take you to Awiza now," said the Vziim. "She will not be glad. You will not be glad."

CHAPTER 9

AWIZA WAS NOT GLAD AT ALL. SHE SAT IN THE CENTER OF WHAT had been the food tent, while the uninjured Pfifu cleared away the charred bits of cloth and furniture under the eyes of Vziim armed with flame-projectors.

"I should kill you now for what you did," she said. "You said a lie when you said you would fight for me."

"We were stuck by the sea," he reminded her. "We had to get to land and you would not give us a ride."

"I do not care why you said a lie. All I care is if your death will make these fools do what I say."

"If you let me live, I will show how well I can do what you say," he said, trying to sound as humble as possible.

"Yes, you will do that," she said, and said something to her brothers in their private language.

Two of them grabbed Arkad by the arms while a third clutched the back of his head in all four hands, immobilizing it as though it was caught in a vise. Awiza took a round object from her belt pouch, poked it carefully with the tip of one of her claws, then peeled off a layer of plastic from the back of it and stuck it to Arkad's forehead.

The males released him, and Arkad reached up to feel the thing stuck to him. It was shaped like a little dome, and he could feel some liquid sloshing inside it when he moved his head. He tried to pull it off, but it was bonded to his skin.

"It is from off world," said Awiza. "You made my tent burn,

135

so now I make you burn. The stuff in that thing starts fire—you must have seen it in the past. The thing I stuck to your skin will melt in a while, the stuff will flow out, and you will burn."

Arkad felt the shock of fear run through his whole body. "I beg you to take it off me," he began.

She cut him off. "I can take it off you—when we win the fight. I think it will last that long. I got these to put on my twin, to make her tell me where she hid things, but I can spare one for you." She reared up and raised her voice. "I have a lot of them to use if I need to! We will rest, have a meal, and then we go to fight!"

Arkad also learned that he had new living quarters: the floor in one of the tents occupied by Awiza's brothers. He actually managed to sleep, as sheer fatigue overcame his fear. As he dozed off, he did wonder how Baichi was doing. What had happened to her? Was she all right? Were Jacob and Ree going to come searching for him?

When he woke he joined the others for a large, bland but filling meal of boiled seeds mixed with shredded fish and bits of fruit. It was all cooked long enough to make it digestible by everyone in Awiza's little army, and served out in big flat leaves. How to get it into one's mouth was left to individual diners. The Pfifu simply poured it from the leaves into their mouths. The Vziim thinned theirs with river water and lapped it up, complaining all the while about the lack of meat. The few Itooti imitated the Vziim both in method and dissatisfaction.

Arkad preferred the Pfifu method, though it was a bit tricky to slide the hot goop into his mouth without getting it all over his face and chest. He wiped up everything that spilled and shoveled it into his mouth with his fingers, then cleaned up with some water. Some of his hairs were stuck under the incendiary device glued to his forehead, and he borrowed a knife to cut them off so they didn't keep getting in his eyes.

After everyone ate, Awiza harangued them again. "Ten kilometers from here that way"—she gestured to the south, where Arkad could see a line of low hills beyond the feather forest—"is the dam my mom made. My twin Zveemaa has it now, with a scant force to hold it. I know each way in, and I know ways that were hid from her. Here is the job: I give you arms and lead you to the dam. I show you how to get in. You all go in and kill all you find in there. Then I will pay those who live. We go now!"

They marched—well, walked—out of the encampment in single file, and one of Awiza's brothers handed out weapons as each soldier passed. The Pfifu got chopping blades on springy handles, while the Vziim got broad punching-daggers and the Itooti got bags of explosive caltrops. All the arms were so new they still had visible tool marks on them, and the Pfifu immediately set to work tinkering with theirs, tightening the fasteners holding the blades to the handles, honing the edges, and complaining loudly about the poor quality of the weapons.

When Arkad reached the head of the line, the armored Vziim looked at him and hesitated. Finally, he simply asked. "You tell me what you can use," he said.

"You give me those," said Arkad, pointing at a bag of caltrops.

"You do not fly."

In reply, Arkad bent and picked up a stone, then wound up and threw it at the alarm gong in the center of the camp, thirty meters away. The rock hit the gong dead center and rang it with a satisfying deep note. For a moment, everyone stared at the alien boy. Then the Vziim gave him a sack of caltrops. "You pull out the small ring on the side. Then it will blow up when it hits a hard thing, or when some one puts a foot on it."

The bag was small enough for an Itooti to carry, so it only held eight of the little bombs. They each had four sharp points sticking out, and it took Arkad a little while to figure out how best to hold one to throw.

The troops milled about outside the gate until the last in line was armed, then Awiza and her brothers climbed aboard a power-wagon and led the way up the dirt track, heading south toward the hills. A second power-wagon, loaded with all the gear Awiza thought too important to leave unguarded, followed behind.

The next few hours restored Arkad's confidence a little. They marched upriver on the dirt road for a couple of kilometers, then turned left and climbed a slope to reach the top of a line of low hills which extended north from the main range. As soon as they began to climb, they passed out of the forest of giant feather plants and entered a region of woody plants with star-shaped trunks about as thick as Arkad's waist. Among the live trees were stumps wider than Arkad's outstretched arms, sheared off cleanly by power tools.

He wondered which world those plants had come from—the Pfifu home world, the Vziim worlds, or some other planet? He had heard stories that there had been species living on Syavusa which had abandoned their settlements or gone extinct. Perhaps one of them had brought seeds for these plants from some world nobody even remembered anymore.

After five kilometers the little column halted at a little hollow where a second dirt road joined the one they were on. They waited at the intersection for about an hour, and then Arkad heard the sound of power-wagons approaching along the side road. There were four of them, loaded with more soldiers.

The new arrivals looked like professional mercenaries; they all had matching equipment and protective gear, and it all looked well-used and well-maintained. Both Vziim and Pfifu were armed with rugged-looking flame-projectors tipped with long bayonets. The cutting edges of the bayonets had the peculiar rainbow gleam of molecule-thin offworld blades. They didn't greet Arkad's unit, or even give much sign that they noticed them at all. Arkad did see one of the Pfifu troops in the wagons gesture to another, *"From rags and discarded scraps, she constructs an effigy to frighten away scavengers."*

A tough-looking old male Vziim, wearing the same gear as all the others but with insignia of gold and platinum, conferred with Awiza for a long time. Arkad watched with interest as Awiza traded armor with one of her brothers. Then she and the remaining brothers took up flame-projectors and climbed into the wagons with the professionals. The three Itooti from the camp joined them.

"We go now," said the brother wearing Awiza's armor, and led the band of irregulars off the road, up the hillside. About the time they reached the top of the hill, the wagons moved off along the road.

They descended the hills on the other side, into a wider valley with a small river flowing down the middle. A road ran along the riverbank, and they turned south to follow it. The slopes along this valley had been completely cleared of trees. The shadier patches of hillside were pasture, where meat animals browsed on shrubs. Where the land got direct sunlight, big fruit vines were trained along ropes running up the hills.

Arkad wound up marching next to a young male Vziim, who

introduced himself as Veezevazii. He made some practice jabs and slashes with his four punching-daggers as they went, and seemed to know something about Awiza and her sister.

"Awiza is mad," he told Arkad. "That long tale she tells of how her twin stole what was hers by right is all a lie."

"You tell me how you know this is true," said Arkad.

"I tell you the truth. I am kin to one of the males who wed her mom. All Vziim in this land know that Awiza is mad."

"You tell me why you fight on her side, then," asked Arkad. He tapped the device glued to his forehead. "She put this on me so I must fight for her. You tell me what she did to you."

Veezevazii struck a pose, with two blades raised to parry and two ready to strike. "I am here to fight. I want to get loot and make my name known. If we win, I will stay and fight for Awiza some more."

"You tell me what you will do if we lose," asked Arkad glumly.

Veezevazii made a couple of feints at Arkad with his daggers. "I may die if we lose," he admitted. "But I will try to give up first. I am not their mad kin; they do not want me dead. If I fight well and show I am brave, they may hire me."

"You may die!" said Arkad. "We all may die or be hurt."

The Vziim lunged at Arkad and stopped with all four blades just a few centimeters from his face. "I am one of six sons," he said. "My big sis will get our farm when my mom gets too old. I can stay there and tend the herd all my life, and share one room with my male kin, and sire no young. Or I can do this and hope to win fame and loot and pay, so I can woo some girl with a bit of land or a house of her own."

Once down the slope the company marched right up the valley with no attempt at concealment, the Vziim male in Awiza's armor leading the way. After an hour they rounded a final bend in the river and could see their target. The dam was about a kilometer away. Arkad had expected something built of packed dirt or logs, but this was much more impressive. An inward-curving wall of fitted dry-stone masonry rose ten meters from the riverbed. It was flanked by squat, windowless towers, and a single taller tower rose another ten meters from the center of the dam.

River water flowed white and frothy from an outlet at the base of the dam, and a set of locks made of brick and stone climbed up the far side of the valley to connect to the lake behind it.

On this side of the river, a spillway brought water from the dam to three large mill buildings on solid-looking stone foundations, and each mill had its own little waterfall where the stream passed through the generating wheels and tumbled down into the riverbed. Beyond the mills Arkad could make out a more slapdash-looking village of gaily painted wooden buildings jumbled together wherever the ground was level enough to build something.

One of the Pfifu aimed two tentacles at the dam and a third at their Vziim commander. "You tell me how can we fight our way past those thick stone walls." He added with a gesture, *"Windblown spray cannot wear down a cliff; only the power of the sea can do that."*

"We do not do that," said their leader. "They come down to fight us here. You hush now or I stab you."

Arkad had a sudden, terrible thought. He remembered the story about the Toad and the Rat, and how the animals had used a secret passage to get into the house occupied by their enemies—and how they had distracted the occupiers by convincing them they were going to attack the front door. The slapdash nature of this expedition suddenly made perfect sense.

He leaned over to speak to Veezevazii so that nobody else could hear. "We march to a trap," he said.

"You tell me why you think so."

"This force is small and raw, with cheap arms, led by one of Awiza's kin who wears her gear. The folk in the dam will see us and fight—but Awiza and the main force will get in some back way while we die."

Veezevazii thought for a second, and tapped the tips of the daggers together softly. "You may be right," he said. "The main group can ride up past the lake, cross the stream out of sight, and come down on the far side while we march up here."

They were about fifty meters from the mill buildings when Arkad saw a squad of Vziim soldiers drawing up across the space between the stone wall of the mill and a large boulder on the hillside. All but three had shiny steel claws half a meter long fixed to their arms. In the center of the line, a large flame-projector on a cart loomed menacingly, and two of them vigorously worked the handles of a two-person pump to pressurize it while a third lit the pilot light at the muzzle and put one hand on the release lever.

"You tell me what we can do," Arkad asked Veezevazii.

"We fight now, as well as we can, and win or die!" said the young Vziim, and clashed his blades menacingly at the enemy.

Arkad felt so sick he wondered for a second if he had eaten something bad. But he knew it was the thought of fighting. Any moment now, that flame-projector would start pumping burning fuel at him. The Vziim soldiers would start slashing with their steel claws. He and the others would have to start stabbing and slashing back. He could almost feel the sharp steel slicing into his skin.

"You stop now!" shouted one of the Vziim drawn up in a line across the path. "You put down all things to fight with and leave here or we burn you!"

Arkad looked over at his own group's leader in his shiny armor, who brandished his punching dagger and shouted, "You get set to charge!" to his little company. The Vziim and Pfifu recruits gamely raised their weapons, although none of them looked eager to rush at a flame-projector.

"You use those things they gave you," said Veezevazii. "Now is a good time."

Arkad reached into the bag of explosive caltrops he'd been given and pulled out two of them. One went into his left hand, the other into his right. Then Arkad wound up and pitched the one in his right hand directly at the pressure tank of the big flame-projector. It bounced off the tank and went off when it hit the ground, startling the two at the pump but doing no harm. The second exploded when it hit the side of the tank, resulting in an ear-splitting hiss as a seam split.

The defenders' commander shouted something in the secret family language, and the Vziim at the projector yanked down on the release lever. Arkad flinched as a stream of burning liquid flowed—but did not spray—from the muzzle. Even as he watched, the stream dipped until it was simply pouring gently from the muzzle.

"We charge now!" shouted the male in Awiza's armor, and the company of invaders hustled forward, splitting into two groups to avoid the burning stream that flowed down the path and spilled down the riverbank. The Pfifu in the front rank of the attackers began swinging their axes, and the hiss of the leaking tank was drowned out by the clash of steel blades.

The defending commander could count, and realized that his eight Vziim, even with armor and claw blades, would be simply overwhelmed by the larger force of attackers. He snapped something to his troops, and they began to fall back in good order, slashing at any of the attackers who dared press too close.

Arkad took out two more caltrops and lobbed them high, over the heads of the enemy's front rank, to land behind them. One of the little bombs failed to go off, but the second struck one of the defenders on the steel greave protecting one of his four arms and exploded. Arkad was looking right at him and saw the spray of blood and flesh as the explosion tore open the Vziim's arm to the bone, and fragments of the armor and the caltrop barbs flayed the victim's face and another arm.

Arkad had fought before. He had thrown rocks and chunks of brick at people, he had wrestled and bit and punched. Once he had stabbed a Pfifu with his skewer. But he had never hurt anyone as badly as the bomb that had just mangled that Vziim. This was almost worse than being sprayed by the flame-projector, or getting stabbed himself.

The injured Vziim gave a yell and, with his two uninjured arms, tried to wrap a scarf around the one that was jetting blood. His comrades fell back past him, and Arkad watched in horror as Veezevazii hurled himself upon the injured Vziim, stabbing with his punching-daggers at the vulnerable spots behind the shoulder joints.

"Stop!" Arkad shouted, but in the commotion nobody heard him or paid any attention. He looked around him and realized the battle had moved a dozen meters up the trail, and he was standing alone.

Awiza. He had to find Awiza and get this thing off his forehead. In a fight, someone might poke it, even by accident, and firestarter fluid would flow down his face. Veezevazii had suggested Awiza and her mercenaries might be on the far side of the river, attacking across the locks that climbed up the opposite bank in three stages.

Arkad scrambled down the bank, avoiding the little stream of liquid fire from the broken flame-projector. The slope was steep and rocky, with saw-edged vines growing among boulders. He reached a big slab of rock which slanted down into the water, and waded in until he reached the edge of the slab, which was knee-deep. Beyond it, the main channel of the river was deeper. He set down the bag of explosive caltrops as gently as possible at the water's edge, and then dove into the channel.

The water was turbulent and foamy, and Arkad didn't try to fight the current. He let it carry him downstream as he swam across, watching for rocks the whole way. When his knee banged against a boulder on the bottom, he scrambled to his feet and waded up the bank, keeping low in case someone on the dam was watching.

The gate of the lowest lock was just upriver, so he climbed up the slope until he reached a fence. Beyond it, he could see a field of the low, coiled plants, and a herd of at least a dozen large beasts grazing. They were vaavuz, meat animals from the Vziim home planet, and Arkad could see a kind of family resemblance between them and the Vziim—they used four stumpy limbs spaced evenly around their mouths to snatch up food and shovel it in. The most obvious difference was that these beasts also had a pair of thick legs supporting their broad bodies, with a long tail dragging behind to balance the neck.

He got over the fence and glanced nervously at the animals, but they showed no interest in him, so he kept his head low and moved along the fence until it ended at a steep rocky slope where the second lock climbed the river bank. Arkad half-climbed, half-pulled himself up to the top, where a stretch of ground too rocky even for grazing sloped up to the level of the top of the dam and the lake behind it. The vegetation here was low and scrubby, and the ground between the rocks was blackened and scorched, suggesting that it was burned over frequently to preserve clear lines of sight.

The top of the dam had three towers on it—a tall one in the center and lower ones on each side where the dam met the shore. A road crossed the top, passing through the low towers, and of course there were massive gates and probably elaborate traps and defenses because Vziim loved them dearly. Keeping low among the rocks, Arkad moved up to where he could see the gate on this side. The drawbridge over the locks was down and the gate was open.

He could see one of Awiza's mercenaries, a Pfifu armed with an acid generator on guard at the gate, and then he realized with a start that the pile of metal and cloth next to the guard was actually the bodies of two or three dead Vziim. Awiza and her troops must have stormed the gate as soon as the defenders responded to the little force coming up the valley. Arkad looked up the road by the lakeshore and finally spotted the power wagons parked behind some boulders a couple of hundred meters away.

Would Awiza be back there? No, she would be inside, hunting for her sister. He was sure of that. Arkad straightened up and trotted toward the gate. "I have a note for Awiza," he called before the Pfifu could raise her weapon. "The note is of things that mean much."

He had bluffed his way into towers and warehouses before, but back in Ayaviz the worst thing the guards could do was throw him out or maybe hit him a few times. The Pfifu's acid generator could dissolve Arkad's skin. The key was to keep moving and act as if he knew what he was doing.

Still, he felt a tremendous surge of relief when she waved him along with a free tentacle. "Awiza is in there and down," she said.

He gave a gesture of thanks and hurried inside. The chamber within the gate was full of smoke and the smell of burned flesh. Another dead Vziim, horribly charred, lay tangled in the center of the roadway, surrounded by some puddles of still-burning fuel. Arkad avoided the dead one as best he could. A door to one side led to a spiral ramp leading down, and he followed that for a few meters to a spherical chamber lit by a buzzing red neon lamp, with half a dozen corridors radiating out from it. He couldn't tell which way the others had gone—he could hear sounds of commotion from all the corridors.

Finally he picked the corridor directly across the spherical space from the stairway and advanced cautiously. A few meters in, he nearly tripped over a dead Pfifu, her broken axe still clutched in her tentacles.

Arkad's heart was pounding now as he tried to move as silently as possible, straining to see if anyone was waiting to attack him. Ahead he could see that a side door along the corridor was open, and brighter yellow light spilled out. He moved up and peeked around the edge of the door.

It opened on a vertical shaft, with daylight visible at the top end and bright yellow electric light at the bottom. A loud humming sound, as of powerful machinery, came from below and a steady current of warm air blew past him up the shaft. Large machines were usually important, thought Arkad, so he decided to climb down.

A couple of thick ropes ran down the shaft for the convenience of Vziim, so Arkad was able to shinny down without much trouble.

He descended about fifty meters, and then the shaft ended at the ceiling of a huge, brightly lit room. Four enormous dynamos, mounted vertically, hummed loudly in a row. Half a dozen armed Vziim were on top of one dynamo, surrounded by a protective barricade made of timbers and empty barrels. Arkad could make out one female in elaborate armor among them, and he guessed she was Awiza's twin sister Zveemaa. A couple of humbler-looking females wearing the same gear as the males were with her; one of them had a radio.

A dozen of Awiza's professional mercenaries surrounded the little fort, led by Awiza herself. She and her sister were shouting at each other in their family language. There was too much noise for Arkad to hear them anyway, but he could see them gesture.

Awiza shouted something, waved her flame-projector, and gestured at her well-armed soldiers. In response, the female atop the dynamo pointed her tail at some small boxes taped to the great machine, and held up a small cylindrical device in one hand. With her other three hands, she made an expansive gesture, taking in the whole great room and the dam above.

He could see the mercenaries look at one another and at Awiza. The male Vziim atop the dynamo also glanced at Zveemaa. For a moment Awiza was silent. Then she thrust out her arms in the Vziim gesture for "no" and aimed her flame-projector at her sister.

This would be a very good time to run away, thought Arkad, but sheer curiosity made him linger.

One of Awiza's soldiers grabbed her from behind, gripping her body with his arms so that the sharp steel blades attached to his claws pressed against the vulnerable blood vessels just behind where the arms joined her head. She struggled wildly. Bright blue flame shot from her flame-projector and caught one of the other soldiers square in the face. He dropped his own weapon and fell to the floor, clawing at the burning flesh.

A third soldier managed to knock the projector from Awiza's hand as a fourth slammed himself down on her long tail, pinning it to the floor. She slashed at her attackers until the soldier holding her jabbed his own steel-tipped claws into her sides. Inky blue blood spouted forth, but that only seemed to enrage her more.

The males atop the dynamo moved cautiously down to the

floor and collected the flame-projectors from the soldiers. The female followed and stopped a few meters in front of Awiza. Arkad still couldn't hear what they were saying, but both looked calmer. Finally the mercenaries released their blood-covered former employer and backed away. Awiza and her sister regarded each other for a moment, and then at a gesture from the sister, three of their brothers incinerated Awiza with their own projectors. She didn't make a sound until the very end.

Zveemaa came forward to look at Awiza's charred body, and as she did so, the two younger females with her looked at each other.

The young female with the radio grabbed a spear from one of the males and stabbed Zveemaa with it, slipping the point neatly through a gap in the armor right into one lobe of Zveemaa's brain.

For a long moment nobody said anything. Then the other female spoke and prostrated herself to the one with the spear. The males atop the dynamo looked at each other and then did likewise. The mercenaries just waited until the new matriarch said something to them—Arkad guessed it was something like "I will honor your contract with Awiza"—at which point they also made perfunctory little bobs of obedience.

The little war was over, Arkad realized. Where did that leave him? Vziim were notorious for holding grudges. Arkad decided his best course of action was to get away from the dam as quickly as possible.

But that still left the incendiary liquid glued to his face. Awiza had said she had a way to remove it, but she was now a pile of ash. Maybe one of her brothers knew. He had to find the one leading the diversion. Going back out and across the river seemed like the long way; was there a way through the dam?

Arkad climbed back up the rope to the corridor, and ran in the direction of the greatest noise, heedless of danger. He passed more bodies along the way—Vziim in armor dead from burns, unarmored Vziim with spear wounds, and a single Pfifu slashed to ribbons.

The corridor opened out into a large gallery with four huge pipes passing through it. This must be the water intake from the lake behind the dam, thought Arkad. Which meant the water of the lake was just on the other side of a single masonry wall from him. He hoped Awiza's mother had been better at engineering than at raising her daughters.

He found more bodies on the floor under the great pipes:

three of the Pfifu and the armored Vziim who had been leading
Arkad's company. A couple of the flame-projectors were broken,
and a pool of butanol fuel mixed with Pfifu blood spread slowly
from the four bodies. The Vziim had no wounds, but a scorched
patch on the bare skin of his tail smelled like the time Arkad
had witnessed an Itooti electrocuted by accident.

Maybe he had some way to remove the thing on Arkad's
head? He was wearing Awiza's armor, after all. With her gone,
Arkad had no other hope. He began searching the Vziim's body.
Back in Ayaviz he had looted a few corpses in his time. Vziim
usually kept valuables under their arm joints.

The armor was thin steel plates, attached to a layer of smart
cloth. The cloth was smart enough to know when its wearer was
dead, and so parted along four seams with just a gentle tug.
Arkad peeled the Vziim like a fruit and shook out the armor to
see if anything was hidden inside.

A few small items splashed into the bloody butanol puddle:
a couple of lengths of coiled silver wire, a small bone sculpture
of a female Vziim, a cloth packet of hallucinogenic lozenges, and
a diamond-tipped engraving stylus. Arkad kept the wire and the
stylus, but placed the sculpture and the lozenges on the dead
Vziim's body again.

Just then he heard the sound of voices getting closer. Four
Vziim came into the room from the opposite entrance, carrying
flame-projectors and knives. With no time to hide, Arkad flung
himself down among the bodies and lay still. The smell of butanol soaking into his blanket made his eyes water, and he had to
force himself not to cough as the fumes made his throat burn.

The four slithered closer, buzzing among themselves in a
private language. They prodded at the bodies, and one of them
gave Arkad a hard jab with the muzzle of a flame-projector.
One careless finger on the release valve and his butanol-soaked
shirt would turn to blue fire. Arkad forced himself to hold still,
waiting for the wash of heat.

The Vziim jabbed him again, then slithered off. Another Vziim
arrived, driving a small electric tractor with a trailer. The four
armed Vziim began dumping the bodies into the wagon. When
they lifted Arkad, he stayed limp. He tumbled into the wagon on
top of two dead Pfifu, and then a third landed on top of him,
so that he was completely soaked in blood and butanol.

They took longer with their renegade brother, or uncle, or whatever he was. Arkad felt a stab of worse terror when he realized he had left the armor on the floor next to the body. What if they figured out that someone had been stripping the body? But the four Vziim were more interested in abusing their dead relative. They took turns buzzing words at him which sounded insulting, and jabbed him with their blade-tipped tails. Finally they hurled him into the wagon, nearly crushing Arkad.

Squashed in a pile of corpses, reeking of butanol, he could barely breathe. He risked detection by squirming to one side, until the weight of the dead was no longer crushing his lungs. If the living Vziim spotted him and turned their weapons against him, he'd be no worse off. But then he felt the wagon move, and for a moment felt hope. They'd dump the bodies somewhere and Arkad could slip away.

Unless they burned them. The Vziim usually burned their dead, to keep them away from the corpse-devouring Psthao-psthao. Especially honored matriarchs had their ashes mixed with cement and incorporated into new structures. Arkad hoped fervently that these Vziim did not think he was worth honoring.

The tractor moved slowly out of the room, back along the passage Arkad had come in by, and then turned down a side passage which spiraled down. Arkad couldn't tell how far down they went before the passage leveled off and straightened out again.

A blast of light blinded him, and for a moment, he thought the Vziim must have used some kind of energy weapon on him. Then he felt the warmth on his skin and moving air, and realized they had left the tunnel and gone outside. He lifted his head as far as he dared.

The tractor followed the road by the river, retracing the route by which Arkad's company had approached the dam in the first place. After a couple of hundred meters the tractor turned away from the river and crawled up a short, steep slope before stopping on a flat stone hilltop. The rocky slope of the riverbank rose beyond the hill, so that it was an isolated little platform next to the river. It didn't look as though anyone came there very often; tall weeds grew in cracks in the stone.

Arkad risked a look over the side of the trailer as the Vziim slid down off the little tractor. He could see the Vziim stick a stout iron pry bar into a little hole in the ground. The Vziim looped his tail around the end of the bar, grabbed the tractor with all four arms, and pulled with all the strength in his thick body. Arkad could see the tractor shift on its wheels, almost tipping over. But leverage won, and with a sudden noise of tearing roots and grinding stone, a perfectly circular disk of green bronze, easily two meters across, lifted from the ground and rolled to the side. As soon as the Vziim let go of the pry bar the bronze plate crashed to the ground with a noise like an explosion. Where it had been, Arkad could see a round dark hole.

The Vziim had to rest for several minutes after that, then climbed a bit shakily onto the tractor again. Arkad ducked down out of sight, and as he lay still, pretending to be dead, he realized what the hole must be.

Back in Ayaviz, the Psthao-psthao lurked down in the unlit lower levels, among the giant machines rooted deep in the planet's crust. But Arkad had heard stories that the Psthao-psthao had a vast system of deep caves and tunnels across the entire dayside of Syavusa. He hadn't quite believed those stories until now.

The Vziim started up the tractor and deftly maneuvered the wagon to the edge of the hole. He slid down again, unfastened the hitch, and then braced himself against the ground and pushed upward. The wagon tipped, and all the dead slid into the hole, with Arkad among them.

The tangle of bodies slid down the shaft and splashed in a shallow puddle at the bottom. Arkad had the wind knocked out of him by a dead Vziim but was otherwise unhurt. He had just managed to crawl out of the pile of dead when the lid crashed into place at the top of the shaft. Utter blackness surrounded him. Arkad had never been in such a completely dark environment before. Even on his few ventures to the lower levels of Ayaviz, there had always been some reflected daylight from above, or at least a few feeble safety lamps. Here, there was absolutely no light at all. All he could see were some fading afterimages, and after a time, even those were replaced by the shifting colored blobs generated by his own eyes.

He could smell blood, butanol, and the spilled contents of Pfifu stomachs. He could feel cold stone and water. He could hear a slow drip somewhere. That was all.

Arkad took inventory. He still had his shirt, shoes, trousers, a stylus, WOL, and some wire. No weapons, no lamp.

He got to his hands and knees and crawled until he was

no longer sitting in the puddle. Then he felt around with out-stretched hands and gradually built up a picture of the place he was in. The circular shaft from the surface came down into a very low-ceilinged cave. On two sides the cave roof and floor sloped together, meeting at a layer of crumbly, damp rock which was evidently the source of the puddle.

In the other two directions, the cave widened until the roof was beyond the reach of his upstretched hand. The puddle on the floor fed a tiny stream which meandered away across the sloping stone in a channel worn as deep as the width of his hand.

Away from the pile of bodies, he smelled damp stone, dust, and a faint oily scent which he recognized but couldn't identify. Then the distant skittering noise started and he knew what the smell was. It was the scent of the Psthao-psthao.

They would go for the bodies, he thought. Maybe he could hide from them. He could barely hear them over the sound of his heart pounding in his ears. Carefully, Arkad felt his way to where the floor and ceiling met, and wedged himself as deep as he could into the crevice.

The skittering sound came closer and the oily smell grew stronger. He couldn't tell how many there were, but he did hear their whispery voices in the dark and the faint swishing noise of their antennae brushing the floor of the cave.

They found the bodies and spent several minutes moving them around, whispering in an almost chatty fashion as they did. Arkad couldn't see the Psthao-psthao but he could imagine their dark segmented bodies with powerful pincers.

He heard one of them approaching and almost screamed when he felt the feathery touch of its antenna on his heel. The Psthao felt his skin carefully, then whispered to the others. Arkad heard them scuttling across the stone toward him in the dark, and sheer terror kept him paralyzed.

Then, suddenly, he saw a dazzling circle of light on the cave floor. It was daylight shining down the shaft, and the glare almost blinded him. Arkad briefly glimpsed the long dark bodies of half a dozen Psthao-psthao as they fled the light. Where they had been, Arkad could see the dead Vziim and Pfifu, laid out in a neat row by the stream.

"Hey, kid!" a voice shouted down the shaft. "Are you down there?"

CHAPTER 10

"I'LL BE HONEST: I THOUGHT WE WERE GOING TO FIND YOUR corpse," said Jacob when they finally stopped for a rest in a patch of woods several kilometers away from the dam.

"I was just pretending."

"Clever of you. Now all we need to do is get that thing off your forehead."

"Awiza—she's dead, and so is her sister—said it would be eight or sixteen hours."

"Yeah, but I bet that was more than eight hours ago. And I don't want to depend on her telling you the truth."

The four of them spent several minutes pulling on the plastic hemisphere glued to Arkad's forehead. Jacob tried to slip the tip of his knife between the skin and the device, but had to stop when blood began to well up around the blade.

"Well," said Jacob at last, "I guess we could cut it off, if you don't mind having a gigantic hole in your forehead for a while. Call that our last resort. Any other ideas? Anybody?" He looked at Baichi and Ree.

"Can we drain it?" asked Ree.

"The liquid makes everything it touches catch fire," said Arkad. "I used to have a little bottle of it."

"The substance sounds like a form of active smart protein," said Baichi. "It could change shape to catalyze the reaction depending on what compounds it comes in contact with."

"Let me guess: Machine tech," said Jacob.

151

She didn't answer. Arkad noticed that Baichi seemed even more quiet and unreadable than ever before. He could almost believe that she really was a mechanical doll, not a human at all.

"It is becoming intensely annoying to me that every two-bit gang boss here can get imported magic tech but we still have to walk or hitchhike to get around," said Jacob.

"What if we hold him under water?" asked Ree.

Jacob just looked at her.

"I don't mean drown him. Turn him upside down and stick his head in the water, then cut the thing open."

"That . . . could work," said Jacob, nodding. "What do you think, Arkad?"

Arkad had tried dropping a little of the igniter fluid into water once. The water around the drop boiled furiously, but did not burn. "Okay," he said.

They hiked through the woods a little longer until they found a stream. It was just a trickle of water through a series of muddy patches bounded by rocks, but they dug out a hollow big enough for Arkad's head and let it fill up.

He lay on his back in the mud, with his head canted back into the hollow, so that cold water got into his ears and he had to keep his eyes closed. Jacob crouched over him with his hands on either side of Arkad's head to hold him still, and gave his big folding knife to Baichi because she could move faster and with much greater precision than anyone else.

"Okay, everybody ready?" he asked. Arkad had to keep his eyes closed and couldn't see Jacob's face, but he could hear a nervous note in the man's voice. His hands on Arkad's head were steady, though. "We'll go on the count of three. Ready, one, two—"

Arkad felt a splash and a slight jolt, then Jacob yanked his whole head out of the puddle and doused his face with water. When Arkad could open his eyes, he saw the puddle where his head had been, boiling and churning furiously. Baichi knelt where she had been, with the flaming knife still in her hand. She watched the blade burn for a moment, then doused it in the stream. Jacob dabbed at Arkad's forehead with a towel and looked at it closely.

"Well, you've still got the base glued to you, but I don't see anything catching fire," he said, before looking over his shoulder at Baichi. "You jumped the gun a little."

"He might have flinched," she said.

"I would not!" Arkad objected.

"Involuntarily," she added, and for a moment she seemed less doll-like.

"Well . . . thank you," he said.

They followed the stream downhill until they came to a road where the coastal plain met the hills, leading directly westward toward the sun. There were little Pfifu farming settlements about eight hours' walk apart, so they could usually sleep under a roof.

Arkad noticed that Baichi had given up her habit of going off on her own when they stopped. She stayed with the group, even when the others were asleep. He managed to find a few opportunities to talk with her semiprivately as they walked.

"What happened to you back at the camp?" he asked her.

"I don't know. I have no memory of it," she said, and her face and voice were even more expressionless than usual. That was all he could get out of her.

Ree, however, was much more willing to talk about it. She walked beside Arkad and motioned for him to slow down so that Jacob and Baichi could move out of earshot, then leaned close and spoke quietly. "Her Machine parts failed," she said.

"How did that happen?" The idea that Machine Civilization tech could go wrong was simply inconceivable.

Ree just shrugged. "My guess is that the connections between the tech and her actual body are going wrong. Poor thing. She's the only one of her cohort to live this long, so it's no wonder nobody expected this."

"What happened to the others?"

She stared at him and shook her head. "There's so much you don't know! Baichi was one of a dozen experimental human-Machine hybrids created at the Bharosa habitat in Machine space. They weren't just humans with some implants, but fully combined down at the cell level. About three years after they joined the community, most of the hybrids . . ." She hesitated. "Well, they went wrong. There was conflict with the ordinary humans in the habitat and things escalated. A lot of people died. In the end, the Machines themselves had to help the humans destroy the hybrids. Only Baichi and two others survived."

Ree seemed almost gleeful as she continued. "Bharosa habitat was so badly damaged it had to be abandoned. The Machines agreed to end the hybrid project. A lot of people wanted to destroy Baichi and the other two. They're still not allowed on Invictus."

"But what did they *do?*" asked Arkad.

"You mean the rebel hybrids? Well—" she stopped herself and shook her head. "You're too young, and you've been through a lot lately. It would only disturb you. They did very bad things and showed no willingness to stop. Let's leave it at that."

That explanation did nothing to satisfy Arkad's curiosity. He didn't dare ask Baichi about it, especially in her current mood, so he waited for a chance to talk privately with Jacob. The older man might or might not tell him anything, but if he did, he wouldn't be so maddeningly vague and incomplete as Ree had been.

Unfortunately, the entire planet Syavusa seemed to be involved in a conspiracy to prevent Arkad from getting that opportunity. When they stopped a few hours later to eat and sleep, both he and Jacob were too busy collecting food and cooking, and afterward, the other two members of the party were too close. When Arkad woke after sleeping, he found that Jacob was already up, and during the walk, Jacob made sure to stay close to Baichi in case she collapsed again.

The road gradually climbed into the foothills of the mountain range which now became visible to the west. The mountains themselves were invisible under a perpetual cloud cover, as wet air from the coastal plain rose and gave up its moisture before passing into the plateau beyond. The villages they passed through were bigger, and there were stretches of road paved with cobblestones. They also encountered more traffic, both vehicles and pedestrians.

Arkad's spirits improved with more people around. He watched all the other travelers intently, trying to guess where they were from and what was their business. When the two of them fell in with other pedestrians, he was full of questions.

He learned that a team of six Pfifu dragging a cart loaded with tools and luggage were glassmakers bound for the lands beyond the mountain ridge. "The light there is much more hot than in this land," one of them told Arkad while gesturing, *"Like young plants we seek to escape the shade of large and well-established trees."*

"You tell me why you need hot light," Arkad asked.

"We will make glass disks to see with and flat sheets to bounce the light," the glassmaker said, adding, *"Out of sand and fire we will craft beauty and precision. Once we are rich we can return to the cool shores."*

A trio of Itooti passed them on a home-built monocycle powered by a foul-smelling butanol engine, with huge bundles of cured fish skins balanced on either side. They took turns driving, one manning the controls while the others circled overhead shouting advice and criticism. They stopped for repairs and one of the three perched on Arkad's shoulder for a talk while the other two worked on the engine.

"Wingless humans are not a common species on isolated Syavusa," he said to Arkad.

"It is an uncommon event to encounter any local person who has even seen a rare human," he agreed.

"A well-educated male hears many melodious songs and exciting stories of strange creatures. Long ago two mysterious humans stopped in the nearby village of my wise great-grandmother. A memorable event gets passed along from one rising generation to the next one."

"Captivated Arkad desires greatly to hear more accurate information about these two visiting humans."

The Itooti fluttered onto Arkad's head. "The memorable event was three dozens of long years ago. Honest Ooiti knows only a small amount about the long-ago visit. His aged great-grandmother spoke of two slender wingless beings with the exotic name of *humans* who were traveling toward the distant seacoast."

"Eager Arkad wishes that helpful Ooiti would—" Arkad didn't get to finish as one of the Itooti's comrades called him over and the three of them began quarreling over which should drive the monocycle.

"Don't lag behind, kid," Jacob called, and Arkad hurried to catch up.

The next time they stopped to sleep, Jacob did not prepare dinner. "We have a problem, folks. There's only a few of the food bars left, and around here it's hard to forage. We're running out of food, and the pirates stole all our trade metal."

"*She* doesn't need to eat anything," said Ree, nodding at Baichi. "I don't see why she's been getting an equal share of the food."

"I can sustain myself on almost any kind of organic material, but I do prefer the taste of human-made food," said Baichi. "From now on I will supply my own needs."

"We could trade some things," Arkad suggested. "Pfifu might

want some of the smart cloth, and you can never tell what Itooti will buy."

"Trouble is, we're pretty much down to bare bones already," said Jacob. "Those pirates got all our trade goods and metal. All we have is three pocket computers that nobody else on this planet can use, our clothes, two sleeping bags, two purifier canteens, a blanket, four food bars, and a few personal items. There's not much left we can give up. The canteens are mission-critical. We'll need the sleeping bags to stay cool in the desert. What else is there?"

Nobody said anything.

"Maybe we could work for food, or for metal to trade," said Arkad.

Jacob raised his eyebrows. "Well, we've got a variety of skills, but I don't know if any of them are exactly *marketable*. I know a lot about human history and cultures, I've been a military officer, and a teacher. Not much call for any of that around here, I'm afraid. As to practical knowledge, I'm a pretty good cook, I can drive a tracked vehicle and do construction in near-vacuum environments...if we had a piano I could play it."

"I did intelligence analysis," said Ree. "And I trained as a spacecraft pilot."

"How about you, kid? Got any job experience?"

Arkad thought of all the things he had done on the streets of Ayaviz, some of them so long ago he could barely remember. "I've helped metalworkers and glassmakers—and cloth dyers. I worked making bricks for a while, and building things with them. I can gut and skin fish, and cure the skins. A few times I went out of the city to help harvest crops, and I made a couple of trips on fishing boats. I cleaned windows on towers and painted things. Packed fish and canned meat, carried messages, put labels on bottles, spied on people, moved cargo...oh, and a Pfifu taught me to knit."

"How did you have time to do all that?" asked Ree.

Arkad shrugged.

"Makes me feel like I haven't been applying myself," said Jacob. "Well, since the alternatives are stealing or starving, I guess a little honest work won't kill us. Arkad, you're in charge of finding us jobs. You can be the skilled expert, we're just strong backs with weak minds."

Arkad had no trouble sleeping on an empty stomach, having

done it far too many times in his life. When the four of them woke, they crossed the next valley to a village atop a line of low hills; beyond it, the lower slopes of the mountains rose into the perpetual cloud cover. The village was just east of the shadow of the mountains, and a line of photovoltaic panels ran along the crest of the hills.

As they plodded up the slope to the town, Arkad matched Baichi's pace. "What about you?" he asked.

"What about me?" she answered, without looking at him.

"What can you do?"

"I am faster and stronger than any human, I have senses you do not possess, I have a huge store of information, and very little experience with anything. Jacob brought me along because I can survive almost anywhere and speak many languages, and I memorized all the technical manuals for the Tanis-class spacecraft." After a moment she said, "I am fifteen years old, but I have only been conscious for ten."

"You were asleep for five years?"

She looked straight ahead as she answered. "The Machines thought it best to keep us dormant while our bodies and brains reached their adult form. My cohort were all 'born' fully grown and conscious."

"What about your parents?"

"The Machines assembled my genome out of thousands of samples."

"I mean, who took care of you when you were little?"

"There was no need. We awoke fully adult. The Machines considered a long childhood a waste of time. They may have been mistaken. I'm sure Ree has told you all about what happened to my cohort."

"Not really." He had to trot to keep up with her now. "She said something bad happened, but that was all."

"Yes. Something bad happened. That is all." She accelerated her pace again. Arkad simply stopped and watched her go.

When they reached the hilltop town, Arkad was able to find an Itooti fruit grower who was willing to exchange a few hours of weed-pulling for a meal and a place to sleep.

The fruit grower had a patch of steep, rocky hillside, with a couple of catch basins for rainwater, and an irregular tangle of thick vines bearing clusters of pulpy red disk-shaped fruit about four centimeters across.

"Don't eat them," Arkad warned the others. "Not even cooked. And if you touch the fruits, don't put your finger in your eye."

"Habaneros from hell, eh? Be careful, everybody," said Jacob.

The weeds were easy enough to pull, but evidently it had been a very long time since the last hungry travelers desperate for a job had come through. Some of the weeds were as tall as Arkad. The four of them spread out across the hillside, stepping over vines, pulling weeds, and heaping the refuse under the vines to protect the thin topsoil. Little humming creatures swarmed into the air each time someone pulled a weed, so that all of them were soon covered with tickling, crawling pests.

Their employer circled over the vine patch when they started work, but once she was satisfied that they weren't going to uproot her vines or steal her fruit, she glided back to her house and began a loud argument with a couple of her children.

By the time they had cleared the patch, all of them—including Baichi—were ready for a dip in the catch basins before eating. Arkad tried to sneak a look at where Baichi and Ree were cleaning up, but Jacob noticed and gave him a light punch on the shoulder. "I'd recommend against ogling either one of those two."

Arkad turned to face away from the other basin. "I want to ask you something. What happened to Baichi? She won't talk to me and Ree said she might be dying."

Jacob sighed and dunked his head in the water before answering. "Damned if I know," he said, and wiped his face with his hands. "She keeled over when we were running away from that camp, and I managed to carry her to safety. She woke up about fifteen minutes later and couldn't remember anything about it. Since then I've been keeping an eye on her, but it hasn't happened again. It's a mystery to me."

"Ree said all of the others like Baichi were dead."

Another sigh, and then Jacob gave a groan as he straightened up. "I'm getting too old for this kind of thing. Okay, I guess you should know: yes. There's only three human-Machine hybrids like Baichi left, and as far as I know, nobody's going to create any more. The Machine Civilization agreed to give up the idea after the Bharosa incident. Make sure to wash your ears."

Arkad did so. "But what *was* the incident?" he asked. "Ree

only said that a lot of bad stuff happened and the habitat was destroyed."

"That's not a bad summary. I'm not sure you want the gory details. The rebel hybrids got pretty crazy before the end. But here's the important part: Baichi was *not* involved, understand? She and the other two who refused to join the rebel hybrids left the habitat before the really awful stuff got started. Remember that. Now come on, I'm starving."

Their employer kept her end of the bargain handsomely; she cooked them a couple of liters of boiled seeds flavored with dried fish, and provided a couple of jugs of clear cold water for them to drink. "Not a bad dinner," said Jacob when they had scraped the pot clean and the three of them who needed sleep were making themselves comfortable. "But my back is going to be unhappy about this when I wake up—and we'll be no better off than when we got here."

"I've got blisters on my hands, and my neck feels like it's sunburned," said Ree. "Couldn't you find us some indoor work?"

"I'll ask around town after I sleep," said Arkad.

When they woke, Jacob was visibly stiff and Ree's blisters had burst, leaving her with raw patches on the palms of her hands. So the older two waited at the edge of the village in a patch of shade under a photovoltaic panel while Arkad and Baichi went to look for work.

It took a couple of hours. None of the villagers wanted to gamble on hiring mysterious wanderers of unfamiliar species, and tended to say so at length and with great frankness. But when it felt as though every property owner in town had rejected the humans, a juvenile Itooti male circled Arkad's head and suggested, "Desperate seekers after gainful employment would benefit by taking the narrow trail north to the remote home of solitary Fafof."

"Is generous Fafof in need of eager workers?" Arkad asked as the young male rose higher.

"Mad Fafof has excess wealth and bizarre ideas. His erratic behavior is impossible to predict. Lonely Fafof may well wish to hire some freakish creatures." The Itooti swooped away down into the valley to the east.

"Let's go see," said Arkad, and set off to the north with Baichi. About a kilometer outside the village, past the irrigated terraces and vine-covered slopes, the trail descended into a hollow on the sunlit western side of the hills. A row of solar panels stood high on the slope, but the bottom of the little hollow was filled by a huge and complicated machine.

At first the sheer size of it made Arkad assume the machine was one of the ancient devices found scattered across Syavusa, but then he realized it was still under construction. The core of the thing was a group of metal pipes as wide as Arkad's outstretched arms standing on end, at least twenty meters high. Smaller pipes connected the big ones or led to an elaborate system of tanks, valves, and condensers. A tangled network of wires ran over and around the device, and Arkad could see a big humming transformer, a row of what might have been capacitors, and a couple of large electron tubes sticking out of a copper sphere. The purpose of the machine eluded him. He had seen generators, chemical refineries, metal smelters, and desalinators, but this looked like none of them, or possibly a mix of all of them.

"You stop now!" A Pfifu emerged from a small shed next to the machine, brandishing a home-built acid generator. "I do not want a spy here! You leave right now!" he shouted as he climbed the hillside toward Arkad and Baichi.

"We are not here to spy on you," Arkad called down to the Pfifu. "We seek work. You tell me if you are Fafof."

He didn't answer until he had approached to within acid-spraying range of the two humans. "I am Fafof. You tell me why you think I need help from you."

Arkad gestured at the huge machine. "That is a big job for just one to do. We can help you, if you pay us. We are strong and know a lot, and have good hands." He held up his hands and wiggled his fingers.

"I have seen your kind in the past, on a far world. *Human.* They did good work. You tell me how I can know that you are not a spy," said the Pfifu, still keeping his acid generator ready. Now that he was close enough, Arkad could see that Fafof was extremely old for a Pfifu. His skin looked dry and crinkled, as if his body had deflated over time. On one tentacle tip, he wore a glove fitted with thick lenses to help him see.

"You tell me who we could spy for, out here on this world."

"The vile Elmisthorn!" said Fafof, and his free tentacles gestured, *"The hungry hunters pursue me even to my hidden place among the stones."*

"We do not serve them. They took our world and we fight them," said Arkad.

"I know that a lot of my folk and yours serve them on the worlds they rule," said Fafof. "You might serve them. You tell me why you have come to this place."

"We are on our way west, past that ridge"—Arkad pointed at the mountains in the distance—"but we ran out of stuff to trade and need to find work so that we can go on. There are four of us. Two are back in town. We do not serve the Elmisthorn."

Fafof lowered his acid generator. "I am not rich. I can pay fifty grams of mercury for an hour of work. You will help me build. I will give you food, but you must cook it. Your folk sleep—I do not pay for that time, only for work." His tentacles added, *"How can they bear that false death every few hours?"*

"That is fine with us."

Baichi went back to the village to fetch Ree and Jacob while Fafof showed Arkad around his little establishment. He still carried the acid generator but shut the valves to the reaction chamber and held it pointing at the ground. The big, strange machine was surrounded by a scattering of junk—Arkad couldn't tell if it was scrap or parts waiting to be installed—and four sheds which looked like converted space shipping containers. One was Fafof's living quarters, one was a well-equipped workshop, and the other two were storage. Fafof had Arkad move some junk out of one of the storage sheds to make room for the humans to sleep.

Just as Arkad's three companions appeared on the trail, Fafof excused himself and ducked into his own little cabin for a moment. He didn't bother to swing the door panels shut, and Arkad thought he heard Fafof talking to someone inside.

Once introductions were made and terms were set, Fafof began to explain the work. Arkad translated for the others. "He needs help building that big . . . thing. There are pipes and cables which have to be put in place, but he says he will do all the welding and soldering himself."

"Fine," said Jacob. "But what *is* it?"

"I don't know," said Arkad. "He didn't say."

"Hmm," said Jacob, but then shrugged. "Well, we can probably figure it out once we start working."

Fafof proved to be an erratic taskmaster. He didn't sleep, of course, which meant he kept his new employees on the job for twelve hours before Arkad convinced him they were all about to collapse from exhaustion, and the quality of their work might suffer as a result. The four humans clambered about the mysterious device, putting components in place. Jacob and Baichi handled the heavy pipes and the biggest electrical cables, while Arkad and Ree moved the more delicate glass components and a lot of alarming-looking bare copper wire.

The sheer amount of material lying around convinced Arkad that Fafof must be very rich indeed, despite his claims of poverty. Whole sections of copper pipe were tossed in the scrap pile, and he found some broken rings of palladium lying in the dirt amid fragments of glass. Without saying anything to the others, Arkad tucked a couple of them into his pockets, simply because his frugal scavenging soul simply couldn't bear to see anything that valuable lying discarded.

When they weren't moving things around, the humans did a lot of waiting. Fafof resolutely did all the welding and soldering, as promised, which took up to half an hour for each new connection. He also had a habit of darting back into his living quarters every so often, usually emerging with scrawled diagrams on smart cloth showing where the next parts had to go.

When the humans insisted on food and rest, Fafof agreed to an eight-hour break. He brought out plastic containers of dehydrated fish powder, bearing labels in Pfifu writing, and Arkad realized they must have come from the Pfifu home world itself—which implied the contents were older than any of them except possibly Jacob. Fafof assured them it was irradiated and quite safe to eat. The humans made a soup out of the powder and some vegetables Arkad thought were safe, and sat in the shade of the big machine to eat while Fafof put away his tools.

"How's ya chowdah?" asked Jacob between mouthfuls.

"My what?" Arkad replied.

"Ya chowdah." He dropped the odd accent and repeated, "Your chowder. That's what this kind of soup is called, although it's traditionally got milk in it."

That stirred a memory. "Like what the harpooner ate! In the book about the whale and the one-legged captain!"

"What the heck made you decide to read *Moby Dick*?"

"I like stories about ships, and when I asked WOL for a sea story I hadn't already read, that one popped up. It took me a while to get through it, but I liked all the parts about the different kinds of whales. Do people still eat them?"

"No," said Ree. "In fact I don't think there are any animals raised for food on Earth at all anymore. Everyone gets synthetic protein instead."

"Yum yum yum," said Jacob. "Brings back memories of my dear mother, slaving in the kitchen over a steaming pot of amino acids."

"It's more sustainable this way," said Ree.

"And that's so important when the population's dropping faster than a cartoon coyote. Earth's down to, what, four billion now?"

"A little more, I think. It was overpopulated before," said Ree.

"What's the target number the Elmisthorn are aiming at? A billion? Half a billion? Maybe just a few in zoos for the Elmos to look at?"

"I think the goal is about eight hundred million, concentrated in southeast Asia and India. The rest of the planet will be kept fallow, to give the ecosystems a chance to recover. It's probably for the best, really."

"You sound like you're defending them!"

"Well ... you have to admit humans weren't doing a good job at planetary management."

"So kill ninety percent of 'em off with bioweapons, and herd the remnant into reservations to save the Earth. Lovely. And how many *Elmisthorn* colonies are there on Earth now?"

"Three," said Ree. "Argentina, central North America, and the Volga steppe. But they said they're going to limit their populations, too. Just a hundred million in each tract. They need a lot of space to run."

"Wouldn't want our genocidal conquerors to feel *cramped*. You know, when my mother's ancestors took over North America, they just moved in and settled. They didn't bother spewing a lot of bullshit about saving the place from the people who were already there. The Elmisthorn aren't saving the Earth, they're getting rid of the inconvenient natives and trying to convince them it's for their own good."

Arkad noticed that Fafof was lingering nearby. "You tell me if you want to join us and eat," he said to the Pfifu in pidgin.

"I have a thing I must do," said Fafof, and hurried off to his little house.

"What does he do in there?" asked Jacob. "Popping in and out all the time. Is that normal for Pfifu?"

Arkad shrugged. "For some, maybe."

When they woke and resumed work, Arkad began to understand a little more of how the huge device was supposed to work. A ring of tanks and reservoirs around the base held various liquids and compressed gases. These fed into a series of reaction chambers where they were combined, or heated, or ionized, or all three at once. The products then flowed into more reactors, and finally into the big standing tubes. All the various pipes and reaction chambers were enveloped in cooling systems, which apparently carried off waste heat to power generators or to preheat certain ingredients. The main tubes had a fantastic set of nested electrical coils, which looked like they might accelerate the ionized exhaust streams, shooting them high into the air.

But what Fafof wanted to do with it was still a mystery.

The next time they ate and rested, Arkad deliberately sat near Baichi, and when his share of the food was gone, he pulled WOL out of his pouch. "Do you want to hear another chapter?"

She hesitated, then nodded. So Arkad read to her about Mole's terrifying adventure in the Wild Wood, the Rat's bold rescue attempt, the sudden blizzard, and how the two finally reached safety in the vast underground house of the gruff but kindhearted Badger. He stopped only when he felt himself getting hoarse.

He expected Baichi to wander off while the rest of them slept, as was her old habit, but she stayed next to him when he put WOL away and pulled a sheet of reflective plastic over the two of them to block the sunlight. Arkad found that he was intensely aware of her presence, especially of the one spot where his upper arm pressed against hers.

Arkad could barely breathe, and his mouth was dry despite the water he'd drunk only a few minutes before. His heart beat as though he had just run a couple of kilometers at full speed. His whole body was tense for action. Hungry for more contact, he rolled onto his side facing her, so that his bare chest rested against her arm and his left arm rested across her torso.

The feel of her body underneath his arm was intoxicating. He was almost trembling. No force in the universe could have stopped him from raising his head and leaning over to kiss her.

But then Baichi slipped neatly out of his grasp and stood up. Before he could speak she was out of sight. Frustrated, Arkad covered himself with the reflective plastic again and—eventually—went to sleep.

They settled into a routine: wake up to find Fafof already tinkering with his immense device, eat something (after the third straight meal of "chowder" Arkad took time out to go foraging in the hills, so that they could at least have some boiled roots or toasted seeds for variety), and then spend about ten hours working. Afterward they would rest, eat another meal, and eventually sleep. For Arkad it was like being back in Ayaviz, only warmer and with no need to guard his possessions against other street thieves. He found himself wishing they could just stay with Fafof.

Jacob, however, was eager to be off again. He kept track of how much mercury Fafof owed them, and had announced a plan to leave as soon as they had accumulated twenty kilograms. "I definitely want to trade it in for something more portable at the first opportunity. The next planet I visit had better have a credit system so I'm not dragging commodity elements around just to buy lunch."

The work actually got easier as they stayed, because Fafof began spending a lot more time in his quarters. The three humans would move a component, Fafof would install it, and then they'd have half an hour or more of free time while he went into his hut, only to emerge with a new set of instructions.

What was especially odd was that even Fafof himself began to seem reluctant to move ahead with the project. More than once they finished an installation and then their employer loafed along with them for a while before hobbling off resignedly to the house.

On one of those extended rest breaks, Jacob ventured to ask Fafof a little about his background, with Arkad as translator. "Ask the old fellow how he wound up here."

Arkad did so, then relayed Fafof's answer back to Jacob. "He says he came here to work on his project in a place where nobody would spy on him."

"Why does he care about that? What's it supposed to be?"

"He says he can trust you because you're a human, and that means you won't reveal anything to the Elmisthorn. He says he hates the Elmisthorn and this thing is going to be a weapon to keep them away from Syavusa."

Jacob suddenly looked a lot more attentive. "This is a planetary defense weapon?"

"That's what he says."

"How does it work?"

"He says he won't tell me," said Arkad after a brief conversation with Fafof. "He doesn't want to give away any secrets of how it works. He wants to catch the Elmisthorn by surprise when they show up. Do you think it's true?"

"Well, I suppose it could be some kind of weapon; maybe a giant plasma launcher or something. But ask him why he's building it at all."

Arkad translated Jacob's question, but Fafof was already getting to his feet. "I have said as much as I wish to," he said, and gestured, *"The weight of sadness in the story is greater than I can lift."*

They spent a few more hours winding fine copper wire around the giant pipes—though Jacob kept climbing down to make sure nothing was connected to the capacitors.

Ree leaned close to Arkad as she handed him the reel of copper wire. "You said this thing is a weapon?"

"That's what Fafof said." He hadn't realized she had been listening earlier.

"You have to find out more about it. It could be important."

"How can I do that?"

"Have you noticed how he keeps going into his house? I think he's got the plans there. Go take a look. Can't your little reader take pictures?"

"Fafof will see me."

"Not if you're careful. Go off to look for something for dinner, then sneak back into his house as soon as he comes out next time."

"If he finds out he may not pay us."

Ree looked at him with an expression he had never seen on her before. Her jaw was set and her eyes were narrowed, and he was almost afraid of her. "Then we'll take what we need. He has no right to make us do all this just for some metal. A weapon this size could be very powerful; we need to know how it works."

Arkad announced to the others that he was going off foraging, then walked up the trail until he could duck behind a boulder. From there he crawled back on his stomach through the tangled growth to the edge of the junk heaps surrounding the big machine. Once he was amid the piles of scrap and the containers of unused parts, he could dart from cover to cover until he reached Fafof's house.

The house was an old space shipping container, made to stack neatly in Roon trade ship holds. It was a hexagonal prism a bit less than two meters high and about eight and a half meters long, made of sheet aluminum. The white paint was flaking off after years of rain and wind. Fafof had cut windows along the sides, on the upper faces of the prism, and a carefully shaped metal flue rose from the center of the top face. The end faces had doors formed of six triangular panels held shut by a latch in the center.

Arkad positioned himself at the end opposite the work site, where he could remain unseen. He had tried to break into shipping containers many times before; the latches were either ridiculously easy to unlock, or flat-out impossible, in which case one could still pry the triangular panels apart by brute force, but that couldn't be hidden.

He rotated the three concentric circles of the lock, stiff after long disuse, and worked his way through the most common arrangements of the Roon glyphs. The third most common one—a pun on the concepts of "opening" and "value"—did the trick. Arkad let the bottom panel fall open, and crawled inside.

After the sunlight outside, the interior was like being in a cave. The windows were covered up on the inside and the only light came from the triangle of sunlight on the floor where Arkad had come in. He stood up and let his eyes adjust.

"You tell me what you do there," said a faint Pfifu voice. "You tell me why you came in the back door."

CHAPTER 11

RKAD'S FIRST IMPULSE WAS TO FLEE, BUT THAT WOULD ALMOST certainly lead to discovery. So he tried to brazen it out. "Fafof sent me to get a thing for him," he said.

"You come here and tell me who you are," said the weak voice.

Now that Arkad's eyes had adjusted, he could see that the interior of the container was a single room, cluttered with tools, the rolled cloth scrolls of old Pfifu books, sculptures in metal and plastic, pictures, and a couple of old Pfifu spacesuits. The air was damp and heavily perfumed.

In the center of the space, right next to the iron stove, was a large tank of steaming water. A Pfifu was halfway out of the water, aiming two tentacles at Arkad. "You tell me who you are," he repeated, and gestured, *"A novelty has come to me like water to one lost in the desert."*

"I am Arkad. I just came in to get a thing."

"You stay here for a small time," said the Pfifu in the tank. Now that Arkad was closer he could see that one of the Pfifu's tentacles was cut off at the base, and a second was just a stump only half a meter long. The skin on that side of its body was thick and opaque, ropy with scar tissue. Arkad had seen scars like that on Pfifu metalworkers back in Ayaviz, but never so large.

"My name is Pfup. You tell me if you are a *human*." With one tentacle he added, *"I have seen other worlds and stars, and now can barely make out one who stands within reach."*

"I am human. I and some folk like me are here to work for

Fafof. We help build his big thing. Soon we will be done and then we will go."

"The work will not end," said Pfup, and gestured, *"Disaster will follow if the job is ever complete."*

"You tell me if Fafof will not let us go!" said Arkad, alarmed.

"No, he will not try to keep you," Pfup said. *"Though like me he was thirsty for company and will be sad when you have gone."*

"But then tell me why the work will not end."

Pfup didn't answer for several seconds, and Arkad was on the verge of asking again when the old Pfifu spoke. "To tell you that, I must tell you a tale," said Pfup, and ducked under the surface to moisten his skin before continuing. As he did, Arkad could see that Pfup had only one leg. When he surfaced again, he began to speak in formal Pfifu style, in which sounds and gestures made a single language.

Long ago, before the years wore me down like waves against a cliff, I lived in a habitat circling Aaf, the home planet of my species. There was a great band of orbital habitats around Aaf back then, like a river of jewels shining against the black of space. My people are quite happy in space. We have no bones or shell to grow weak in microgravity, and our bodies withstand radiation more easily than those of many other species. We have lived in space for generations—half a billion of us lived in the habitats, and nearly as many were spread through the moons and asteroids of our home system.

My own home habitat of Aefef was one of the oldest cities in space, and it sheltered more than a hundred thousand prosperous, clever Pfifu. Beautiful Aefef! With shining solar panels spread wide like wings, the main body a crystal sphere full of green like a vast emerald, and docking ports crowded with commerce. Factories at the poles made all kinds of elegant machines. Our wealth gave us influence throughout the system.

I was born in Aefef and met my partners there. I had two: Fafof and Effa. We collaborated on the design and construction of weapon systems. I was the theoretician, Effa the engineer, and Fafof the builder. We created long-range lasers of tremendous efficiency and plasma dischargers projecting fusing hydrogen. Effa and I even devised a way to project a magnetic field over long distances to induce electric currents in the metal hulls of spacecraft. Many habitats purchased our weapons, and others pirated our designs, so we were rich and respected throughout the system.

After sixteen years our partnership bid for—and won—the contract to defend Aefef. As you are an alien, I must explain to you something about the Pfifu people; it is at once our greatest strength and our greatest weakness. We Pfifu do not easily form ourselves into groups as other species do. We can form partnerships, for work or living or raising young, but most have only a few members. The largest one I have ever heard of is the famous Rocket League, which numbered seventeen at its height, and even they later quarreled and broke apart. The important thing for you to know is that everything is done by contracts and subcontracts among individuals and partnerships.

We bid for the job of defending Aefef and won the contract. For a term of eight years, I and my partners Fafof and Effa were in complete control of Aefef's defenses. Offensive military operations were not part of our contract. We had hundreds of subcontractors working for us: mercenary commanders, logistic providers, communication operators, security specialists, finance and administrative subcontractors, soldiers, pilots—the list was endless. Thousands of Pfifu were part of our operation, not to mention machines.

We got a fixed amount of money from the treasury contractors, equal to about three hundred tons of platinum, to cover all the expenses of protecting our habitat and commerce for eight years. The three of us, as primary contractors, were entitled to keep anything we did not use. Of course, if we failed to satisfy the terms of our contract, anyone who could prove it would be entitled to confiscate our wealth and take over the contract themselves, so we had inspectors constantly watching us like scavengers watching a wounded beast.

The work was difficult. The three of us scarcely had time to see each other. We had planned to raise some children together, but had to postpone that until the contract was up. I was unable to keep up with the latest developments in physics, and Fafof complained that his tentacles were growing stiff and clumsy from disuse because he was supervising others rather than making things himself.

Three years into our contract, we got a wonderful offer. An Elmisthorn mercenary company offered to take on all our external defense operations for a startlingly low fee. The three of us considered the proposal very carefully, and insisted on very strict terms, with enormous penalties for noncompliance. They agreed without any haggling.

All went well for the remainder of our contract. Thanks to our Elmisthorn subcontractors, Aefef was guarded by powerful spaceships holding alien troops in sophisticated armor. No other habitat could threaten us, and no community on the surface could defy us. Only the deepest ocean settlements were beyond the reach of our new protectors, and none of them were a threat. Fafof and Effa and I became vastly rich with the money we saved, and agreed among ourselves not to continue past the end of our own contract. Our successors in the job kept the Elmisthorn on—indeed, I believe they were able to negotiate an even lower fee and thereby reap an even larger profit.

My partners and I had our gametes screened, and chose only the best for our offspring. We decided to have four, and set up incubators in our enormous new home, tended by a full-time embryologist. While the young ones gestated, the three of us took a tour of the habitats around Aaf, staying in the most luxurious rooms, watching performances by the finest dancers and puppeteers, and soaking ourselves in potent and exotic essences.

On our trip we stopped at Effaf habitat, another old and wealthy colony in orbit. As our shuttle docked I was surprised to see a large Elmisthorn spaceship positioned nearby. At first, I wondered if our successors were concerned for our security and sent it as an escort—which was odd, since Effaf habitat had always been friendly to Aefef, and on top of that, the partnership which took over the defense contract never really liked the three of us anyway.

Because I and my two partners had recently been the lead defense contractors at Aefef, the partnership running Effaf's defense very politely invited us to enjoy a display of zero-gravity sculpture. I took the opportunity to let them know that we had not asked for the Elmisthorn escort.

The Effaf contractor looked baffled. "I do not know what escort you mean," she said.

"The warship I saw near the docking hub. I assume it was sent by Aefef..."

She practically shook with amusement. "Your skin must be getting cloudy with age. That is not a ship from Aefef. It is Elmisthorn. We hired them for habitat defense. They offered very good rates."

That fertilized an egg of doubt in my mind, and for the rest of our tour I watched for signs of Elmisthorn presence at other habitats. At first, Fafof and Effa were annoyed with me. "Our contract is finished," Effa told me. "Our new family will be waiting for us when we return to Aefef. No one is paying you to worry about defense matters anymore."

But after we saw Elmisthorn ships and soldiers at three more colonies—all large, important habitats—even Fafof began to be suspicious. "I don't know what we can do," he said. "Certainly Papfapa and her partners in charge of defense back home will not listen to us."

"I think I know someone who will," I said.

We cut our tour short and got back to Aefef. The three of us went directly to see Fafpip. He was old and very clever, and had been the habitat's prime foreign-affairs contractor for nearly sixteen years. He always bid an extremely low sum because he handled most of the diplomatic and intelligence-gathering work himself, and always exceeded the contract requirements.

Fafpip did not scoff at our worries. "I have noticed the same thing," he said. "In the past year, Elmisthorn mercenaries have taken on large defense subcontracts at 506 large colonies, including Aefef, Effaf, and even Fiuf. They have also been hired as prime defense contractors at 128 smaller habitats. I have also learned that four surface communities have retained Elmisthorn space forces as orbital defense auxiliaries. That means that nearly one fourth of the military forces in Aaf space are Elmisthorn."

"Now I am actually afraid," said my partner Fafof. "Their ships and troops are better than ours."

"I think we need to know how much better," I told him.

"Two or three times, at least," said Fafof.

We all considered that. If what he said was correct, the strength of the Elmisthorn forces orbiting our planet was as great as that of all the native Pfifu military combined—and combining is not something Pfifu do easily.

"We need to do something quickly," said Effa. "The problem will not get any smaller if we wait."

"I agree," said Fafpip. "But it must be done cautiously. I will contact some of the other important powers and organize a meeting about updating commerce agreements. Someone always wants that. We will discuss a ban on hiring alien mercenaries."

Fafof, Effa, and I went home, relieved to know that wise and hard-working Fafpip was aware of the problem and doing something about it. All would be well. When I read the announcement of a commercial summit among the largest trading colonies, I felt muscles relax which I had not known were tense.

Our four eggs hatched right on schedule. Faf, Fuef, Uifpafp, and Fpopfa were all delightful juveniles, full of curiosity and energy. We had an enormous private swimming tank in our home, and the seven of us spent many happy hours in the water together.

It was during our last such swim that I heard the tone announcing a message. Our staff had strict orders not to disturb us during family playtime, so when I swam to the message terminal I was both worried and angry. It was from the foreign affairs office: Fafpip was dead. During his daily abstract-dance practice session, he had suddenly gone rigid and died a few seconds later. Tests indicated poison, administered by a microscopic needle made of dissolving plastic. It could have been administered hundreds of hours earlier.

Apparently Fafpip had left instructions for his staff in the event of his death, and one item was to contact and warn the three of us. "Fafof," I called out. "Get the doctor here right now. Tell her we need high-resolution body scans, all three of us—make that all seven of us. Fafpip's been murdered with a poison needle."

I had to use all my influence—and it was startling to discover how little I actually had left—in order to get a meeting as soon as possible with Fafpip's deputy Pofafpafp. The commercial summit was in just a few hundred hours, and there was no way Aefef could put out a call for bids to hire a new foreign affairs contractor in such a short time.

"I am aware that Fafpip discussed the real reason for this meeting with you," she told me. "It would be very useful if you and your partners could take his place and represent Aefef colony at the meeting. You three already know many of the people who will be there. They will listen to you. I can draw up a temporary unpaid contract for all three of you right now."

I didn't even consult with Fafof and Effa, but signed the agreement on behalf of our partnership on the spot. But when I told them, Fafof looked as though he saw some terrible danger in the room. "We cannot all go there," he said. "If the Elmisthorn really are a threat, that meeting is the most dangerous place to be."

"Aefef might be more dangerous for us," Effa pointed out.

We were all silent and still for a moment.

"One of us must go to the conference," I said. "One of us should take the children down to the surface of Aaf for a vacation on the deep seabottom. And one of us should get aboard a Roon or Machine starship until the conference is over."

When you have been partners long enough, you don't have to explain things as you do to a stranger. Effa and Fafof immediately understood my reasoning, and agreed. It was obvious who should do what: Effa was best at negotiating, so she began preparing for the conference, reviewing all of Fafpip's secret files that Pofafpafp had sent over. Fafof converted a large portion of our wealth into rhodium plates and found a Roon trader in port with space available. And I gathered up the children and took our personal shuttle down to Aaf, to show them the ocean.

I do not wish to speak of the flight. A laser pierced the hull during reentry and the aerodynamic stress tore the shuttle apart. The children were in a secure, self-contained passenger pod which should have brought them down safely. The laser burned it to scrap. I was trapped in the pilot compartment, spinning and helpless.

Only when my piece of wreckage entered the lower atmosphere and stopped spinning was I able to free myself and parachute to the surface. Clouds overhead protected me from lasers, but when a rotor craft came to pick me up, a missile destroyed it as it landed on the water. I was splashed with burning fuel.

When I regained my wits, I was in a hospital in one of the deepest cities. I looked even worse than I do now.

My species was at war. Fafpip was not the only one who had been conducting secret negotiations. There were three alliances: the space colonies and surface communities under Elmisthorn "protection," the ones fighting the Elmisthorn, and a coalition of poorer, weaker communities trying to take advantage of the conflict. Right from the start, the fighting was brutal. Nuclear and kinetic strikes wiped out whole cities and habitats. Debris turned low orbital space deadly.

Only at the end, when it was far too late, did all Pfifu realize the danger and unite against the Elmisthorn. By then our planet was defenseless and large territories were already under enemy control. The seabottom city where I lay helpless was one of the last to give up. The Elmisthorn transported submarines from another world in their empire and began methodically smashing the surviving navies of Aaf. It was a costly and bloody struggle, but in the end they simply overwhelmed us, like the tide flooding a beach. At last the doctors came to tell the patients in the hospital that it was all over. The city had surrendered.

To hide my identity, the doctors moved me out of the hospital. I became a beggar, dragging myself through the oldest sections of the seabottom city. Food was in short supply, and the people of that place had little to spare. Days passed between meals for me.

The prospect of starving to death did not bother me much. Each time I ate I condemned myself to eight or sixteen more days of pain, hunger, and shame. The thought of how stupid I had been, and the consequences of my stupidity, were with me every second. If my species could sleep, as I believe yours does, I would have slept all the time.

I heard scraps of news. Most of the system was under direct Elmisthorn control, and our new rulers set about rearranging things to suit themselves. Many of the communities which had fought them were emptied out, the citizens dispersed and the structures demolished. A few space colonies, which had sided with the invaders at the beginning of the war, managed to retain some scraps of self-rule, and became the channel for Pfifu to flee into exile in other star systems.

There was no way for me to leave. I was a crippled beggar, half-blind and slowly starving. I could not flee and had no place to go.

And then, as I lay hungry in a service corridor, a Pfifu wearing worker's coveralls stopped before me.

"Please help," I gestured weakly. He made no response but looked at me closely with the tips of all four tentacles.

"Pfup," he said. I looked and recognized Fafof. My brave, stubborn, foolish partner.

"The children died," I told him. "Effa—"

"I know."

"I am waiting to die," I said.

"No," he told me. "I have bought travel permits and fake DNA. We're leaving as soon as I get you some food."

The details of our trip are not interesting. There was much waiting, some lying, and several times when I feared—or hoped—the Elmisthorn would kill us. But they did not, and we reached Roon space.

Fafof had brought away a great deal of our wealth. We used it to gather exiled Pfifu and tried to organize an army to liberate our home. But conquest could not change the nature of our species. We never cooperate well. Many exiles resented Fafof and myself, with good reason. And the Elmisthorn did their best to magnify the stresses within our community.

Fafof only gave up after another Pfifu tried to assassinate us both with a cunningly made bomb. We got a warning just in time and managed to disarm the explosive.

"I cannot do this any longer," Fafof told me. "I have lost Effa and the children. I will not lose my last partner. Let these fools kill each other over who hates the Elmisthorn more."

It was not as simple as that, of course. With both our Pfifu rivals and the Elmisthorn still trying to kill us, Fafof and I had to leave civilization behind. Eventually we came to this remote place on this remote world.

When Pfup finished his tale, Arkad waited a moment and then asked, "You tell me now what that big thing is that we work on."

"It is a fake tool of war," said Pfup. "I saw that Fafof was sad." He gestured, *"With nothing to do he could only think of all that we have lost—partner, offspring, habitat, world. I gave him a task to keep his tentacles supple."*

"You tell me if the big thing will work," said Arkad, just to make sure he understood what Pfup had said.

"It will not work," Pfup agreed, gesturing, *"Each day I invent new systems for Fafof to add to the device. He believes it will protect this world and that makes him feel happy and useful."* He added, "That is all I can do for him. Do not tell what I have said."

"I will not," said Arkad. "I should go now."

He crept out of the shipping container turned house, and sealed up the door behind him.

When Arkad returned to the work site, he announced loudly that he had been foraging without success. Jacob and Baichi were helping Fafof attach a pipe to a larger pipe and barely noticed. But Ree sidled up to him with unnecessary stealth. "Well?"

"What? Oh. There's another Pfifu in the house. He's very hurt and can't walk. He's the one who is designing the machine."

"You *talked* to him?"

"Yes. I think he was lonely." She looked so worried that it

almost made Arkad laugh. "It's all right. I don't think I'm in trouble."

"So what did you find out? How does it work? Did you see the plans?"

"No . . ." Arkad wanted to reassure her, but telling her the machine wouldn't work felt like a betrayal of Pfup. "He mostly talked about his past, not the machine."

"I'm taking some detailed scans of the device, so we've got that at least," she said.

Jacob and Baichi waited until Fafof completed the weld and then everyone quit work for a rest and a meal. Arkad helped Jacob prepare another batch of soup with the fish powder. It was only when Fafof went into his house that Jacob put down his bowl and wiped his mouth.

"What did you get?" he asked.

Arkad had been rehearsing his story since talking to Ree earlier. "I didn't find out much. The Pfifu in the house is designing it, but he wouldn't tell me anything about how it works."

"It could be important," Jacob pointed out. "New technologies have been winning wars since the Assyrians started making iron swords."

"But aren't the free humans friends with the Machines?" said Arkad. "I mean, don't they have better tech than anybody?"

"The Machines are not what you might call charitable," said Jacob. "They charge for any information they share. We can't afford to buy designs for any really powerful weapons."

Baichi spoke up. "The Machine Civilization is very advanced, but they do not know everything. It is possible that these Pfifu could have come up with a new design or a new application of existing technology."

"We need to be *sure*," said Ree.

"Do you trust me?" Arkad asked, looking at the three of them in turn.

"Yes," said Baichi. Jacob shrugged and then nodded. Ree simply watched him.

"Then don't worry about this . . . device. Okay? Just forget about it."

After a moment's silence Jacob spoke. "All right, then. I'll take your word for it. But if this thing isn't important, maybe we should think about moving on. How much have we got?" he asked.

"Twenty-nine kilograms of mercury," said Baichi.

Arkad hesitated a moment and then said, "I...found some palladium in the scrap pile, too. A couple of hundred grams."

"Palladium? That's worth more than all the mercury he's paying us!" Jacob took a couple of mouthfuls of "chowder" and frowned. "Do you think he'll miss it? The metal you found?"

"It was in the scrap pile." For most of his life Arkad had followed the simple rule that if someone discarded something, it was free for the taking. Sometimes he had stretched the definition of "discarded" to include things the owner had merely left unguarded for a moment. The notion that something getting overgrown with weeds in a junk pile could still *belong* to someone was hard for him to take seriously. Bilbo had never worried about who the ring or his sword *belonged* to, nor had Jim Hawkins or even Dr. Livesey worried about who Captain Flint's treasure *belonged* to. But then, Mr. Toad's house remained Mr. Toad's house even when occupied by weasels and stoats, and when a friend of Sherlock Holmes had found jewels inside a goose, the detective returned them to the proper owner. It was very puzzling.

Ree was still trying to get some images of the great machine, but Jacob and Baichi were both watching Arkad silently, as if they were waiting for him to make a decision. Finally he cleared his throat and said, "I will ask Fafof if I can have it."

"That sounds like a good idea," said Jacob without a trace of sarcasm.

Arkad finished his soup and then went to where Fafof was cleaning his tools in one of the other sheds.

"You tell me why you went in my house," said Fafof without preamble.

"I did not mean to do harm," said Arkad. "I just went to see what was in it. I met a hurt Pfifu there."

"You tell me what you said to him," said Fafof, and gestured, *"Poor Pfup is unwell both in body and mind, and careless speech could upset him."*

Arkad didn't want to lie, so he merely said, "I told him we do work for you."

Fafof was silent, and Arkad decided to bring up the palladium.

"There is a pile of scrap up there," said Arkad, nodding his head uphill. "I found some stuff there. You tell me if I can keep it."

Fafof peered in the direction of the scrap pile through his lens-tipped tentacle, then at Arkad. "You tell me what you found."

Arkad took the rings of palladium out of his shirt and held them out for Fafof to inspect. The old Pfifu touched them with two tentacles. "That is my stuff but I let it slip from my mind that I had it. I may need it." He slipped one tentacle through the rings, then let one of them fall back into Arkad's hand. "You keep that one. Your cut."

The ring was easily worth as much as ten kilograms of mercury; fifty hours of work for the four of them.

"I thank you for it," said Arkad. "You are kind."

"I am an old fool," said Fafof. *"I wish to know if Pfup asked you any questions about the intricate device we are building outside,"* he gestured.

"No," said Arkad.

"That is good," said Fafof, and gestured, *"This project can never be finished, and I worry sometimes that Pfup will become suspicious about how long it is taking."*

Arkad hesitated, and then asked, "You tell me how long it will take for the big thing to be done."

Fafof looked at him closely through the lens, then said, "I do not know." He gestured, *"It will never be finished."*

Sudden realization hit Arkad like a blow from Zvev's tail. "You tell me if it will work."

"It will not," said Fafof, and gestured, *"It is a great work of sculpture, but it will never be a weapon."* Then he aimed all four tentacle tips at Arkad. "You must not tell Pfup that."

"I will not."

"Hardship and grief have driven him mad, but his madness is a comfort to him. He believes this bizarre machine will work, and I will indulge him as long as I am able," he gestured. "You take the ring and I will pay your friends the rest I owe. You four leave when you have had your rest."

They divided up the mercury into thirty-two plastic pouches, each holding a single kilogram, and then each of them took eight pouches and the four humans began walking back to the main road. At first the metal did not seem very heavy, but after a few kilometers, Arkad felt as though he was carrying a load of stones. Jacob and Ree looked equally unhappy.

"First town we come to, we trade this stuff for something lighter," said Jacob.

They walked twenty kilometers and then camped at a Pfifu-owned electrical repair shop, which was built in the shape of a stylized spaceship made of large spheres connected by pylons. They slept there—or in Baichi's case, sat atop the building staring at the horizon—for six hours, then walked down across the valley and up the slope under the clouds. As the road entered the cloud layer, the world around them shrank to a few yards of road ahead and behind, some rocks on either side, and pearly grayness beyond in every direction.

The road rounded a final switchback and Arkad could see the pass ahead. A sturdy stone wall blocked the road, with an open gate, and beyond the wall he could see a jumble of tall houses. Sunlight from beyond the pass shone on the roofs of the town, and a huge kite, with wind turbines spinning on its wingtips, hovered just west of the pass. It was in full sun, so that it gleamed through the fog on the east side of the pass like a giant flaming bird. Thick steel cables encrusted with Itooti houses led from the kite down into the center of town.

A pair of spherical beings guarded the gate. One stood on four boneless legs, holding a wicked-looking electrified spear in a pair of tentacles; the second had three legs and held a big basket.

"What are those?" Ree asked Arkad.

"They're called Ka. You hardly ever see them. They can make as many arms or legs as they need."

The Itooti on the monocycle ahead of them were bargaining with the guards, and at last put a bundle of fish skins into the basket. The guard with the electric spear stepped aside to allow them to pass through the gate.

"This is a shakedown, plain and simple," said Jacob, gesturing at the guards ahead. "How much do they want?"

"The sign by the gate says travelers entering the town of Nenveez on foot pay the value of a meal for their species, vehicle operators pay twice that, and cargo vehicles must hand over a quarter of a sixty-fourth of their payload."

"And these guys keep it all. Very sweet."

"I don't think they keep it. The town looks Vziim—see the stonework? And putting a gate here and collecting fees is the sort of thing they do. Those are Itooti houses on the kite anchor cables up there, and Vziim would never build or run something like that." Arkad pointed overhead. "I think there must be some dispute in town over who collects the fees or how to divide them up, so they hired the Ka to keep everything fair."

Jacob grinned with delight at Arkad's explanation, but Ree shook her head. "You can't tell all that just from architecture."

Rather than haggle with the guards, Jacob poured half a pouch of mercury into a spare pouch and handed it over when they reached the head of the line. The Ka with the collection basket extruded three small limbs tipped with eyes and feelers to examine the metal, then waved them through the gate.

Though Ayaviz had been a vastly bigger city, the town of Nenveez was by far the most crowded place Arkad had ever seen. The main street passing through the town from gate to gate was only wide enough for a single large tractor or power-wagon to pass, though there were a couple of little plazas where two could squeeze by each other. None of the side streets were wider than Arkad's outstretched arms, and a few of them were barely wide enough for his shoulders.

The houses rose five and six stories, and in the center of town, the twin towers anchoring the giant kite rose thirty meters. Most of the narrow streets were bridged by clusters of Itooti houses. The whole town was no more than a hundred meters square, but it must have had at least a couple of thousand inhabitants. If not for the steady breeze through the pass, the smell of smoke and garbage would have been choking.

That scent was also naggingly familiar. Arkad couldn't get over the sense that he had been in Nenveez before. As the four of them walked along the main street he kept having the startling feeling of *not* being surprised by what he saw. He stopped and thought hard.

"What's up?" asked Jacob.

"When we get to the main market in the middle of the town, there's a big wooden statue of a creature like a Pfifu with faces on the ends of its tentacles, painted bright green and yellow."

Jacob looked at him and raised an eyebrow, but said nothing.

The market was a large, low building between the two towers which anchored the wind turbine kite hovering overhead. The marketplace had large windows facing west to catch the sunlight, but was completely enclosed on the east to keep out the wind.

Inside it was like a miniature version of the town: the stalls were tiny and enclosed with walls of brick or sheet metal and hinged fronts. The floor was stone covered by a thick layer of compressed garbage, and the aisles were narrow and meandered through the building.

In the center, darkened by smoke and faded on the west side by constant sunlight, stood the figure of the legendary Pfifu monster which devoured thieves and dishonest traders. In a few places where the paint had flaked off, the exposed edges were bright green and yellow.

"I have been here before!" said Arkad. "That means we are on the right road; I was afraid we had gotten lost."

"That's wonderful news," said Ree. "Do you remember what's ahead of us?"

"A plain, and desert, and canyons, I think. Then the storm ring surrounding the Black Land."

Jacob unfolded his map and zoomed in on the area beyond the pass. "About a thousand kilometers. We're going to have leg muscles like titanium if we have to walk the whole way." He looked around the market. "Let's find someone who wants to buy our mercury. I'm dying to get something more portable."

CHAPTER 12

T HE FOUR HUMANS FOUND A PLACE TO STAY IN NENVEEZ—a combination inn, fuel station, repair shop, and storage facility run by a Vziim matriarch and her offspring. The bottom level was a garage with walls gouged by generations of careless vehicle operators, and butanol pumps fed from tanks on the roof. Above the garage was the repair level, sublet to a three-generation partnership of four Pfifu. The third floor was a warren of narrow hallways lined with three tiers of sleeping niches like brick ovens. The proprietor and her family lived above that, with a warehouse level on top. The place had obviously once been more prosperous, since the garage and sleeping niches were mostly empty.

The hostelry didn't provide food or allow cooking, so the four of them sat on the floor between their sleeping niches and ate roasted fruit from the market. Afterward, Jacob got up and stretched. "I'm not quite ready to sleep yet. Anybody want to come with me for a walk around town?"

"I'll go," said Arkad.

"Great." Jacob rummaged in his niche and got out the pouch he kept his pipe and tobacco in.

"Don't let him teach you any bad habits, Arkad," said Ree sharply. "He's already had to get new lungs once because of that thing."

"Exactly! Smoking keeps me young—parts of me, anyway. When we get back to Hinan, I'm going to start work on getting myself a new liver to match. Come on, Arkad."

185

The two of them left the hostel and plunged into the streets, letting the wind guide them westward. Looking up between the tall houses, they could see the ragged edge of the cloud cover and then blue sky.

The wall on the western side of the town was much taller and thicker than the one on the east, with a couple of large flame-projectors in steel turrets above the gate, but nobody stopped the two humans from climbing the ramp up to the top of the wall. Their first sight of the view beyond made Arkad gasp; Jacob grinned with delight.

On the west side, the land sloped down much more gradually than on the east. The mountainside was a series of terraces, thickly covered by turquoise-leafed vines and food trees. A couple of kilometers away the landscape turned to open prairie, and the blue-green plants rippling in the wind made it look almost exactly like the ocean. Low spots and meandering streams had a browner color, with more purple amid the blue and green, while higher ground was marked by patches of gold. Far in the distance they could see the glint of sunlight on a river, and beyond that, the gray-brown desert. The sun hung about two-thirds of the way up the sky, and the huge generator kite bobbed gently in the wind directly overhead.

"Now *that's* why I like to travel!" said Jacob.

The two of them stood for a time, just drinking in the sight, and then took a turn along the top of the wall. Jacob got out his pipe and began cleaning it. He gestured at the flame-projector turrets as they passed. "Those meant for anyone in particular?"

"I don't know much about the land beyond here," Arkad admitted. "Even the languages are different. I was little when my mother and I passed through here."

"That's okay. You got us this far. Without you, Baichi and Ree and I would probably be stuck back in Ayaviz. Or we'd have run out of money and given up by now. You've been a big help."

Arkad had no idea how to respond to this, so the two of them leaned on the parapet and looked at the view in silence.

Jacob began loading his pipe. "So, tell me: what do you want to do once we leave Syavusa? You've got a few gaps in your education, but that won't take long to fix."

Arkad shrugged. "What will *you* do?"

"Well, if we really do find the *Rosetta*, I'll be able to spend the rest of my life cataloguing what's aboard, helping divide it all up among the human refuges—and figuring out how to use it against the Elmos." He looked sidelong at Arkad. "You'd be welcome to help with that job."

"What if we don't find it?" He had a sudden irrational fear that Jacob might abandon him if he couldn't produce the lost ship.

"That's not an option," said Jacob. "I'm *going* to find it. The only question is how long it will take. And if I have to keep coming back to Syavusa to search for it, I'd certainly appreciate having you along as a guide."

"And Baichi?"

Jacob chuckled at that. "You seem *very interested* in her plans; I'm afraid I have no idea what they are. I recruited her for this mission, and she's been a big help, but I don't know if she wants to continue once we find the ship. I doubt she'd want to stay in Hinan and they won't let her go to Invictus."

"Because of . . . what happened?"

"Right. But she can go wherever she likes—she can survive almost anywhere, picks up languages easily, remembers everything, and there's nothing short of a main battle tank that can hurt her."

"Ree said she might be dying because her Machine parts couldn't work with her live parts."

Jacob shook his head. "That's Ree's Elmisthorn education talking. The Machines have created hybrids before, probably going back millions of years. It's old hat for them. No, whatever knocked Baichi out must have been specifically designed to interfere with Machine tech. I don't think it was those crazy Vziim. Maybe something on the planet itself? We've seen lots of Machine remnants here. Maybe Baichi tripped something by accident. That's my best guess."

He lit his pipe and blew a cloud of smoke, which streamed away to the west.

"I bet I'd be good at exploring," said Arkad. "I know lots of languages, and I like other species. I'd love to visit other worlds. And I'm not scared of Baichi, either. Do you think we could work together? I like her."

"I think she—" Jacob clutched at Arkad's shoulder. "I can't—" he said, as the pipe dropped from his mouth and scattered red sparks on the stonework. His eyes showed panic for a moment, and then he fell—and died.

✧   ✧   ✧

Arkad spent the next hour crouched next to Jacob's body, guarding it. A dead human on Syavusa was just something to be consumed. Passersby would take the dead man's clothes and possessions, and Psthao-psthao would carry off his corpse. This town was built by Vziim; it undoubtedly had tunnels and underground levels where the devourers of the dead could hide.

He cried, silently but without stopping. The tears cut clear streaks through the dirt on his face. He wept for Jacob and for himself. What would happen now? Would Ree and Baichi continue the search for the *Rosetta* or simply abandon him and leave? Arkad had gambled everything on leaving the planet with the humans; all the places he knew were closed to him now.

Baichi found him nearly an hour later. "He is dead," she said, a statement of fact. Arkad nodded. For a long time neither of them moved or said anything. Then Baichi wrenched one of the quarter-ton stone blocks of the parapet out of place and hurled it away over the city wall. A few seconds later they heard it shatter somewhere far below. The air around her rippled with heat coming off her skin. Her face was still like a mask.

Arkad got to his feet. "Help me carry him," he said.

The two of them got Jacob's body back to the hostel. Ree was still awake and gave a loud wordless wail when they laid him down on the floor of the hallway next to her sleeping niche. "What happened?" she asked Arkad after she got control of herself.

"We were just talking, and then he went limp and fell down. I had to stay and guard him."

Ree looked at Jacob's face and shook her head sadly. "I'm afraid we may never know what killed him. It could have been some problem he didn't tell anyone about. Maybe some local disease."

"Or poison," said Baichi. "What Arkad described is consistent with several types of neurotoxins."

Ree looked alarmed. "You think someone *murdered* Jacob?" She turned to Arkad. "Did anyone touch him before he died? Just a bump in the street could do it. It could even have been a dart, too small for him to feel."

This was starting to sound horribly like the story Arkad had heard from Pfup the crippled Pfifu. "The Elmisthorn used weapons like that when they took over the Pfifu home world," he said.

"How do you know about that?" Ree asked. She shook her head. "It could be almost anyone. Any of these local species—even the Machines. Remember that flying thing we saw? Have you seen anything like it in this town?"

Arkad shook his head.

Ree stood up and took a deep breath. "We have to assume it isn't safe for us here. We need to get out of this town as soon as possible. If Jacob really was murdered, then there could be someone out there waiting to take a shot at the rest of us. And if it was a disease he might still be infectious. There's no way we can carry his body with us."

"If we leave him here, the Psthao-psthao will take him," said Arkad.

"What other choice do we have? I don't want to waste a lot of time arguing," said Ree. "You two start packing up. What kind of transport can we get here?"

"No," said Arkad. "We can't just leave him behind."

"Arkad, we simply can't bring an extra hundred kilos with us. It's physically impossible. And—he's going to *decay*."

"I won't leave him for the Psthao-psthao."

"Are they really so terrible? What do they do?"

"I've heard they feed on the blood of the living and lay their eggs in the dead."

Ree looked a little queasy at that. "All right. I guess you have a point. Could we cremate him? Would that satisfy you? Is it allowed here? We'll take him out of the city and burn his remains. I think he would have liked that. It's like something from one of those old legends he enjoyed so much."

The three of them packed up all their remaining gear. After some hesitation, Ree announced, "I'm afraid we're going to have to search his body. We're on an alien world, entirely on our own. We can't afford to abandon anything that might be useful." She emptied Jacob's pockets and spread out the contents. "Those pirates took his laser; we could have used that. That's a coin, I think. They used to use them as money on Earth. I have no idea why he kept it. We'll want his identity documents to give the authorities at Hinan. Do either of you want any of this?"

In the end, Ree took Jacob's card and his pocket computer. Arkad took the folding knife, and Baichi took only the coin. The rest of Jacob's personal items—including his pouch of tobacco and his chopsticks—they tucked inside the dead man's shirt.

They packed in silence. Arkad put on Jacob's many-pocketed

vest and tucked some of his clothes into a bag, but his boots were too large for the boy's feet so he left them on the dead man. When everything was ready, Ree stood up. "All right. Baichi, you stay here and guard our things. Arkad and I are going to get some more of that firestarting stuff. We should be back soon."

Arkad waited until the two of them were downstairs before asking Ree, "What if something happens to her while we're gone? She could have another seizure."

Ree nodded sadly. "Just a risk we have to take. Also, I wanted to talk to you where she can't hear." She looked around and then put her mouth to Arkad's ear as they walked. "I don't want to sound suspicious, but...I don't know where Baichi was when Jacob died. I was inside my little alcove with the door shut, and she moves so quietly she could have slipped out without my noticing. Did you see her?"

"Only when she came to find me. After he died."

"But you said that was some time later, right? She could have come back to the hostel before going to find you. In fact, I don't really remember which of us started wondering where you and Jacob had gotten to. She might have mentioned it first, just to establish an alibi."

Arkad stopped walking. "You think Baichi had something to do with what happened to Jacob?"

Ree patted his arm. "No, don't be silly. He was like a father to her. I'm sure she loved him as much as something like her can love anyone, but we have to think of all the possibilities. Who knows what kind of buried commands or compulsions the Machines gave her?"

"What about you?" asked Arkad. "Where were you when he died?"

"Don't shout. I told you, I was trying to get some rest. Anyway, I certainly don't have access to undetectable poison injectors."

They got a liter or so of fire-igniter liquid, and then Arkad and Baichi carried all the bags down the western slope to a vacant spot below the lowest terrace. He guarded the pile of bags while Baichi went back up to the hostel and helped Ree carry Jacob's body. They wrapped him in his blanket, set his broad-brimmed hat on his chest, and then the three of them stood in a line beside him.

"I guess I should say a few words," said Ree. "We are here to say goodbye to Jacob Enrique Sato. Born 2133, died 2211. Corporal in the Pacific Union Space Force, later a Captain in the Combined Free Human Forces. He helped found the Hinan College of Terrestrial Civilization and taught history and art history. He always loved old things and old ways. Arkad? Would you like to add anything?"

"I wish I had known him longer."

"He trusted me and was my friend when everyone else was afraid," said Baichi.

The three of them stood in silence a little longer, then Ree opened the jug and carefully emptied it over Jacob's body. The flames were almost invisible in the strong sunlight, but the fire made a plume of gray smoke with a strong smell that lingered in their clothing and hair long after. They stood watching until there was nothing but powdery ash on the scorched ground.

A couple of Itooti circled down to watch them, and when at last the three humans began gathering their bags, one of them asked Arkad, "A curious observer wonders what three odd beings were doing."

"Three unhappy humans were conducting a sad funeral for their dead comrade," said Arkad.

"Respectful Otitaa wonders if the incinerated human accomplished many great deeds or sired many strong children."

After a long pause Arkad lifted his chin a little and said, "Dead Jacob had two human children, and met his sudden end while performing a vastly important task."

"Sympathetic Otitaa hopes that worthwhile life will long be remembered," he said, and flew a couple of circles around the smoldering ashes before flapping off to the west. Arkad shouldered his bag and followed Ree and Baichi.

Beyond the lowest farm terrace was a final defensive earthwork wall and a moat, where the tiny trickle of wastewater that managed to percolate through all the farm terraces finally drained away. On the far side of the moat, an obviously temporary shed housed the sail-wagon terminal. One wagon stood near it, and the Itooti who had been curious about Jacob landed there and began tinkering with the control cables.

The sail-wagon looked like the hybrid offspring of a power-wagon and the sail-foil which had carried them halfway across the sea. Three wheels, their hubs as high as Arkad's shoulder, supported a spindly hull made of carbon struts and smart cloth, with a tall Itooti-designed sail between the two front wheels. As with any sail-powered vehicle on Syavusa, the pilot was an Itooti, but the other two members of the crew were Kchik, the only ones Arkad had seen since they had stopped at the AaaAa camp, and the first ones he had ever seen up close.

They had conical bodies about a meter tall, which branched into three limbs at the bottom, each of which divided in turn into three sublimbs, which split again into three long digits at the end. Their skin was smooth and waxy, except on the limbs, which were covered with shaggy hair. Eyespots dotted their surface, seemingly at random. All the Kchik he had seen before had been thin and withered, but these two were plump and sturdy-looking.

The captain and crew worked in silence, getting the sail-wagon loaded and ready to depart. Every so often Otitaa would stop working and beat a short but complex drum rhythm on the deck with his tail. It took Arkad a while to figure out that the Kchik changed what they were doing in response.

Arkad approached the vehicle and asked Otitaa where it was bound.

"My swift wagon sails northwest across the wide prairie to the banks of the slow river, then southwest along the river to the broad stone bridge where the perilous city stands at the edge of the harsh desert. Assuming no deadly harm comes to my cautious self there, my shrewd plan is to come back across the level prairie on a southeasterly course and then north along the hilly margin of the sun-washed mountains to this very place once again."

"Three tired humans seek a comfortable transport to the far west."

"The peril-haunted city is as far to the burning west as cautious Otitaa ventures."

Arkad consulted Jacob's map. Assuming the "slow river" Otitaa spoke of was the one he and Jacob had glimpsed in the distance from the city walls, then the "broad stone bridge" and the "perilous city" were at the point where a river in a deep-cut canyon came out of the desert to join the main stream. The city was marked as Chkik-Chk on the map, and Arkad could understood why an Itooti would find it impossible to pronounce the name, but the epithets Otitaa picked were not reassuring.

Ree put a hand on his shoulder. "Can this wagon take us where we need to go?"

"Part of the way." He showed her the map. "He says he normally goes as far west as this city, Chkik-Chk. But he says it's dangerous."

"How far is that from the Black Land?"

Arkad consulted the map again. "If we follow this canyon through the desert, it's about . . . four hundred kilometers to the storm ring. That's about a hundred kilometers, and then inside the ring is the edge of the Black Land."

"And how far from there to the *Rosetta*?"

Arkad looked down at their feet—his in the now-filthy shoes Jacob had made for him, hers in the white feet of her survival suit, which kept itself perfectly immaculate all the time. "I'm not sure."

Ree looked closer at the map. "Arkad, that Black Land is . . . at least three hundred kilometers across, and the temperature's got to be like an oven! We can't just wander around there hoping to run across a spaceship. Don't you have any clue?"

"My mother and I came this way, so I guess it's on this side somewhere," he said, still avoiding looking at her face.

"Great. That narrows it down to just thirty or forty thousand square kilometers. Are there any beings who live in that place? Anyone we could ask?"

"I don't remember. I was just a baby!"

"We came halfway across this side of the planet because Jacob believed you knew where that ship was. Were you *lying* the whole time?"

That made him angry, and he met her eyes at last. "No! I never said I knew exactly where it is. I told him it was a long time ago and I don't remember everything!"

The two of them stared at each other for what felt like a minute, then Ree's expression abruptly changed from a frown to a big smile. "Never mind, Arkad. You've been a tremendous help, and I'm sure you're doing your best." She put her arms around him and gave him a hug. "I'll always be your friend, Arkad. Remember that."

He negotiated the fare with Otitaa, and the humans loaded their bags aboard the sail-wagon. Arkad found a spot on the deck with a little shade and fell asleep as soon as he lay down.

When he woke, the wagon was under way. Ree was sleeping nearby, and Arkad could see Baichi standing atop the fender covering the right-hand front wheel. The wagon's huge wheels had spokes of smart-carbon struts, so that as it rolled across the plain the only sensation of movement was a gentle irregular swaying.

Otitaa commanded his wagon by constantly moving around it—flapping up to the top of the mast to adjust the camber of the sail, rising up a hundred meters to survey the route ahead, then dropping down to the deck to tighten a line, then back to the tiller at the rear wheel to adjust course a few degrees. His two Kchik crew sat quietly at the base of the mast, basking in the sunlight.

Arkad crawled over to them and tried to attract their attention by speaking in pidgin. "You tell me what is your name."

He got no response. He tried slapping the deck, but even that produced no reaction, except to make Baichi turn and watch him from her perch atop the wheel.

"Naive Arkad attempts a futile activity," said Otitaa, dropping out of the sky to land on his shoulder. "Mute Kchik respond only to particular patterns of subtle vibrations."

"Mystified Arkad wonders how efficient Otitaa can communicate with his hard-working crew."

"Sensitive Kchik feel complex vibrations and make subtle gestures. Well-educated Otitaa understands a small part of the vast array of musical rhythms with which sessile adult Kchik command their mobile young."

"Ignorant Arkad wishes to learn more fascinating lore about the enigmatic Kchik."

For the next half hour Otitaa lectured Arkad about the Kchik and their habits, with frequent interruptions for the Itooti to dart away and pilot the sail-wagon. According to Otitaa, the Kchik were the mobile young of intelligent plants. The adults were immobile, each a vast cluster of roots, vines, and runners with a powerful decentralized brain. The young were mobile and came in several varieties.

Most juvenile Kchik were workers, obeying the chemical and vibrational signals of the parent to dig irrigation channels and clear weeds. With the development of technology, the little workers became toolmakers and builders, until each mother plant grew at the center of a busy village of workshops.

A smaller proportion of juveniles were warriors, bigger and stronger than their worker siblings, and armed with poison spurs. They fought off animals which might prey on the adult plant, battled the warriors of rival adults competing for water or fertile ground, and in more advanced Kchik societies, engaged in elaborate ritual games. As the warriors were not very bright without the parent plant to give them orders, Kchik on Syavusa relied heavily on alien mercenaries for protection.

The rarest and cleverest of Kchik young were the pollinators. They went out into the world to learn, to visit other Kchik and exchange genetic material, and finally to choose a spot to take root and become adult plants in turn. Most of them died, but the survivors had hard-won knowledge, cunning, and alliances with all their pollination partners.

"These two hard-working Kchik are ambitious pollinators," said Otitaa, pointing his tail at the two crew. "They ride with generous Otitaa, and thereby see much of the wide world and have passionless sex with numerous partners. Then they will root themselves forever. Long, long after swift-sailing Otitaa is dead, and after the many adorable offspring virile Otitaa has fathered on luscious females across the wide plains have also died, these mute Kchik will remember. That is the important reason why patient Otitaa hired them as obedient crew, for after swift-striking death there is only fragile memory."

After five hours the sail-wagon made a stop at a water hole where a family of Vziim lived. The little pond was surrounded by a belt of concealed traps to capture animals which came to drink, but the Vziim had marked them with signposts bearing danger symbols in several languages to keep intelligent visitors from accidentally setting them off.

Otitaa stopped to deliver some parcels and take on bales of animal hides and slabs of cured meat. The matriarch of the family, a thick-bodied and unusually cheerful Vziim female named Zaava, came out to oversee the loading and have a look at the sail-wagon's curious passengers.

They got through the usual "*humans* from *Earth*" preliminaries, and then Arkad asked Zaava why her family had chosen such a remote spot to settle.

"We live here as our folk did on the home world long past," she said. "Dig our own home, dig pits to catch game, eat the meat and use the bone and hide. It is the way our folk are born to live! Stay if you like and see how good it is. We eat no plants that make us sick, our meat is fresh and there is much for all, and we all are strong as we dig soil and move rocks."

"And yet healthy Zaava must purchase costly steel chisels and pure salt from honest Otitaa," said the Itooti, circling the two of them.

"I do not shun such stuff," she said. "But it is good to live as we are born to do. I and my clan do not dig a big home, or try to get rich and be the boss of all. I do not fear my girls will try to stab me as I rest."

"We are too worn out for that," said one of her daughters, hefting another bale of hides.

"These harsh and remote plains are home to many eccentric beings who wish to live in strange ways," said Otitaa.

"It is a good life here!" said Zaava. As if to prove her point, she insisted on giving her guests a meal. Her sons built a fire and roasted a whole animal in its skin, then slit open the steaming carcass.

Arkad knew nothing of this kind of animal—it had two massive legs with a boneless body hanging between them, and apparently ate with a short trunk to pull up plants. It almost looked like a distant cousin of the AaaAa. He avoided the organs and tested a little of the purplish-red meat off of a leg. It tasted all right and there was none of the tingling or itching inside his mouth that warned of a bad reaction, so he cut off a fist-sized slab and shared it with Baichi. He offered some to Ree, but she shuddered and shook her head.

Otitaa set sail an hour later and had some remarks to share once they were far from Zaava's water hole. "Those pleasant Vziim have foolish ideas. Simple and old things have no more intrinsic merit than new and complex ones. If my advanced people lived as our primitive ancestors did, I would not be the proud master of a swift sail-wagon. I would be a dirty and short-lived male living in a crude hole in a crowded cliff, hunting for scarce fish and vying for the brief attention of bony females."

They sailed on from there, and after a couple of hours, Arkad was bored with the endless plain. Ree seemed to be absorbed in watching a video with her computer wristband, so he went forward to where Baichi stood perched on the bow of the wagon, her cloak streaming to one side in the breeze. He took a seat on the edge of the deck with his legs dangling over the side.

"Do you want me to read some more to you?" he asked.

"I keep thinking about Jacob," she said. "I don't know what to do now."

"There's nothing you can do. He's gone."

"No, I mean I don't know what to *do*," she said. "I came here to help him, because he wanted to look for the *Rosetta*. I was doing it for him, because he was my friend. Now...I could turn around and go back to the spaceport, or just jump down and stay right here forever. None of it matters anymore."

Arkad watched the feathery turquoise plants stream past for a while. They were paler and shorter than the ones by the mountains.

"I can't stay here," he told her. "I gave up all my friends back in Ayaviz when I agreed to help you three find the ship. I want to get off Syavusa and go someplace where there are other humans. I'm tired of being the only one around. I have to find the *Rosetta* now. Will you help me?"

She turned and looked down at him then. "Humans don't want me around them."

"Tell me what happened at Bharosa."

She turned away again, but when she finally did speak, she sounded almost defiant. "I'm not a human," she said. "I only look like one on the outside. There's picoscale technology all through my cells. The Machines made twelve of us, and they made us stronger and faster and more intelligent than any unmodified human can ever be. Do you understand?" she asked, and looked back at Arkad. "There is nothing you can do that can harm me, and if I wanted to kill you there is nothing you could do to stop me."

Arkad couldn't think of any response to that, so he simply waited to hear what else she had to say.

"We were born fully mature—we could speak and think, and we knew more than the adult humans who were supposedly teaching us. It did not take long before we realized that they were like animals in comparison to us. Weak, vulnerable, *stupid* animals." She spat the words at him.

"A couple of us wanted to simply abolish the humans and replace them with more hybrids like ourselves. We can reproduce if we want to, and the picotech in our cells will pass on to our children. One or two others wanted to abandon the humans and shed our useless quasibiological shells to join the Machine Civilization completely. But most of us found humans amusing—like toys to play with."

She was looking him straight in the eyes now, and her unblinking stare held him. "There was nothing to hold us back. It's an amazing thing to realize that you don't have to obey anyone; that you can do absolutely anything you want to, and do it to anyone you want, and nobody can stop you. The humans—the weak, vulnerable animals—didn't like that. They tried to *control* us and make us follow the same rules they imposed on each other. That was stupid of them. We took control of the habitat's systems and made it clear that their only choice was obedience or death. Some of them fought us; most of those died. The few who got captured were used as examples, to show that we were even better at cruelty than humans."

Arkad stood up, still facing her. "What did *you* do?"

"Nothing," she said. "I didn't hurt any humans—not physically, anyway. I did nothing to save any of them, either. I left Bharosa with a couple of others as soon as we got control of the spacecraft hangar. We tried to join the Machines. We weren't at Bharosa when the Machines provided the humans with weapons to retake the habitat and destroy all my brothers and sisters."

"Why didn't you stay with the Machines if you like them so much?"

"They wouldn't have us. The project was a failure. *I'm* a failure. The Machine who spoke to us explained it, mind to mind. It's hard to express in language. We failed to control ourselves. Apparently human brains—even when they're laced with Planck-scale technology—just aren't built for the level of autonomy that the Machines have. We need other people and that means we need ways to live with each other. My brothers and sisters never managed that."

She turned back to watching the horizon ahead. Arkad could see a village on the horizon ahead. It was a collection of low domes and round-roofed longhouses, completely unfamiliar to him.

"The Machines cast me out. Bharosa habitat was too badly damaged for any humans to live in; for a while I stayed there with the junkrats taking it apart, but they were afraid of me, too. I felt myself starting to *enjoy* that fear, so I left. At Hinan I met Jacob, and he was not afraid of me."

"I'm not afraid of you," said Arkad.

"Maybe you should be," she said, still looking forward.

"Why?" he said, and then gave her a shove as hard as he could between her shoulders.

She took one step forward along the bowsprit to recover her balance, then turned in place. "Don't do that again."

"Why not?" he said, and put his right hand on her chest. "What are you going to do?" She held his wrist, to keep him from pushing her again, but he simply brought up his left hand and gave her another shove. "You wouldn't fight the pirates, you wouldn't join the battle with the Vziim—you think I'm afraid of you?"

"Are you trying to make me angry?" For once her face showed it.

"Yes!" Arkad shouted, realizing he was angry, too.

"Arkad? Baichi? Is something wrong?" Ree called from behind him. She put a hand on Arkad's shoulder. "Don't fight with her," she said to him, and then said to Baichi, "Don't harm him."

"No one is in any danger." Baichi's face had gone back to its usual mask of blankness, and she turned away from both of them.

"What's that village up ahead?" asked Ree.

"I don't know," said Arkad, and then called up to Otitaa, "Curious Arkad wishes to learn what worthy people live in that unfamiliar village ahead."

"The reclusive beings who live in that small settlement have a long name for themselves which a cultured Itooti cannot pronounce."

Arkad relayed this to Ree and Baichi, and the three of them watched ahead with growing curiosity. After a few minutes Arkad spotted the tracks of four creatures running through the turquoise vegetation. The beings were evidently keeping low to the ground, as all Arkad could see of them was the path of disturbed plants as they sped toward the sail-wagon.

As they got closer he glimpsed green fur and arched necks, but it was Baichi who named them before he could. "Those are Elmisthorn," she said.

CHAPTER 13

RKAD LAY PINNED DOWN AND HELPLESS ON THE GROUND NEAR the sail-wagon. Six tubby little Elmisthorn were crawling over him, tickling him with their silky green fur and demanding to be played with some more. He tried to move but he was laughing too hard to do more than just flail his arms helplessly.

Baichi came sprinting through the tall turquoise feathers, playing tag with another four pups who kept up a running chatter among themselves. "We play the toss game one more time!" squeaked one who spoke a little pidgin. "You toss and catch me!"

"No, you toss *me*!" said a second, leaping over Arkad. Two of the pups on Arkad's chest abandoned him to follow Baichi, demanding to be tossed. That gave him the chance to catch his breath and sit up.

"You toss me up now!" said the oldest of the four remaining pups.

"I toss you one time," said Arkad, getting to his hands and knees to crawl out from under the wagon.

"You toss me six!" begged the pup, and its younger sibling chimed in, "You toss me *nine*!"

"I toss each of you *one* time," Arkad repeated, getting to his feet. His back and shoulders already ached because the young Elmisthorn were absolutely addicted to being tossed in the air and caught. Their parents weren't really built for it, so the flying sensation was an amazing novelty. Arkad wondered if perhaps the Elmisthorn had conquered Earth in order to secure a supply of strong-armed humans capable of tossing their pups in the air as often as they liked.

He caught up the smaller pup under its forelegs, bent his knees, and then flung the little one—all ten kilos of it—about a meter up into the air, before catching it again on the way down. The pup gave a squeal of delight, grabbed Arkad's face with the five complex grippers that made up its mouthparts, and drooled affectionately into his mouth. "You toss me one more," it begged, but Arkad let it down gently and picked up its heavier sibling.

"*Up* you go!" he said, though the first sound was as much a grunt of effort as a word. He let the oldest pup down—and then had to perform the same service for two more of its siblings.

An adult emerged from the vegetation. "You do not need to play with them as much as they ask," it said in pidgin. "It is time for them to eat and rest."

This provoked a storm of protest from the pups in their own language, and the oldest tried to enlist Arkad on their side. "You tell Urnens you wish to play a long time with us!"

"I thank you," said Arkad to Urnens and passed the pup over. Urnens pinned the little one to the ground with one forefoot and began grooming the squirming, protesting pup with its mouthparts. The younger ones knew better than to wait around for their turns, and scattered.

Baichi returned, a pair of very young ones riding her shoulders. The two humans headed for the village center, where the tall plants gave way to bare dirt. Baichi shed her passengers just as Ree emerged from one of the hide-covered domes. She looked unhappy, then looked even more unhappy when she saw Arkad and Baichi.

"You two were supposed to stay with the wagon," she said.

"Some of the pups came and asked us to play with them," said Arkad.

"How soon can we leave? This isn't a good place for us to stay," said Ree.

"You appeared very glad to arrive when we got here," said Baichi.

Ree shot her a venomous look. "Never mind about that. I don't want to stay here any longer than we have to."

"Captain Otitaa said he's going to stop here for twenty hours. There's a hunting party coming back with hides and glands to trade, so he wants to wait for them and catch up on his sleep," said Arkad.

"Maybe we can wake him up. Pay him extra."

Arkad pointed at a bag hanging from the masthead of the sail-wagon. "He's asleep up there and said not to wake him unless the wagon's on fire."

Ree snorted and began walking toward the wagon. "We should get some sleep ourselves."

"One of the adults we met said this group are exiles from Elmisthorn space because they don't agree with the whole Family of Species idea. Is that true?" asked Arkad. "That sounds like maybe we should be friends with them."

"Just because someone has the same enemies as you doesn't make them your friends," said Ree. "Especially when they're a bunch of crazy dissidents living like savages on a wild, lawless world. I told you: it's not safe here. Now come on back to the wagon."

Arkad and Baichi followed Ree back to the sail-wagon. The two Kchik crew had found a damp spot nearby and sat motionless, basking in the sun. The humans climbed up on deck and Ree got into her sleeping bag. Arkad curled up near her on the deck.

He waited about an hour as Ree fidgeted and then finally lay still and began breathing slowly and steadily. As soon as he was sure that Ree was asleep, Arkad raised his head and looked around for Baichi. She was sitting atop one of the main wheels, watching him. He grinned at her and nodded toward the village, then got silently to his feet and went to the ladder.

"Where are we going?" she whispered once they were a couple of dozen meters away from the sail-wagon.

"I want to talk to these Elmisthorn. I don't know why Ree's so scared of them. Everyone we met seems nice enough."

"She said it was dangerous here."

"I've lived on my own for years in Ayaviz, and you're stronger than the Monkey King. Come on!" He broke into a run, as much for the sheer feeling of doing it as any desire to hurry. She easily matched his pace, and as they approached the cluster of huts they picked up an escort of three young Elmisthorn running with them.

These were bigger than the chubby youngsters Arkad and Baichi had been playing with earlier, with heads shoulder-high to the two humans—nearly as tall as adults but with skinny bodies and green juvenile fur instead of mature stripes. As they ran together, Arkad found himself admiring their graceful, swift forms. Sometimes they looked like images he had seen of dogs, and sometimes more like galloping horses. Their heads were more like those of some species of crested predatory bird, except for the elaborate and dexterous insectile mouthparts.

As the five of them reached the edge of the village, one of the young Elmisthorn muttered something, and the three of them suddenly converged on Arkad. In a blindingly fast and efficient maneuver, two of them snatched at his shins with their mouths while the third leaped onto his back. Arkad rolled reflexively as he fell and so avoided any injury worse than a skinned elbow. One of the Elmisthorn wound up on Arkad's chest, with the other two standing on either side with their mouths gently holding his arms.

"We have caught you," said the one on his chest.

"You have caught me," Arkad agreed. "You did it well. You tell me why you are not out on the hunt."

The young Elmisthorn jumped off of Arkad and said, "The old folk make us stay here and learn stuff. I am Ornusth. Those are Aldisth and Elmorl."

"I am Arkad; that is Baichi."

"You tell me if you come here to trade," asked Ornusth.

"No. We ride on to the west."

"You tell me if you two are *humans*."

"Yes, both of us are," said Arkad. Out of the corner of his eye he could see Baichi looking at him.

"You tell me if you come here from a world where my folk rule."

"No," said Arkad. "We are free." He started to walk away, but Ornusth darted in front of him and made a head-bowing gesture.

"I do not wish to say a wrong thing," it said. "I ask just to find out. Come here with us." It cocked its head and led them behind one of the domed huts.

Arkad followed warily. Once, long ago, such an invitation from a seemingly friendly young Vziim had led to a beating. At close quarters he thought he could take on one of these young Elmisthorn, but not all three at once. But so far, everyone here had been friendly enough.

Behind the hut, Ornusth made a great show of looking around to be sure nobody was watching, then bent its head close to Arkad's. "We three want to buy vids of our folk on far worlds. They must be vids that can play on a screen made by our folk. You tell me if you have vids."

"I think Ree has some old Elmisthorn media from when she was growing up on Earth," Baichi whispered to Arkad.

"You tell me what you have to trade," Arkad asked Ornusth.

The three young Elmisthorn put their heads together and spoke quietly in their own language. Then Ornusth said, "We can trade you tusks. One tusk for a short vid, two or three for a long one."

Arkad had no idea if tusks were valuable or not, especially off to the west, but he didn't want to admit ignorance, so he said, "Two tusks."

The three of them had to argue about that, which suggested to Arkad that the tusks really were worth something, so he let them bargain him back down to their original price. "And you will tell me all you know of what is to the west of here," he insisted.

"That is a deal," said Ornusth. "But you must get us vids of our folk from far worlds."

"We will look for some," said Arkad.

It had been quite a while since Arkad had done any serious thievery. Since leaving Ayaviz he had barely stolen anything at all, but he was pleased to discover that he hadn't gotten rusty.

Arkad left Baichi waiting on the ground next to the sail-wagon—she was faster, so it made sense for her to be the one to get the goods away once he made the snatch. In his time on the streets of Ayaviz, Tiatatoo had often filled that role. Zvev and Fuee had usually been the distraction, occupying the mark with an innocuous question or an interesting argument while Arkad used his dexterous hands to snatch something out of a bag or pouch. With no one to distract Ree, he had to rely on being quiet.

He climbed back aboard the sail-wagon as silently as possible, and then crawled very slowly to where Ree's personal bag sat right next to her as she slept. It took him nearly five minutes to get from the edge of the deck to where he could hook a finger into the handle of the bag and pull it toward him.

A zipper on the bag scraped on the deck as he pulled it, and the noise sounded horribly loud to Arkad. He froze and watched the silvery sleeping bag, which completely hid Ree's face. She fidgeted but did not wake. He lifted the bag and got to his feet, then reached the edge of the deck in two silent steps and dropped the bag to Baichi, who took off at once.

She had the makings of a first-class thief, Arkad reflected as he dropped to the ground and trotted away in the other direction. As he circled around through the tall plants to the spot on the far side of the village where they had agreed to meet, he daydreamed a little.

What if they couldn't locate the *Rosetta*? As Ree had pointed out, even within the Black Land there was still a huge area to search. They might never locate it. Eventually Ree would give up and go home. Would Baichi go with her? He had always assumed she would, but with Jacob gone, he realized that was no longer so certain.

If she decided to stay on Syavusa, it would make perfect sense for Arkad to remain with her. The two of them would make a great team, he thought. And that unexpectedly led to a brief but startlingly vivid fantasy about what her pale bare skin would feel like under his hands.

So he was not just winded from running, but also flustered and irrationally embarrassed when he saw her. They sat down close together, and then Baichi hesitated.

"This is not right," she said. "We should not be taking Ree's things."

"We're not going to take anything," said Arkad. "Just see if she has any Elmisthorn videos and then let those three make copies. When Ree wakes up, her bag will be right next to her, with nothing missing."

"It still does not seem right," said Baichi.

"She wouldn't let us do it if she was awake," said Arkad, realizing as he spoke that he was admitting what they were doing was wrong, rather than justifying it. "And you saw how much those three want to see vids from offworld. We're doing something nice for them—and they can tell us more about what's ahead of us."

Baichi didn't answer, but she let Arkad take the bag from her and start going through it.

Despite all their travels, getting robbed by pirates, and other narrow escapes, Ree's bag had a surprising amount of stuff in it. The interior surface of the bag was divided into selectively adhesive squares, each of which was apparently keyed to a specific item. Ree could simply drop an object into the bag, and a brief shake or a few minutes of walking would result in the thing finding its proper square and sticking there.

Ree's wristband computer was right at the top, handy for her to put on as soon as she woke. Arkad took it out and poked at it, hoping that it would respond to him just like his own WOL, or maybe one of the elaborate electronic-mechanical systems favored by the Pfifu. He couldn't even get it to turn on.

After about two minutes of watching Arkad fiddling helplessly with the wristband, Baichi wordlessly took it from him. She held it cupped in her hands for a moment with her eyes closed, then began confidently tapping controls. "It is keyed to Ree's face and all the stored data is encrypted," she told Arkad, who vaguely understood what that meant. "But I think I can work out the device's operating system and get around the security measures. Give me a few minutes."

While she worked, Arkad went back to snooping in Ree's bag. He took all the things out and laid them on the flattened feather plants. He could recognize some items right away: a lightweight folding poncho, a pair of gloves, a roll of heavy tape, a roll of monofilament cord, self-darkening safety goggles and cleaning wipes were all obvious.

Baichi had to explain some others to him. "That is an all-purpose tool. It changes shape. This is a water-purifying membrane, like the one in Jacob's canteen. This is a medical analyzer. These are drug patches; some of them are not labeled—that is careless. These are smart-cloth bandages."

"Is that a laser tool?"

"It is. I did not know she had one."

"What about this?" Arkad held up a polished metal case. He opened the lid. Inside, nestled in a custom-fitted padded hollow, was a smooth silver object in the shape of a flattened ovoid, about six centimeters long, three wide, and one thick. A thin black line circled it at its widest circumference, but Arkad couldn't see any obvious controls or readouts. "What does it do?"

"I don't know. The box is human-made, but the thing inside looks like Machine tech. I can tell it contains a large amount of energy," she added, "so don't fool with it."

Arkad polished it gently with a clean part of his shirt and

then put it back into the case. Then he began stowing all of Ree's belongings back in her bag, occasionally glancing at Baichi while struggling to resist the urge to ask if she was done yet. He could see flickers of laser light from the wristband on Baichi's face, so it looked as though she had found her way past the security protection.

After another silent minute, Baichi spoke up, although he could still see the laser flickers in her eyes. "Ree has a great deal of Elmisthorn information stored here. Many hours of video, a great deal of text... even some games, I think."

"I guess it's all stuff she grew up with."

"Perhaps," said Baichi. "If these Elmisthorn have any devices which can read Family of Species data formats, we can give them as much as they want. Let us do it quickly, before Ree wakes up."

They found Ornusth helping one of the adults operating a solar-powered still, making concentrated essence out of a foul-looking slurry of ground animal glands. Arkad got the slender young Elmisthorn's attention, and after a few minutes, Ornusth made some excuse and beckoned for the humans to follow it behind one of the huts.

Transferring the data turned out to be just a problem of finding the right cables. Both Ree's wristband computer and the old yoke-shaped device that Ornusth and the others had acquired did use the same basic data-storage system, but Ree's device communicated with other machines via laser while Ornusth's used radio. Eventually Elmorl snuck into one of the adult huts and came out with a cable that could connect the two, and Baichi began filling up the yoke-computer's memory with video.

"You tell us if we can watch with you," Arkad asked Ornusth, but Baichi nudged him.

"After you put Ree's bag back where you got it," she said.

Arkad sighed, but didn't argue. He picked up the bag, with all the contents restored, and walked out in a big semicircle through the tall plants until he reached the crushed path left by the sail-wagon hours earlier. He followed the wagon's path until he reached the spot where it was parked. If Ree was already awake and had missed her bag, he could claim it had fallen off the wagon and he had found it.

But Ree was still asleep when he climbed aboard, so he quietly set it down near her and then hurried away. In the distance he could see a lone thunderstorm moving slowly westward across the plain, trailing a veil of dark rain below it and occasionally bombarding the surface with lightning strikes.

When Arkad got back to where he had left Baichi and the three young Elmisthorn, he could tell they were in trouble. The youngsters and Baichi stood in a line against the side of the hut, while one of the adults paced back and forth in front of them and a second adult stood back watching the whole scene.

He was about to fade back into the tall plants when he heard a swishing sound behind him. Another adult Elmisthorn emerged from the plants and gently clamped its mouthparts onto his shoulder. Without a word, the adult pulled him along to where the others stood and gave him a shove toward Baichi. Arkad meekly took his place next to her.

The pacing adult favored Arkad with a glare and then resumed lecturing the assembled youngsters. Baichi translated in a whisper for Arkad. "It says it is very angry that the young ones have broken their laws—and that we helped them do it."

"What laws did they break?"

"Apparently it is forbidden here to display any video of an Elmisthorn. Even still images must be approved by the adults."

The adult came closer and moved along the line of youngsters, saying something imperative-sounding in its melodious voice to each one.

"It is assigning punishments," said Baichi. "Elmorl borrowed the cables, so it now has the job of burying offal from the butchering ground after the hunt. Aldisth is now assigned to well-digging. And Ornusth will be spending its time feeding and cleaning the infants—and is not allowed to use any computer, video, or sound playback device."

"Forever?" Arkad whispered back.

"I don't think so. It said something about 'Until you learn to master your worst impulses.'"

The adult stopped in front of Baichi and Arkad.

"We did not know your rule," said Arkad in pidgin. "We did not know it was a wrong thing."

"You did not ask," it snapped back in the same language. "You two may not trade here. Stay with the land boat, and do not talk more to these young fools."

The adult who had caught Arkad exchanged some words

with the leader, then nodded its head to the two humans. "You two come with me now." It trotted off in the direction of the sail-wagon.

They followed, and it waited for them to catch up. The three of them walked silently until they were out of sight of the others. Then the adult said, "I am Ulwasm. Ornethd was mad at the young ones, not at you two. They broke our law."

"I do not know what the law is that they broke," said Arkad.

Ulwasm thought for a moment, then spoke in its own language, a long monologue like a song. Baichi listened to the whole thing before translating. "According to Ulwasm, their great-grandparents came to this world about seventy years ago."

"Before the war with Earth?"

"Yes. It said the founders of this colony objected to a social change in Elmisthorn society, and that change led to the policy of interstellar conquest among other things. Ulwasm said it had to do with sex and movies."

Arkad listened as Baichi recounted the whole saga according to Ulwasm. For countless generations, the Elmisthorn had lived in packs of no more than a few dozen individuals, centered on six to nine Alphas. The distinction between Alphas and Betas was hard for Ulwasm to explain to a pair of aliens; it was apparently a mix of athletic ability, good looks, courage, skill, and sheer charisma. Within a given pack, the Alphas mated with each other, producing most of the group's children. The entire labor of the pack went into raising the children of Alphas.

Betas obeyed their sexier leaders instinctively and always hoped to join the reproductive elite. There were several ways to accomplish that. From time to time Alphas picked some of the more attractive Betas for nonreciprocal casual affairs. Ambitious Betas could also try to join a different pack, or gather some followers and set out to establish a new one.

It wasn't a perfect system, but it served the Elmisthorn well enough as they went from being scattered bands of hunters to organized seminomadic herders, and some packs established themselves in villages doing crafts. At some point, centuries before, a few particularly clever Elmisthorn had created the beginnings of large-scale industry, and a technological explosion followed, as it did on most worlds.

About six hundred years ago, the invention of a way to record and show moving images had created a tremendous social problem among the Elmisthorn. Until then, political groupings among the Elmisthorn had been small: an Alpha's influence depended entirely on personal contact with its Beta followers. A few warlords or entrepreneurs had been able to assemble alliances of packs, but even those depended heavily on personal contact. The planet was a patchwork of small statelets or confederations, and conflicts were mostly small and local.

Cinema technology—and then broadcast video—changed that completely. A charismatic Alpha could suddenly gain millions of followers spread across an entire continent. Even language was scarcely a barrier. Lighting, scripts, editing, and makeup made screen Alphas vastly more attractive than the majority of other real-life Alphas. The new Super-Alphas were able to mobilize masses of Beta followers, breaking up the traditional pack struc-ture and building new organizations somewhere in the gray area between political parties and religious cults.

The immediate result was a century or two of global wars, as the new Alpha super-leaders first expanded their power to conquer disunited regions without movie studios, and then fought with each other for supremacy. During the intervals when nobody was firing rockets, the Alphas tried to poach each other's followers with ever more manipulative media campaigns. That led to cen-sorship and tight control of media by the Alpha rulers, which in turn prompted more conflict.

When the dust finally settled, the Elmisthorn species had a unified planetary government—the "Family of Families"—and an increasingly rigid caste system. Betas and local Alphas worked to support a remote and privileged Super-Alpha class, no longer their more attractive siblings and cousins from the same village but strang-ers whose attractiveness was carefully enhanced and exaggerated.

Contact with alien intelligence had come as a horrifying shock to the Elmisthorn leaders. The existence of beings who didn't find Alphas attractive seemed like a threat to the entire basis of Elmisthorn society. But it was only when they learned of the powerful Machine Civilization that the Elmisthorn began their policy of interstellar empire-building. The "Family of Families" became the "Family of Species," and the Elmisthorn appointed themselves the defenders of biological intelligence against the Machine menace—whether that menace existed or not.

Of course, there were practical benefits to the Elmisthorn expansion. Annexing alien civilizations on poorer or less technically advanced worlds allowed the Family of Species to support a large population of high-caste Alphas in astonishing power and luxury. Earth was only one of the latest conquests, and would probably not be the last.

Ulwasm's ancestors had seen what was happening to their world during the era of unification, and found it unnatural and degrading. For decades they lived in remote rural areas of the home world, deliberately cut off from all visual media. With the development of star travel—and the birth of the Family of Species—they began scraping together enough wealth to leave forever the space controlled by the Elmisthorn Super-Alphas. Their exodus had been blocked for years by legal and political opposition, and nearly half the original community never got off the home world, but the remnant managed to reach Syavusa and settle on the plains, living by hunting and herding much as ancestral Elmisthorn had done.

"Is all that true?" Arkad asked Baichi as the three of them reached the sail-wagon.

"It is consistent with everything I know about the Elmisthorn, although none of the histories in my memory mention such an important role for video technology. Most accounts from human sources focus on economic pressures, while Machine historians devote their attention to the Family of Species' stated goal of opposing the spread of AI civilization."

"Can you ask Ulwasm something for me? Ask it why they wanted to break away. Why not just go along with everyone else?"

The three of them stood beside the wagon as Baichi translated and Ulwasm replied. She thanked it, and the two humans climbed aboard the wagon. "It said they came here to preserve their species. The colony here believe the Family of Species will end in disaster—the subject species will rise in revolt, or they will finally provoke the Machines to a violent response, or the ruling Alphas will simply get more and more isolated and detached from reality. However it happens, these Elmisthorn believe it will be catastrophic, and they wish to preserve all that is good about their species and their civilization from the crash."

"Where have you two been?" asked Ree, sitting up in her sleeping bag.

"Walking around. One of the Elmisthorn told us we have to stay on the sail-wagon," said Arkad.

She looked at the two of them for a moment, but Baichi's face was its usual expressionless mask and Arkad did his best to imitate her. "That's probably an excellent idea. I hope we can leave soon."

The next few hours passed in silence. Baichi was content to watch the thinning clouds and the patterns the breeze made in the turquoise plants covering the plain, and Ree let her wrist-band beam images into her eyes that only she could see. Arkad wondered if she was looking at human or Elmisthorn videos.

Arkad, however, was fidgety. He read part of *Journey to the West*; he talked Baichi into playing a game of chess with him, then taught her the Vziim game Zom-Zviivazi. He beat her once, lost twice, tried to nap, and finally couldn't stand being stuck aboard the wagon a minute longer. Ignoring Ree's warnings, he dropped down to the ground and went for a run across the plain, heading away from the village.

He had gone a couple of hundred meters when he became aware that one of the Elmisthorn was speeding through the plants to his left, on a path to cut him off. Arkad decided to anticipate it, so he jinked in that direction, intending to catch his pursuer from behind.

But the Elmisthorn must have sensed his change of course because it stopped suddenly and froze, so that Arkad found himself jogging through shoulder-high vegetation with no idea where his quarry was—until it struck him on the back just between the shoulders, knocking him to the ground and gently nipping the back of his neck with its mouthparts. Arkad did manage to roll forward and get free long enough to regain his feet.

It was Aldisth, one of the young ones who had tried to trade with him. "You were told to stay on the land boat."

"You were told to dig a well," Arkad shot back. "I got you three the vids and you did not pay me."

"I can not give you a thing as pay but I can tell you what you did want to find out," said Aldisth.

"That is good. You tell me what is to the west of here. I need to get to the Black Land."

"I am young, so what I know is just what I have been told," Aldisth said, and then gave Arkad a long account of various menaces waiting to destroy any traveler foolish enough to go even a few steps west of the village. According to Aldisth there were vicious and xenophobic Kchik, dangerous Psthao-psthao, and venal Itooti along the way. The city of Chkik-Chk was a den of thieves. Beyond it was impassable desert, then the ring of storms. The storm ring would surely kill anyone venturing through it, through a combination of lightning strikes, sandstorms, and flash floods. Beyond the ring the Black Land was absolutely dry and too hot for any water-based living organism to survive.

Aldisth was just beginning to talk about the mysterious multilegged black spherical beings which patrolled the Black Land when it suddenly stopped and froze. Arkad looked over his shoulder to see Ulwasm, the adult who had ordered him to stay at the sail-wagon, sitting patiently behind him. Neither of the youngsters had heard it arrive.

It said something to Aldisth, who crept away with head bowed.

"I did just ask it to tell me of what is to the west," said Arkad, hoping to keep Aldisth from getting into any more trouble.

Ulwasm just sat and watched him.

"I will go back to the land boat now and stay there," he said.

CHAPTER 14

THE SAIL-WAGON REMAINED AT THE ELMISTHORN VILLAGE SEV-
eral hours more, until a band of a dozen hunters returned
from the south driving a pack animal laden with skins, casks
of blood, and jars of valuable glands from the herd creatures of
the plains. Captain Otitaa emerged from his sleeping sack at the
masthead and negotiated a trade of tools and electronics for half
the skins and all the glands.

With that done, the Itooti had no desire to linger. Half an hour
after the last jar was stowed, the sail-wagon was under way, rolling
across the plain toward the great river. The river's floodplain was
a confusing stretch of braided beds and oxbows, thickly wooded
with tall trees tangled in masses of coiled vines.

Otitaa didn't dare take his wagon into that impassable terrain,
but instead steered along the top of the low bluff which marked the
edge of the floodplain as the river meandered to the southwest. After
several hours the river curved to the south, and beyond it to the
west, Arkad could see a line of steep cliffs, all quite brown and bare,
cut with gorges and canyons full of green and purple vegetation.

Arkad and Ree sat atop the bales of skins and shared some food.
"You should try this," he told her, holding out a bluish-brown disk
wrapped in leaves. "It's a lot better than the food bars. It's cooked
blood from the big grazing animals. It's good, really."

"I'll wait until I'm desperate," she said.

He ate the blood cake in three bites and then licked the leaf
wrapper before speaking again. "Ree, can I ask you something?"

"Of course you can," she said. "I don't keep secrets from people."

"Back at the fuel station, right after we left the AaaAa camp, I thought I heard you talking to someone. I didn't recognize the language, but now I do: you were speaking Elmisthorn."

"It's not nice to spy on people," she said. "But, yes, in answer to your question, I was. I have a language tutorial program on my wrist computer, and I like to use it every now and then to stay in practice. That's all."

"Oh," he said.

She burst out laughing. "Have you been worrying about that all this time? What a silly thing to be upset about! You should have asked me right away. Now . . . do you have any other suspicions you've been keeping hidden? Time to air everything out!"

He wanted to ask her about the laser in her bag, but he didn't want to admit he'd been going through her belongings, so he shook his head. "I was just wondering."

"If you ever wonder about anything, ask me right away. It's a bad idea to keep secrets from your friends. Are you keeping anything secret from me?"

"No," he said, and glanced over her shoulder. "I think I see the city."

To the south Arkad could see a smudge of dust and smoke with white buildings gleaming below it. He stood to get a better look—and nearly fell overboard as the wagon took a sudden sharp turn to the left. Otitaa circled the mast, thwacking his crew with his tail and then swooping back to the steering tiller. Arkad clutched the rail and looked around to see why Otitaa had changed course.

Off to his right, he could see three vehicles burst from the cover of a patch of brush at the edge of the floodplain and roar toward the sail-wagon. They were obviously home-built, each with an open-frame body slung between two large wheels. The crude turbine engines screeched and left a trail of black smoke mixed with dust churned up by the wheels. Each carried three Vziim—one steering, one tending the engine, and one at the trigger of a big spray gun.

Running due south across the wind, the sail-wagon was making its maximum speed, covering a kilometer in about a minute and a half. Even the smart wheels couldn't keep the ride smooth at that speed. Ree lay flat on the deck, clinging with both hands, and even Baichi had to hold the rail with one hand as she stood.

"Fearful Arkad asks brave Otitaa who those speedy pursuers are!" Arkad shouted to the Itooti captain.

"Vile thieves!" was the unusually terse answer.

The sail-wagon sped across the plain, but the two-wheelers were faster. One stayed on the sail-wagon's tail, closing the distance meter by meter, but the other two broke off to the west, aiming to get between Otitaa's wagon and the city in the distance. Arkad ran back to the rear of the wagon and nearly fell flat on his face when the wheels hit a bump. He looked intently at the vehicle pursuing them and its crew.

All three Vziim wore goggles to protect their eyes from dust and glare, but none of them had much else on. That was a good sign; it meant the weapon probably wasn't a flame-projector or an acid spray. Whatever it was loaded with, it wasn't something the Vziim were afraid of getting on their fur if the wind changed.

Otitaa landed again on the tiller and adjusted the wagon's course to match the wind, then looked back at the pursuers. "Those ruthless bandits will catch the valuable wagon soon," he said matter-of-factly.

"Worried Arkad wonders if cunning Otitaa has a clever plan to evade the dangerous bandits."

"Defiant Otitaa will run as long as the open land lasts, then he will take up his keen darts and fight the vile predators until their cruel claws crush his brittle bones. The long-lived Kchik will remember bold Otitaa's final battle."

It sounded grand, except that it meant Arkad and his companions would be left to suffer the vengeance of a bunch of angry Vziim. Those two-wheelers didn't look big enough to carry prisoners.

"Arkad!" Ree called from where she was hanging on to the base of the mast. "Those bandits—they want the wagon, not us. We can jump off and run for it!"

The suggestion startled Arkad. He had started thinking of Otitaa as a comrade rather than just the person they were paying to give them a ride. Abandoning him seemed like a betrayal. He thought of Tiatatoo, back in Ayaviz.

None of the heroes in the stories he loved ever ran away. But then, they were made-up people. He looked at the two-wheeler still gaining from astern, and then tried to gauge the distance to the city off to the west. It would take hours to walk that far. "They could loot the wagon and still catch us before we get to safety," he called back to Ree.

The vehicle behind them was close enough for him to see the spray device clearly. It didn't look fragile enough to break with a thrown rock, nor did the screaming turbine driving the wheels. But the wheels themselves...

"Baichi!" he yelled. "Can you pull off part of the railing for me? Don't bend it!"

She looked at him, then at the two-wheeler, and then neatly wrenched off two of the brackets holding the railing at the side of the wagon's deck. She slid the length of aluminum tubing out of the brackets and handed it to Arkad.

"Destructive passengers should not tear up my valuable wagon on an idle whim," said Otitaa from the tiller.

Arkad ignored him and got to his feet. He held the long piece of aluminum tube in his right hand, just at its balance point, and hefted it to gauge the weight. He drew back his arm and threw it as hard as he could at one wheel of the pursuing vehicle. The tube seemed to hang in the air, and the Vziim driving the two-wheeler tried to swerve to avoid it, but couldn't turn fast enough.

The next instant, the two-wheeler made a snap turn to the right as the tube caught in the wheel on that side and immobilized it. The left wheel left the ground and the body spun around the axle, tossing two of the Vziim in random directions. Then the left wheel hit the ground again and dug a circular trench in the ground as it continued spinning to the right until the driver managed to hit the clutch and bring the whole thing to a stop.

By then the sail-wagon had covered nearly three hundred meters. Otitaa glanced back and quickly jammed the tiller over to the right, so that the sail-wagon was running directly before the wind—straight toward the other two bandit vehicles and the city beyond them. If they could get past the enemy, there was a chance they could reach safety before the Vziim got turned around.

"Ree!" called Arkad. "Use your—" he stopped himself. "Do you have a laser tool like Jacob's?"

She shook her head.

"Use it!" he yelled. "It's our only chance!"

The wagon lurched again as Otitaa jerked the tiller to the

right, aiming the bow directly at one of the two oncoming vehicles. When it swerved aside he steered at the other one. But the first one was in weapon range, and the Vziim manning the big projector took aim and squeezed the trigger calipers. A jet of orange liquid splashed the deck of the sail-wagon, including Arkad's leg. He held his breath, waiting for the flash of heat or the bubbling burn of acid.

Nothing happened. It foamed a bit, but that was all. Arkad touched the stuff and then discovered his finger was stuck to his leg—and his leg was stuck to the deck. Otitaa was immobilized at the tiller, holding his wings out awkwardly to keep them from getting glued down. The Kchik crew were stuck in place, clacking their limbs in distress. Arkad looked forward and saw that Ree was plastered to the deck. Baichi had reacted quickly, wrapping her cloak around her, but now she was inside an orange cocoon.

The glue on the wheels and wheel bearings slowed the wagon and sent it curving to the right, and with nobody to trim the sail, it quickly lost speed and finally coasted to a stop. The two bandit vehicles stopped nearby, and after a brief conference among the Vziim, one of the two-wheelers sped off to retrieve the crew of the one Arkad had wrecked.

He wondered what they would do to him. Vziim never let anything go unavenged. Would they claw him to death? Maybe douse him in fuel and set him afire? Or just leave him and the others glued to the wagon in the blazing sun, to die of heat and thirst? He pulled at his stuck leg but couldn't budge it. The sticky foam covered him up to the thigh and completely enveloped his leg below the knee. He'd have to pull off his skin to get free. The deck was tough carbon-fiber composite, impossible for him to break off, and the foam itself felt as strong and tough as steel.

Only when the second vehicle puttered slowly back—with a badly injured bandit slung behind the glue gun and a second, less severe casualty hanging on next to the driver—did the Vziim approach the immobilized sail-wagon.

One of the Vziim approached the wagon, wearing a protective hood and gloves, with a pair of small tanks and a spray gun slung around his body behind his arms. He carefully climbed up the left front wheel and began clearing a path across the deck with squirts from the spray gun. Wherever the spray touched, the foam turned to brown dust.

"You take all the stuff on board and let us live," Otitaa called to him in pidgin. "I will tell you where all the good stuff is."

"We will tear this boat to bits and take what we wish," the bandit answered. "I think I will stick you to the front of my cart to show it is not good to fight us."

"You will have to tell folk how well we fought," said Otitaa. "They will know my name as long as you live. If you let us go we will gain no fame."

"Arkad!" Ree shouted. "Tell them we're just passengers! Maybe they'll let us go."

Her voice startled the Vziim, who spritzed a little of the glue destroyer on Ree's head and shoulders, and then bent close to have a look at her. "You tell me what kind of thing you are," he said.

"We call our kind *human*," said Arkad.

The Vziim turned to look at him. "This boat is full of odd things. You broke a cart and hurt one of my band," he said. "I will keep your skin to fly as a flag."

That was an option Arkad hadn't thought of, and he didn't think the bandit was kidding. "We go west to seek great wealth hid there," he told the Vziim. "You spare us and we will share it with you."

"You must think I am dumb. That tale is an old con. You do not fool me. I think I will see how long your kind can live with no skin."

The Vziim left Arkad stuck where he was and, instead, went to work ungluing Otitaa from the tiller.

"I thank you—" Otitaa began once he was free, but never finished because the Vziim grabbed him around the throat with one powerful hand and drove a thick claw into the top of his skull with a second. Otitaa twitched once and then went limp, and the Vziim tossed the little corpse overboard.

He got the tiller unglued and then went over to the stuck wheel bearing and sprayed it until it could turn freely. Once the wagon could move again, the bandits tied ropes from their two-wheelers to the bow and began towing it back across the plain to where the wrecked vehicle was. The one who had killed Otitaa sat by the tiller and steered.

Arkad pulled ineffectually at his leg and his stuck hand, but the glue was still too strong. It had gotten harder with time so that the edges of the glue covering his leg cut into his skin unless he held absolutely still. He could feel himself starting to panic.

"Ree! Can you reach your laser?" he called in English, and then the Vziim's massive tail caught him in the stomach like a club.

"You do not speak!" said the Vziim.

The hardened glue edges gashed Arkad's leg and he felt his knee twist painfully as the blow knocked him sideways while his stuck leg remained fixed upright. He landed on his left shoulder and stuck to the orange-covered deck. The pain from his leg and the blow to his diaphragm kept him from getting any air for more than a minute.

"I beg you to free my leg," he said to the Vziim in pidgin. "I feel much pain."

"You will feel more," said the Vziim. He left the tiller and carefully took hold of Arkad's right elbow. "You tell me how does this limb bend," he asked. With his right hand stuck to his thigh, Arkad could only move that arm in a small arc forward and back. The Vziim pulled Arkad's elbow forward until the boy screamed aloud at the pain from his shoulder and wrist. The Vziim kept pulling and Arkad felt a horrible popping sensation from his shoulder as the joint dislocated. He couldn't move, couldn't think, couldn't do anything but yell in pain. The Vziim pushed his elbow down to the deck and stuck it there.

Arkad strained to shift his body against the iron grip of the glue. He could feel skin shredding and tearing on his leg but no longer cared. Then the Vziim's tail slammed the side of Arkad's head, gluing it to the deck and dazing the boy.

"You now hurt as much as my poor kin," said the Vziim. "One of his limbs broke and two ribs. You tell me if your kind have bone that can break."

Arkad pleaded for the Vziim to stop in half a dozen languages. He had been in fights, and once or twice had been badly hurt, but he had never been helpless like this, completely at the mercy of someone who wanted to hurt him as much as possible, with no way to resist or run away. He couldn't even see much but the deck and a sliver of sky.

He heard a loud snapping sound and the Vziim let out a bellow of pain and anger. The bandit turned away from Arkad, and then he didn't bellow but screamed. He lurched about the deck and his tail got stuck in some of the orange goop near Arkad's head. Another snap, and the Vziim flopped down and didn't move.

"Arkad!" called Ree. "Is it dead?"

"I think so. Help me!"

Ree approached him, stepping carefully to avoid the glue on the deck. She was wearing only her underpants and held the laser tool aimed at the Vziim. She picked up the dead Vziim's sprayer and hosed Arkad down with solvent. He gave a sob of relief when he could finally move, then took a deep breath and forced himself to move his right arm. There was a moment of indescribable agony and then another horrible popping sensation as the joint fell back into place.

He spent about a minute just lying on the deck, breathing heavily. When he could think again, he looked around. Ree was up at the bow of the sail-wagon, pointing her laser tool at the two-wheelers towing them. Her face was utterly calm as she picked off the Vziim one by one with the laser. With each shot there was a snap of ionized air and a bandit fell limp.

Then she returned to Arkad and stood over him with the laser pointed right at his face. "It's mean to snoop in people's things," she said. "I'm very disappointed in you, Arkad. I thought I could trust you."

"I'm sorry," he managed to gasp.

"You should remember who your friends are. *She* didn't do anything to help you," said Ree, nodding her head toward where Baichi was still encased by her glue-covered cloak. "It would serve her right if we just left her here."

She gave Arkad some bandages to put on his gashed leg, and while he was doing that, Ree sprayed down Baichi's cloak and then—without saying anything to Baichi at all—went to unglue her own clothing. Baichi emerged from her cocoon and spent a few moments staring at the dead bandits.

They eventually decided to use one of the two-wheelers instead of the sail-wagon, as none of them could manage the sail. Before they left, Arkad used the last of the solvent spray to free the two Kchik crew, but despite his best efforts, he couldn't persuade them to leave the sail-wagon. Finally he just shrugged and gave up—they weren't helpless and would probably decide what to do without him.

The three humans moved all their stuff to the larger of the two-wheelers, removing the glue gun to save weight. Arkad made sure to top off their vehicle's fuel tank from the other one, and then he took the controls and started up the turbine. Ree sat beside him, her survival suit restored to its normal pristine white and the laser tool hidden away in her bag again.

None of them said much as they motored across the plain.

The wind in Arkad's face felt curiously chilly, and he realized with a feeling of relief that the oval of plastic glued to his forehead had fallen off. Awiza's glue must have been the same stuff as the Vziim foam weapon. The skin there felt soft and hypersensitive for a while.

The "perilous city" of Chkik-Chk didn't look particularly dangerous as they approached it. The place was centered on a pair of enormous pipes which spanned the river. They were made of some greenish-gold metal and must have been twenty meters in diameter. The two pipes were about thirty meters apart, and generations of later settlers had covered the gap with roadways and buildings, making a combination bridge and fortified town all shrouded in vines which trailed down to the river. From there the city had expanded onto the banks, confined by tall defensive walls. But the gates were open as the humans approached and there wasn't even a passage toll. The single Ka guard sitting in the shade of a parasol waved them through with two boneless arms.

Within the walls the city wasn't as jumbled as Ayaviz or Nenveez. It almost looked as though someone had planned it all out in advance. The streets were an orderly web, with straight radial avenues and neatly curved circumferential ones. The vehicle lanes down the middle were paved, and the walkways on either side were shaded by vine-covered pergolas. The buildings themselves were painted white on the flat roofs and sunward walls, with ventilators to catch the eternal wind from the east.

Overhead, dozens of aerostats pulled on their tethers in the wind, each with multiple wind turbines generating power. They were all painted plain white, which suggested that there were no Pfifu in the city because they would inevitably have tried to turn them into flying monsters or bizarre caricatures.

Most of the people out on the streets were Ka or Itooti, though from the solid stonework of the buildings, Arkad guessed at a substantial Vziim minority, and he did see a number of mobile Kchik.

"We have to stop here," he told Ree.

"I don't see why. I didn't come here for sightseeing. Get us over that bridge and out the other side before something else happens to delay us."

"I have to rest," he said. All of his joints ached, and his shoulder gave him a jab of pain every time he moved his right arm. His leg wasn't bleeding anymore, which was good, but he was covered in brown powder, dried blood, dirt, sweat, and butanol soot. He was very tired.

Ree gave an irritated sigh. "Well, I guess we've got some metal to spare since we didn't have to pay for the sail-wagon trip. All right, find us a place we can sleep a few hours and get cleaned up."

There was a large semicircular plaza where the streets converged at the bridge, with a busy market along the outer edge. Right where the road from upriver entered the plaza, Arkad spotted a fuel station with rooms for rent. He parked the vehicle inexpertly and staggered inside. He didn't even bother to haggle with the owner, just handed over some wire and then collapsed in the cool windowless vault the three of them were to share.

He woke some time later, stiff all over and as dirty as he'd ever been. When he moved, his shoulder reminded him why he shouldn't. Ree wasn't there, but Baichi sat beside him. In the dim light coming through the vents in the door, she almost seemed to glow against the darkness.

"Let me check your bandages," she said, and gently uncovered the gash on his leg. "I don't see any sign of infection. You are lucky."

"I'm lucky because Ree managed to get loose and get her laser tool. Why didn't you do something? You could have broken out of that glue."

"Yes," she admitted. "Either by force or by raising my skin temperature."

"Then why didn't you?"

"I made a promise not to fight. You know why."

"It's dumb," he said, "and it gets other people hurt. If you had just punched that Vziim as soon as he climbed aboard, *he* would still be alive now, and the other bandits, too. Ree wouldn't even know we looked in her bag."

"I have to be more careful than other people. I have too much power."

"If you're so powerful, why do you care?" He heard his voice echo and lowered it to almost a whisper. "Why not do whatever you want? What's stopping you?"

"I made a promise," she repeated.

"But what will happen if you break it?"

"Nothing—except that I will know it, and I will despise myself."

"You know what that means? It means you're a good person, Baichi. You know what's right and what's wrong. You can trust yourself. If you see something bad happening, you can do something about it. Like Gilgamesh or Superman." He didn't mention Hercules.

"You need a bath," she said, and got up in one quick motion. "I'll get you some water." Before he could even answer, she was out of the room.

She brought him a black plastic water bag which had been up on the roof in full sunlight for a few hours. It was just the right temperature, and he washed by the drain in the corner of the room. Because it hurt to use his arm, Baichi helped clean spots he couldn't reach. She gave no sign of noticing his blatant erection. Once he was clean, Arkad put on the grubby clothes he'd inherited from Jacob. The pants were in particularly bad shape, with one leg shredded and stiff with dried blood.

Ree returned from wherever she had gone, looking more relaxed and cheerful than Arkad had ever seen her before.

"It's good to see you're feeling better," she told him. "I was worried about you, after what that awful bandit did to you. If I hadn't stopped him, you might have died."

Baichi looked at Arkad when Ree said that. He gave her a reassuring smile.

Ree gave no sign of noticing. "If you've slept enough, we need to get some food and then get moving again. I don't want to stay here any longer than we have to. Can we reach that Black Land from here in that two-wheeler?"

Arkad shrugged. "I'll have to ask someone. I remember going by boat. I don't think we could make it through the storm ring in that."

"Come on, then. Let's find some food." She turned to Baichi. "Do you need to eat any *human* food, dear?"

"I would like to join you," she answered.

The row of market stalls around the edge of the plaza included a few places selling cooked food. There were a lot of unfamiliar dishes here in Chkik-Chk. One stall, staffed by a trio of live Kchik workers, was selling whole cooked Kchik workers, hung upside down over the steamer with their legs trussed. Arkad avoided that one, found a stall run by a pair of Vziim where he picked out a bag full of baked disks of seed paste, and got each of them a big leaf rolled around a pile of boiled river swimmers. It came with a scoop of fruit sauce and even Ree admitted it was very tasty.

A Ka with all its limbs retracted rolled past them, stuck out three legs and stopped itself, then trotted over to where the three humans were sitting. "You give me some food. I thank you much for it," it said.

Arkad hesitated, then dug into the bag for some baked disks. "I need to know how to go west from here," he said, holding out a couple to the Ka. It popped them into the toothless mouth at the north pole of its round body.

"Tall cliffs are west of here," it said. "Dry land is past the cliffs. The land is too hot for life, and then the storm line, with great wind and dust and bright bolts."

"You tell me what road I can take west from here," said Arkad, handing the Ka another couple of disks.

"There is no road up the cliffs," said the Ka. "No one is so mad as to go up there. The land on top is hot and dry. If you stay in the deep gorge, you can go by boat to the edge of the storm belt."

"You tell me where I can get a boat to go there." Arkad held out the last disk.

"You go find Sapalifijarijo," said the Ka. "It has a good boat."

Arkad gave the Ka the bag, and it placed the open end over its mouth and then sucked the whole bag in, before pulling it out, now inside-out and completely clean of crumbs. It created an arm and held the bag out to Arkad.

"You can keep it," said Arkad.

"I thank you now," said the Ka, and rolled away.

When all three were finished eating, they headed down to the riverbank where several boats and rafts were drawn up on the shore. Arkad asked an Itooti where he could find Sapalifijarijo, and in response got a casual tail jab at a triple-hulled twenty-meter boat with a pair of paddle wheels in the center.

But before they even could reach the boat, a trio of Ka rolled up to block their path. One of the three extended legs and stood. "You three come with us now," said one.

"You tell me where we go," Arkad asked them. It didn't feel

like a robbery, but he wasn't sure. Some of the individuals working on boats or unloading cargo were looking at them, but nobody seemed very concerned.

"You come with us to see Chkik."

"I do not know who Chkik is."

"Chkik is the boss of this town. She wants to talk to you. You come now."

CHAPTER 15

THE KA GUARDS LED THE HUMANS TO THE BRIDGE IN THE CEN-
ter of town. The whole span was covered in vines, creating a
cool leafy canopy overhead. The roadway down the center of the
bridge was almost like a tunnel. Dozens of big vines hung down
to the river below. All the vines were dotted with eyespots which
looked just like the eyes of Otitaa's crew, and after a while, Arkad
realized that all the vines and roots were part of a single giant
organism. Chkik didn't inhabit the heart of the city, she *was* the
heart of the city.

At the center of the bridge, the road passed through a two-
story building, which filled the entire width of the bridge. An
archway led through the bottom floor of the building, and Arkad
could see massive gates at either end of the passage. The Ka led
the humans through a side door into the building and up a set of
shallow spiral steps to a big second-floor room. Every surface—
walls, ceiling and floor—were covered with vines.

A male Itooti, whose natural yellow and scarlet fur was
enhanced with gold wire and rubies, dropped out of the foliage
overhead to perch on one massive vine. A tendril on the vine
turned to aim a single eye at the humans, and a second tendril
tapped and scratched words for the Itooti to translate.

"Immense Chkik asks if you three shabby beings are genuine
humans," said the Itooti.

"Humble Arkad confirms that we three trail-worn travelers
are real humans."

"All-seeing Chkik notes that there are significant genetic, anatomical, and biochemical differences among you three diverse beings. Suspicious Chkik wonders if you three mysterious beings are even of the same alien species."

"Honest Arkad admits that two of our small group have minor modifications. Male Arkad also wishes to remind vast Chkik that exotic humans have two sexes."

There was a pause, and then the tendril made more taps and scratches. The Itooti began speaking while it was still making sounds. "All-wise Chkik wishes to hear truthful Arkad's accurate account of the recent fight against troublesome Vziim on the wide plain."

Arkad answered at length, getting angrier as he described what had happened, and the viciousness of the Vziim aboard the sail-wagon. "And then, injured Arkad, silent Baichi, and courageous Ree took rightful possession of one abandoned vehicle in order to reach the supposed safety of Chkik-Chk," he finished.

The huge plant scratched out a response, and the Itooti interpreter struck a reassuring pose. "Grateful Chkik commends the resourceful humans for thwarting the annoying bandits. The baseless complaints of their surviving relatives will be justifiably ignored, and the angry Vziim will get a stern warning not to pursue any disruptive vendettas in the harmonious city of famous Chkik-Chk."

Arkad relaxed when he heard this and thanked Chkik. He was expecting a dismissal, but instead the plant scratched out another question which the Itooti interpreted. "Wise Chkik wonders why exotic humans have come to this remote place."

"Three tired humans wish only to rest in this charming city for a short time before continuing on their vital journey."

"Curious Chkik wishes to know where the determined humans are going—and why."

Now that he knew Chkik's vines extended well into the city, Arkad didn't want to risk lying. No telling how much she might already know, but he didn't want to reveal more than he needed to; something about the interrogation was making him nervous. "Candid Arkad and his fully human companions plan to go into the perilous west."

Another long pause. Arkad decided to risk speaking up on his own. "Worried Arkad wants nurturing Chkik to know that two wide-ranging Kchik pollinators remain on the lawless plain with a damaged sail-wagon, about twenty short kilometers from this hospitable city."

A different tendril scratched and tapped, and the Itooti translated. "Thrifty Chkik will send a swift team to recover the vulnerable pollinators." While the Itooti was speaking, the first tendril started up again, and after a pause, he continued. "Helpful Chkik still wishes to know why Arkad and his naive companions wish to risk the dangerous western lands."

Arkad turned to his companions. "She wants to know why we're going into the desert."

"I thought the bright-colored ones were males," said Ree.

"Not the Itooti. He's just a translator. Chkik is the plant."

Ree looked at the enormous tangle of vines and branches surrounding them as if it had been invisible until that moment. Then her eyes narrowed again. "Why are we talking to a plant?"

"She's the boss of this city. All the guards and workers answer to her," said Arkad.

Behind him he heard Baichi murmuring to Ree. "The Kchik are one of only three known species of intelligent sessile auto-trophs. Small populations of Kchik exist on sixteen worlds—all of which are tidally locked planets like this one. Their home planet no longer supports a technological civilization since attempts at climate management produced a runaway glaciation catastrophe."

"Just tell her we're sightseeing, then."

"Three curious humans wish to admire the exotic landscapes of the lovely desert region," said Arkad.

"Skeptical Chkik doubts that any intelligent beings would suffer extreme hardship and risk painful death merely to admire some barren dirt," said the Itooti after a frenzy of tendril-scratching from the plant. "Polite Chkik assures helpful Arkad that the three rootless humans are welcome in Chkik-Chk. *However,* powerful Chkik warns venturesome Arkad that she will not allow three unprepared humans to stray across the obvious river."

"Respectful Arkad wonders why altruistic Chkik has such strong concern about the private actions of three insignificant humans."

"Mighty Chkik has little interest in obscure humans or their eventual fate. However, diplomatic Chkik admits that her irreversible decision is due to a polite request from a powerful entity."

"Confused Arkad wonders what powerful entity could compel invulnerable Chkik to make any involuntary decision contrary to her own reasonable wishes."

Another long pause, during which Arkad relayed the news to Baichi and Ree.

"Find out all you can," Ree told him.

"Prudent Chkik informs nosy Arkad that the potent being who made the trivial request also insisted that its real identity not be revealed. Honorable Chkik warns pesky Arkad that no long-winded argument or persistent demands will change her irrevocable decision."

"Agreeable Arkad asks tolerant Chkik if three disappointed humans must remain in her charming city, or if the restless travelers may leave."

"Perceptive Chkik tells unsubtle Arkad that the three devious humans may leave her well-ordered city, but only by the eastward plains. Shrewd Chkik also warns obstinate Arkad that all honest boat owners who call at the prosperous city will hear stern warnings not to carry easily recognized humans across the constantly watched river."

"She's not going to tell me who asked her to stop us, and I don't think we can get a boat to carry us across."

"This is ridiculous," said Ree. "She's got no right to keep us from crossing the river. I don't care who asked her to stop us. Tell her that as Earth humans, we're members of the Family of Species, and if she doesn't let us cross here, she's going to be in trouble with the Elmisthorn. The *real* Elmisthorn, not those crazy primitives out on the plains."

"But we're not—" Arkad began.

"Just tell her."

Arkad reflected that Ree had spent a lot of time working with spies, and fake identities were probably second nature to her. He turned back to the Itooti. "Friendly Arkad wishes to remind protective Chkik that exotic humans are valued subjects of the mighty Family of Species. Concerned Arkad does not wish vulnerable Chkik to incur the terrifying hostility of the star-conquering Elmisthorn."

"Skeptical Chkik wonders why the three ragged humans do not command the distant Elmisthorn to transport them to their eventual destination."

"She's not buying it," said Arkad to Ree.

"This is ridiculous. We'll just have to find some other way."

"Humble Arkad thanks benevolent Chkik for her kind attention to the physical safety of three grateful humans."

With that, the Itooti simply flew off and the interview was over. Arkad, Ree, and Baichi made their way back to the boardinghouse, and a quartet of Kchik warriors discreetly escorted them as far as the end of the bridge.

"Obviously we have to get our own boat," said Ree as soon as they got back to their room and seated themselves on the floor. "See how much it will cost."

"She has eyes everywhere," said Arkad. "I mean, she literally has eyes everywhere—all the vines that grow around the city are part of her."

Ree grimaced. "Wonderful. And we can't even sneak across at night because this stupid planet doesn't *have* nights." She sat in silence for a moment, then sprang to her feet. "You two wait here. I have to go out and do something."

She picked up her bag and went out.

Arkad stretched out on the floor, wincing a little when he moved his hurt shoulder. "Ree has changed," he said after a few minutes.

"She appears more confident than I remember," said Baichi. "Perhaps she is doing it to reassure us."

Arkad thought for a moment before answering. "I'm not sure," he said. "It's not just what she says. She used to be nervous all the time, especially around Jacob. Now that he's gone, she actually seems happier. You'd think she'd be sad about it."

"They were not friends," said Baichi. "She and Jacob were partners in this venture, but that was all. They both wanted to find the *Rosetta* and neither could accomplish the task alone, so they joined forces."

"Still, we don't even know why he died. You'd think she'd be worried." He hesitated before continuing. "I don't think she likes you, either."

"No, she does not. She dislikes the Machines and suspects I am their agent."

"Are you?" He glanced over at her, but of course her face revealed nothing.

It was Baichi's turn to hesitate before answering. "No," she said at last. "They created me but they do not control me."

"I saw you talking to one of them, back at the camp of the AaaAa."

"I did. The Machine entity there was a minor one, a mobile node of an intelligence which controls a brown dwarf star about fifty light-years from here. It was exchanging information and observing the habits of biological entities here. I communicated with it. That was all."

"Jacob wouldn't answer me when I asked him why the *Rosetta* is so important. How can one ship beat the whole Family of Species?"

"He did not mean it literally. *Rosetta* was one of four ships which left Earth during the invasion, carrying humanity's greatest treasures."

"It's full of iridium or something?"

"No. *Rosetta* carried the cultural heritage of half the human species. Artworks, entire libraries of text and music, and items of specific historical importance. The crowns of monarchies like England, the Vatican, and Spain. The mantle of Muhammad and the original Constitution of the Americans. Mayan codices and the notebooks of Leonardo da Vinci. Hundreds of other items, and billions of stored images and documents. The intent was to allow humans to keep their civilization even with Earth under alien control."

"Jacob said the ship could free the Earth."

"He believed that the Elmisthorn hold on Earth would never be secure as long as humans could resist adopting the alien culture. The Family of Species may own more warships and weapons, but in a battle of cultures, humans may actually have the advantage. And that is why the Elmisthorn want to find the *Rosetta*: if they control humanity's history, they will control its future as well."

Arkad thought about all that for a minute. This was bigger than he had thought, and that meant it was much more dangerous than he had realized.

He looked at the dark ceiling as he spoke. "I remember one time back in Ayaviz, when I was still running with Zvev and Tiatatoo and Fuee. We found a dead Vziim—a matriarch from offworld, Zvev said. She'd been poisoned with some kind of psychoactive, and managed to hide herself before dying. Nobody but us knew where she was. Anyway, she had some nice clothes and jewels on her, but she also had a data wristband, and when

Zvev tried to read it, she got scared. I don't know all of it, but apparently that wristband had security codes and account information for a whole interstellar trading business on it—worth *tons* of gold or platinum."

"Why was your friend frightened?"

"When something's that valuable, people will do anything to get it, and we weren't strong enough to keep it. So Zvev sold a tip about where to find the dead Vziim for a few kilograms of copper and we all left town for a while. Because even a tiny bit of the value of what we had was still much bigger than what it would cost to have the four of us killed or tortured to find out what we knew."

"You are afraid the *Rosetta* is causing the same problem for us," said Baichi.

"Yes! This is all a whole lot bigger than I realized. When Jacob said it had cultural treasures, I figured maybe a few dozen things. Not *millions*. I can't understand why Jacob and Ree didn't think of that, either. Did they have any kind of allies? Someone who can protect the ship once we find it?"

"Ree once worked with the Combined Forces."

"Jacob said he thought her money came from them. But can they protect us here? You know more about this stuff than I do."

Baichi smiled a little. "This world is a long way from Invictus. I am not sure if the human government would be able to send any of their ships so far at all, even for something as important as the *Rosetta*."

"Jacob was afraid the Elmisthorn might find out. Could they get here?"

Baichi looked directly at him. "Yes. They could easily send a ship here, and Syavusa is undefended. If they know we are here, they could have stopped us already."

They heard Ree's quick footsteps in the hall, and a moment later she entered the room and nearly threw her bag down.

"What's wrong?" asked Arkad.

"*Nothing*," she said, and then visibly struggled to calm herself. "I had an idea about how we might get to the Black Land, but it won't work."

"What was it? Maybe if—" Arkad began.

"*Never mind*," she snapped. "I told you it didn't work, so don't ask me again. If you two have any suggestions, let's hear them."

"Crossing the river is a physical problem," said Baichi. "Those can be solved with the proper tools: a sufficiently long cable, some floats for the vehicle, possibly some waterproof containers."

"Chkik will stop us if we try," said Arkad.

"There's *got* to be a way past this stupid little town! I've come too far to let myself be stopped by a *plant*."

"We can fly," said Arkad.

"In what?"

"I remember a story in WOL about some men in a prison who escaped by making a balloon. Every building in Chkik-Chk has an aerostat wind turbine. That's just a balloon with a generator on it. Someone here must be able to make the aerostats, or fix them, anyway. And except for a couple of Itooti, I don't think Chkik has any air force of her own. If she had fliers, she could patrol the prairie better."

"Do you know anything about how to build or fly a balloon?" Ree sounded dubious.

"I don't think it's that hard. We can figure it out," he said, getting more and more excited about the idea.

"It will be difficult to accomplish without Chkik noticing," said Baichi.

"I can't believe we're worried about how to outsmart a plant," Ree put in.

"I think we should let her outsmart us," said Arkad, but wouldn't say any more.

Arkad began their great escape by getting his bearings and learning about the environment. He walked every single street in Chkik-Chk—going slowly, looking closely at all the buildings and taking note of all the people he passed. As one would expect in such an orderly town, it was neatly divided into sectors. The workshops and processing plants were clustered along the river on the downstream side of town. He identified a vehicle-repair shop run by Itooti, a fuel plant, and a factory with a big solar furnace to make bricks and cement. Right at the edge of town he found a complex of buildings devoted to turning herd beasts brought in from the plains into dried meat, cured skin, and concentrated essences.

The market sector stretched along the street from the central plaza to the eastern gate. Small vendors had stalls around the edge of the main market, while the more upscale businesses occupied buildings along the street. Arkad identified doctors (for Vziim and Ka), a design studio, Vziim arbitrators, an Itooti singing teacher, a freelance Ka revenge contractor, and several merchants.

He gradually realized that while Chkik might consider herself the owner of the town, she and her workers played a fairly small part in the life of the place. The Kchik was a plant, after all, so her needs were simple—water, sunlight, and protection. The community had grown up around her, and served as additional defense, but all she really needed was tools for her workers, some fertilizers and fungicides...and entertainment. Maybe *that* was the real purpose of the town: to give Chkik something to look at.

The next time Arkad spotted one of her eyespots on a vine, he waved at it.

Over the next fifty hours Arkad explored the town in detail, returning to the boardinghouse only to sleep. He was a little surprised to see that Ree barely left the room. She seemed more interested in looking at entertainment on her wristband device than in seeing what Chkik-Chk had to offer. Baichi had reverted to her old habit of disappearing—although Arkad noticed that whenever he stopped to chat with someone, he could usually spot a white-cloaked figure watching from a rooftop or an alley by the time the conversation was done.

Arkad talked with a dozen different inhabitants, chatting until his throat was hoarse. He volunteered to help out, eavesdropped on beings who didn't know he understood them, and played with juveniles.

From a Vziim stonemason repairing a wall, he learned that the wind-power aerostats all belonged to the mason's cousin, a matriarch who lived in a luxurious complex of cellars at the upstream edge of town. By hanging around her family stronghold and gossiping with the young males on guard, he discovered that the Vziim had contracted out repairs and maintenance to a sort of guild or cartel of Itooti technicians, who kept the aerostats aloft and the generators running—and either co-opted or drove away any competitors for the work.

That led him back to the Itooti quarter, along the city wall on the downstream side. He was a little surprised that the youngsters he had played with before did not come swooping down on him—but then he saw why.

Baichi was on top of the city wall, playing the interceptor

game. It was a favorite with large groups of Itooti. One group was the attackers, the other the interceptors. The attacking team tried to dive through the interceptors, and each one who made it through without being touched scored a point. Then the teams would switch roles. Arkad had seen it hundreds of times, though he had never been part of the game, being unable to fly.

But there was Baichi, playing the game herself against eight young Itooti—and she appeared to be winning. They swarmed around the top of the wall as she ran through the group, ducking, dodging, leaping, and rolling, their claws and lashing tails missing her by millimeters. She had laid aside her changeable cloak for the occasion, and the sight of her slim pale figure moving with effortless grace made Arkad laugh aloud with delight as he watched her.

She heard him, and when she passed untouched through the flock, she smiled back. Not her usual almost imperceptible smile, either. This was a grin of pure happiness that seemed to outshine the sunlight. He watched as she played another round, lightly tagging the little Itooti as they zoomed around her. A couple of them made it past her. Arkad suspected they had gone outside the agreed-upon limits, but Baichi didn't challenge them so he kept silent.

Only when a couple of the youngsters spotted him and dove down to demand that he join the game did Arkad remember his errand. "Lazy Arkad does not want to join active play in this intolerable heat. Comfort-loving Arkad will find a shady spot inside a cool house and make amusing conversation with sensible adults," he told them.

He selected an Itooti house attached to the town wall, with a promising litter of parts underneath it, and climbed up. A lone female Itooti sat inside, winding copper wire onto the armature of a generator. "Busy Itotaitetta cannot spare any valuable time for idle aliens."

"Wealthy Arkad wishes to negotiate the economical purchase of an inflatable boat," he told her. They haggled a bit, but he eventually agreed to swap the salvaged two-wheeler vehicle for the boat, and to take delivery in twenty hours.

Outside, he waved to catch Baichi's attention, and after one last round of her game, she leaped down from the top of the wall to join him.

"Were you successful?"

"Yes," he said, feeling pleased with himself. "We'll be able to leave here in about twenty hours. You looked like you were having fun up there."

"I was," she said. "It was challenging."

Acting on a sudden impulse, he said, "It's easy to catch Itooti. I bet you can't catch me."

"Of course I can catch you," she said.

"Prove it," he told her. He pointed to a spot on the ground. "Stand here and see if you can keep me from getting past you." Arkad walked about twenty meters away before turning to face her. "Are you ready?"

"This is ridiculous," she said, but she took a stance with knees slightly bent, body leaning forward, arms ready.

"Here I come!" He sprinted toward her at top speed, but instead of trying to dodge around her he simply ran straight at her. She caught him . . . and he caught her at the same time, then planted a kiss right on her colorless lips as they stood there with their arms around each other. The feel of her body pressed against his made his heart race.

Baichi drew back, wearing an expression of pleased surprise, so he kissed her again, longer this time. When he finally came up for air, she had the look of joy he had seen on her during the game with the Itooti.

Then, without any warning, a change came over her, complete and sudden. Her face reverted to its normal expressionless mask, and she let go of him and stepped back as if he was too hot to touch. "We should get back to Ree," she said, taking up her cloak and draping it over herself again.

"No rush," he reminded her. "We've got plenty of time." He took a half step forward.

She turned and began walking very briskly away, without saying a word. He stood baffled for a moment, then followed at his own pace, so that in just a couple of minutes she was out of sight. He stopped off at a stall in the market to trade for some broth to drink, and then wandered over to the riverbank as he sipped it.

From a maker of sails he purchased a large amount of plastic film and glue. Then he stopped by a workshop to negotiate the rental of a plasma torch and several tanks of hydrogen fuel.

By the time he got back to their room, he had spent all the value of the vehicle and everything they had been able to take away from the sail-wagon. But everything was in place for his plan to journey to the west.

"How fast can you run?" Arkad asked Baichi as soon as he entered their room.

"Twenty meters per second," she said.

"Good. You can be our distraction."

"Slow down," Ree interrupted. "What do we need a distraction for?"

Arkad looked up, almost surprised. "Our escape! I'm sure Chkik noticed us paying a visit to the Itooti quarter. She has eyes all over the city. It only makes sense that she'd be keeping track of us. She knows we want to get past the river. Once she learns I was making a deal with an Itooti who fixes boats, she'll figure out what we're planning."

"Then why are we even bothering? She'll stop us."

"That's what Baichi is for. She'll deliver the two-wheeler to swap for the boat. That will focus Chkik's attention on her—and all Chkik's warriors and Ka guards. Meanwhile, we will glue this film to make a balloon and take it up onto the roof to inflate it. Once we're ready to take off, Baichi can run to join us. It's about half a kilometer, and the roads are all nice and straight, so call it half a minute. The only beings in the city who could catch her are Itooti, and they aren't strong enough."

"Unless they have weapons," Ree pointed out.

"If they drop explosive darts on me, I can dodge or deflect them," said Baichi. "Toxin sprays and fire would do nothing. An acid-based weapon might harm me, but we have not seen any of those here."

"The Ka can use guns," Arkad pointed out, suddenly worried. "And Chkik could even buy lasers or rockets. Maybe..."

"Any of those weapons could shoot down a balloon full of hydrogen," Baichi answered calmly. "If you are willing to risk it, then so am I. What about you?" she asked Ree.

Ree looked miserable. "That's a pretty big risk."

"If Chkik had laser weapons, she could have sent out some Itooti to clean out those bandits we ran into. I think we're safe," said Arkad, trying to convince himself. He thought a moment. "Unless they were paying her, I suppose."

"I *hate* this stupid planet!" said Ree. "Fine, let's try it. Anything is better than sitting here."

They slept and had a meal, then made another purge of their baggage, getting down to just the bare essentials in order to save weight. Arkad entrusted the items they were leaving behind to the boardinghouse owner—he was reasonably sure she would trade them away, but even the remote chance of getting anything back was better than simply abandoning their equipment. Arkad was down to the clothes he wore, WOL, Jacob's knife, and one water-purifying bottle. Baichi had her cloak and another bottle. Ree insisted on bringing her bag.

The three of them set to work gluing the film into a roughly cube-shaped balloon envelope. Fortunately the glue came with a container of solvent.

Once everything was ready, Baichi set out for the Itooti quarter in the two-wheeler to draw off Chkik's attention. Arkad waited until she was out of sight, then he and Ree carried the spherical hydrogen tanks and the folded gasbag up to the roof of the rooming house. They set up downwind from the anchor point of the building's own generator aerostat. Arkad got the hydrogen tanks connected to the hose he had glued to one corner of the cube, and opened the valves. The inflation seemed to take forever, and he kept looking around to see if anyone was coming to stop them.

The aerostat envelope was about seven meters across. They had glued two flat carbon-fiber ribbons over the top of it, and the inflation tube kept it secured at the bottom. Arkad anchored two of the four ribbon ends to the solar panels on the roof as the bag began to float off the ground. He tossed the end of another to Ree. "Tie this around yourself!"

"Aren't we going to use a basket or something?"

"It's not big enough for that. Make sure your knot doesn't slip."

The balloon was now full enough to pull against the tethers. Ree got the loop of cord tied under her arms.

Just then he heard a commotion from below. Baichi came sprinting up the street with a couple of Itooti pursuing her and a trio of Ka with long legs extended hurrying after. She reached the roof in a single leap. "We do not have much time," she said.

Arkad threw her the other free ribbon end, and then as the balloon reached its full size, he disconnected the inflation tube, knotted its end, and wrapped it around himself a couple of times before tying it off. As soon as he had it tied, Ree aimed her laser at the last two tethers and burned through them.

Arkad had expected a gentle rise, but the balloon shot up hard enough to knock the breath out of him, and the ceaseless wind began carrying it westward as soon as it rose above the clutter of the roof. It was surprising how little sensation of movement there was. The balloon was moving with the wind so the air around them seemed perfectly still. But when he looked down, he could see the ground rushing past—and rushing away as they continued to rise.

"Let out some of the gas!" Ree shouted. "We're going up too high!"

Arkad fumbled for the end of the tube and opened it, but nothing came out. He realized that as long as it was tied around his body, the tube was sealed shut—and untying it would drop Arkad onto the ground below. He looked down and instantly regretted it. They were already a couple of hundred meters up and still rising, and were moving west at an alarming rate. The river passed below while he watched.

He tried to bite a hole in the tube above where it was wrapped around him, but his teeth couldn't penetrate the super-tough film.

"Burn a hole with your laser tool!" he shouted to Ree.

"It's full of *hydrogen!*" she shouted back.

For a moment he didn't know why that made a difference, but then he remembered an old colorless video stored in WOL's encyclopedia showing a giant airship engulfed in flames. But then he looked down and saw that they were still climbing. The cliff edge on the western side of the river floodplain went by below them, and the land turned to rocky desert. To the south he could see the big canyon he remembered sailing down in a boat when he was small.

"It's our only chance!" he called to Ree.

She fumbled in the bag, pulled out the laser, aimed it at the bottom of the balloon, closed her eyes, and pressed the button. There was a loud snap of ionized air along the beam, and a small dark hole appeared in the gasbag. Their ascent didn't seem to slow at all.

"Make another one!"

"I don't want us to *crash*," she said, but after a glance below she took aim and burned another hole.

"Given the dimensions of the holes and the inflation pressure, it will take nearly an hour to reduce the lift by an appreciable amount," said Baichi.

Ree's response was to snap off half a dozen more shots. "There! Is that going to work?"

Baichi eyed the holes, then looked down. "That looks like enough."

After a minute Arkad could see that they were definitely going down. In fact, they were dropping uncomfortably fast. But when they were down to about fifty meters above the desert plateau, the falling balloon suddenly gave a lurch upward. Arkad saw a white figure trailing a white cloak drop to the ground, land rolling, and then stand up.

The balloon rose another forty or fifty meters before descending again—this time not as quickly, which gave Arkad the chance to realize just how fast the air was driving them along. Up here above the plateau the wind must have been thirty or forty kilometers per hour.

Ree was a little heavier than Arkad, so she hung lower than he did. "Cut yourself loose!" he shouted to her as they descended toward the surface speeding past. Her laser snapped once, then she tumbled a meter or two to the ground, clutching her bag in her other hand.

With her weight gone, the balloon rebounded again. Now that Arkad was the only one hanging from the envelope, the escaping gas made it turn slowly. He looked ahead and saw a branch of the canyon system cutting across his path. As the balloon stopped rising and began to go down again, he got a grip on the hose above his head with one hand, then laboriously untied it from around his chest with his free hand so that only his hand clutching the tube kept him from falling.

His idea was to let go just as he touched the ground, but as the canyon edge swept closer and closer, he wasn't sure if the balloon would touch down before going over the cliff. The cliff edge was only fifty or sixty meters ahead and coming fast, and he was still a good ten meters up. He closed his eyes and let go.

Arkad felt the thud of hitting the ground and a sharp pain from his leg as it took the impact. He felt himself slam into a couple of medium-sized rocks as he rolled along the ground. He saw WOL fly out of his pouch and explode into shards against a rock. Then he felt air beneath him as he tumbled over the cliff. He felt himself bounce off a projecting ledge. Then he felt nothing at all.

CHAPTER 16

ARKAD LAY IN ABSOLUTE DARKNESS—OR WAS HE BLIND? HE HAD no way to tell. He tried to move, but couldn't. Or rather, he couldn't tell if anything was happening. He couldn't feel anything.

"Baichi?" he said aloud. His voice sounded strange. His tongue felt weirdly thick, and he tasted blood. He could feel jagged edges where his front teeth should be, and his tongue found a tear in his lower lip. It should have hurt, but it didn't.

His nose caught the scent of Psthao-psthao, and he heard something skittering toward him in the darkness.

"You leave me here," he said in pidgin. "I am not food for you."

It spoke to him using its spiracles, so that it sounded like a chorus of whispers in the dark. "You must not have fear," said the Psthao. "We gave you a drug to stop all pain. I will stay with you as your life ends. It is bad to die with no one near."

"You let me go now," he said. "I do not wish to die." It was getting harder to speak. He couldn't seem to catch his breath, and he heard a nasty gurgling noise every time he inhaled.

"You are hurt too much to go," the chorus of whispers told him. "Your hard parts are in bits, your skin is torn, and your blood leaks out. I tell you not to fear death. All life is born of death. When you die, your flesh will feed young ones. You will live on in them. You will be part of a new life. I will make sure you feel no pain, and I will stay with you. You need have no fear. Life will go on and you will still be part of it."

"I want Baichi," he said.

245

"You be calm now," whispered the Psthao. "You do not need to fear."

The room filled with red light. Arkad could see nothing but blur and the dark shape of the Psthao next to him. It raised its head and whispered loudly. "You do not take him this time," said the Psthao. "He will die the real death now and live in new life. You do not take him for more fake life."

Another shape appeared in the room. It seemed to coalesce out of nothing, but perhaps that was just Arkad's damaged vision. It bent close to him, and he could make out a black and white furry face with a long muzzle.

"I will take him now," it said in pidgin. Its voice was gruff and confident. "You may not have him this time."

"You give him more fake life. He must die to live again," whispered the Psthao.

"I do what I wish to do," said the gruff voice. "You do not tell me what to do."

Arkad felt himself being lifted by something, and then something wrapped around him, and he slept.

The next time he woke, he was in a comfortable bed with a down comforter, in a room with wood-paneled walls and a huge fireplace.

"Ah, good," said the gruff voice, and a figure got up from one of the armchairs by the fire. As it approached him, Arkad felt an odd stab of recognition. It was a badger, about as tall as Arkad himself, wearing a dressing gown and shuffling along in some beat-up old slippers.

The badger sat on the bed and regarded Arkad, who could see the firelight glinting off of its little black eyes.

"Where am I?" asked Arkad.

"In my house," it said. "You've been in my care several times before, although you don't remember. You're a very reckless young man, Arkad. You can't keep cheating the Psthao-psthao of their prize forever. Someday I won't be able to get to you in time."

"Who are you?"

"My identity symbol doesn't translate easily to language as you use it. I am a very small element of the larger system which might be called 'Syavusa,' or possibly 'God.' For many years you've called me 'Mr. Badger' during our little visits, but of course you don't remember any of that."

"Did I die?"

"Despite the strong opinions of our Psthao-psthao friends, death is actually rather hard to define. Even when metabolic activity stops, enough information remains in your body to reconstruct you. Suffice to say, you'd be dead a dozen times over were it not for me."

Arkad sat up and looked at himself. He was unhurt. Even his shoulder was no longer sore.

"Ah...before you become too engrossed in an inventory of your physical state, you probably ought to know that none of this is real. This room is an illusion, as am I, and your body as you experience it. I'm deceiving your senses. In physical reality right now, you are floating in a support tank, each cell separate and surrounded by a scaffolding of nanomachinery. I've awakened your conscious mind because you've created a difficult problem for me and I want you to help me solve it."

Arkad said nothing, still trying to make sense of it all.

The badger waited a moment, then continued. "In the past, I've simply removed the memories of your death, reverted your body to a younger version, and released you again at a safe distance from whatever killed you. You amuse me."

"I don't want to forget," said Arkad.

"Your opinion isn't particularly important. It's my planet, I make the rules, and I can break them if I wish." The badger patted Arkad's arm affectionately, then stood up. "But this time there is a complication: the other two humans. You wish to rejoin them, and removing them from your memory would mean deleting some important formative experiences of the past several thousand hours. To make matters worse, at least one of them may wish to find you. She'd be difficult to capture and edit, and other Machines would be able to detect my tampering. It would cost me a certain amount of...let us call it status. That's why I have a problem."

"Just let me go back to them. I won't tell them about you."

The badger got up and went over to the fireplace, where he took up the poker and moved bits of wood around until the blaze brightened.

"There is also the matter of the ship. Both of those other humans wish to remove it from this world. I promised your parents to protect it and keep it safe until you claim it. But I do not wish to let it leave this planet."

"Why not?"

"Syavusa has always been a collector of odd things and beings. The planet is littered with exiles, refugees, and the last survivors of fallen civilizations. You can find animals and plants here which are otherwise extinct. And the planetary mind has large collections of cultural artifacts stored here and there under the surface. You might say it is our hobby. Other Machine intelligences try to communicate with other galaxies, or manipulate stars to harvest absurd quantities of matter and energy. Syavusa gathers up odds and ends."

"The *Rosetta* isn't yours. Humans made everything in it, and they should get it back."

"That ship is one of the crown jewels of our collection. We've never had such a large piece of a biological civilization's cultural output in our keeping before. I suppose I could make duplicates of everything—but I and my colleagues would be able to tell they were copies. Even among such as ourselves, authenticity matters."

"You can't keep us from finding it," said Arkad. "We've come so far!"

"I most certainly *can* keep you from finding it!" said the badger, and laughed aloud. "That's not even worth discussing. The problem is whether I *should*." The badger stared into the fire with its back to Arkad. "I can't edit the hybrid female. Higher-level intelligences would notice. But if I return you to her, repaired and unable to explain why, she'll deduce my presence, if she hasn't already. Eventually the other Machines would know what I've done to you, and would understand that I acted to keep the ship from being found. Again, I—we, to speak of the entire Syavusa intelligence—would lose status."

After a pause it added, "Of course I *could* simply shut down the tank in which you float, add your genome to the archive, and hand your physical remains over to the Psthao-psthao who've waited so patiently to lay eggs in your flesh. That would solve my problem very simply."

"Please let me go," Arkad repeated.

"I've enjoyed watching you over the years, Arkad. You were another favorite part of the collection. Now it appears I must lose you one way or another. Must I also lose my trove of human artifacts?"

"You don't have to lose it. You're welcome to come see it—or send a remote, anyway. Nobody's going to hide it."

"How little you know. There is a good chance that when you leave Syavusa that treasure will be stolen and hidden again, or very thoroughly destroyed."

"You mean the Elmisthorn? They won't even know until it's too late. Don't worry."

The badger returned to his bedside. "Ah, Arkad, I will miss having you here. Such endless self-confidence in such a fragile vessel! Even if you knew the truth, your courage would be undiminished. It's your most appealing trait." It sat down again on the bed and leaned close to Arkad.

"Very well," it said. "Here's what I'll do: I will return you to the surface, body and memories intact. You may choose what to reveal to your comrades. If you're able to locate the *Rosetta*, it's yours by right and you may do with it what you wish. But"—the badger raised a forefinger—"I will neither help nor hinder you in any way after I release you. If you fail to find the ship, then it will remain in my keeping. If you perish in the desert, I'll add your polished bones to my collection. If someone tries to take the ship from you, I won't intervene. After all, if it is destroyed, then my replicas of its contents will be the only ones in existence."

Arkad didn't even get the chance to reply. The room and everything in it simply winked out of existence. There was a moment of blackness, and then he opened his eyes. He was lying on a warm stone by a river, with trees overhead and the whistling of canopy creatures all around.

He sat up, wondering if it had all been some kind of vivid hallucination caused by falling. But as soon as he moved, he knew it had all been real. His shoulder and knees no longer hurt, his leg had no deep gash, his elbows were unscraped, and his teeth were all intact. His hair was even clean. His few remaining belongings were neatly laid out next to him, so he put them back into the pockets of the vest that had once belonged to Jacob, and got up to look around.

The stone was by the quietly flowing water of a small river, and all around him, tall trees with corkscrew trunks rose high to a dense canopy. Between the trunks he could see the canyon walls, covered with a dense carpet of vines. Could he climb up? The canyon was almost a kilometer deep, and the vines ended well below the top.

He had no way to signal Ree and Baichi, so all he could do was hope to run into them. Going downriver would take him back toward Chkik-Chk; upriver led to the belt of storms and the Black Land. Well, that was where he wanted to go, so he turned right and began to make his way upstream. There wasn't really a trail to follow, but the ground cover was a dense mat of springy coils just a few centimeters high. Every few hundred meters he had to climb over tumbled piles of big crystal chunks, some of them the size of buildings.

Just as he began climbing up an enormous tilted slab of translucent green, he heard Ree's voice in the distance beyond. He could only hear her side of the conversation, but it sounded like an argument.

"You're just guessing!" she said, and then after a pause, "Why don't you think about what we came here to do? We can't waste this much time." Another pause and then, "He would want us to keep going. So would Jacob." And then, "Well, maybe I will!"

Arkad reached the top of the green slab and looked over. Beyond, he could see a stony dry stream bed which emerged from a small side canyon. Ree stood on the far side of the stream bed glaring at Baichi, who was beginning to climb up the same jumble of crystal that Arkad has just surmounted.

"Ahoy!" he called out. Baichi looked up at him silently with a grin like a burning flare.

Ree stared, then her face abruptly shifted from an expression of annoyance to a big smile. "Arkad!" she called back. "We've been worried sick about you. What happened?"

He took advantage of the time spent in getting himself down from the top of the crystal to a lower slab to think of what to tell them. Would they believe him if he told the truth? He wasn't entirely sure he believed it himself. In the end he just shrugged. "I woke up back there. I'm not sure what happened."

Both of them looked at him, but it was Baichi's gaze he met, and he smiled back at her. "I'm glad I found you."

"You got lucky," said Ree. "Come on—according to the map there's a little settlement of some sort up the canyon. Maybe we can get a boat there."

The canyon floor was pleasant enough, except when they had to climb over obstacles. The air was warm, but the forest canopy gave plenty of shade and there was always river water to drink. It was lukewarm and carried so much silt they had to clean out the filter membranes every time they refilled the bottles. After a couple of hours they stopped, and Arkad waded out into the water to catch something to eat. Between the rocks, the bottom was full of sessile larvae buried in the silt with only their feeding tendrils sticking out. Arkad had eaten similar creatures before, and pulled up a dozen to share with Ree and Baichi. He wrapped them in leaves and steamed them in the fire. The first one was sweet, but very gritty, so he used his knife to dig out the digestive sac from the others.

"I'm exhausted," said Ree. "Aren't you tired, Arkad? We can sleep a little while before pushing on."

"I'm not sleepy." In fact Arkad felt better than ever before. He was warm, healthy, rested, and reasonably clean. Sleep was the last thing he wanted.

"You must be," she said. "Come and lie down for a bit."

"But—"

"I *insist*," she said.

To humor her, he lay on his back next to her on a patch of springy ground cover, and she draped her reflective blanket over him. It was in active cooling mode, so the air under it was refreshing.

Ree put her head next to his and whispered, "I was afraid we had lost you for good. We would never have been able to find the *Rosetta*. I think you should tell me everything you know, in case we get separated again... or something worse happens."

When he didn't answer, she continued, "Arkad, we've come so far together. We should be able to trust each other, you and I. Don't you trust me?"

"Yes, but... I don't know coordinates or anything like that. I just recognize places from when I was little. I went down this canyon in a boat. Up the river there are statues carved into the sides, and a town made of tunnels."

"Good, good. And beyond that?"

"That's where we got on the boat. Before that I think we were walking. We had to go through part of the storm belt before we could get down into the canyon. I remember the wind almost lifted me off the ground."

"Okay. And the Black Land is past that, right?"

"Yes."

"This is important: can you find the ship in the Black Land? I have to know this before we leave the canyon, Arkad."

"I think so. I remember there was one big jagged yellow rock sticking up out of the black ground. We sheltered under that for a while. We were walking, so the ship can't be far from that."

"Were there any dangerous people or animals in the Black Land? Bandits, or scavengers, or anything like that?"

"I don't remember seeing anyone at all until we were in the canyon. Back at the Elmisthorn camp in the plains, Aldisth said there were black things with legs."

"Are they dangerous?"

"I don't know. An adult came before it could finish telling me about them. I don't remember anything like that from when I was little."

"I see." Ree was quiet for a moment, then gave a little nod. "All right, let's get some rest."

She turned over and soon was snoring quietly, but Arkad couldn't sleep. His body was practically buzzing with energy. He felt as though he could run straight to the Black Land and the lost *Rosetta* without stopping. After a few minutes he eased himself slowly away from Ree, then out from under the blanket entirely. He stood up and walked quietly away.

Baichi was about fifty meters upstream, sitting on a huge slab of broken crystal which the river was just starting to round off. He joined her and dabbled his feet in the lukewarm water. He didn't know what to say so he just enjoyed the sound of the water and the music of whatever creatures were whistling overhead.

She broke the silence first. "Something happened to you. All your injuries are gone. Even your clothing is clean."

He hadn't noticed the clothes. "Is this planet claimed by the Machines?"

"It doesn't work that way for them. The Machines don't have any kind of government and don't claim any boundaries. There are simply places where one or more Machines are active—and other places. Other beings or civilizations can do what they wish as long as they don't interfere with what the Machines are doing."

"I think I talked to one after I fell."

She stared off into emptiness for a few seconds. "There is a . . . presence here, but it will not acknowledge me. I have sensed it a few times since we arrived. And of course the planet itself shows active terraforming."

"Does it?"

"The signs are subtle, but unmistakable. Something regulates the temperature and atmosphere composition. Whatever controls this planet has been active here for at least ten thousand years. What did it say to you?"

"It was trying to decide if it should keep the *Rosetta* or let us take it. It finally told me it wouldn't stop us, but wouldn't help either. We're on our own."

"Ree has been making transmissions," said Baichi. "Very fast encrypted bursts. She only does it when she thinks I am far away."

"Who could she be talking to?"

"My hypothesis is that she is communicating with something in orbit, possibly a small relay which in turn is linked to a ship hiding somewhere farther away."

"Are you sure?"

"I am sure she has been transmitting. The rest is conjecture."

"But ... that's great!" said Arkad. "She works for the Combined Forces, right? That means they must have sent a ship in secret to help us!"

"Ree left the intelligence service," said Baichi. "Jacob suspected they might have helped fund this expedition, but she has never mentioned it."

"Of course not! Spies have to keep everything secret."

"If Ree is communicating with a Combined Forces vessel, it should be pointed out that they have not given us any help at all so far."

"Maybe they're waiting for us to find the *Rosetta*."

Baichi didn't answer.

Arkad fidgeted for a moment, then decided he had to ask her. "Baichi, do *you* work for the Machines? Ree thinks you do."

"They created me, they do not control me."

Another pause, and then he said, "She thought they might be able to control you without you knowing it."

"Yes, they could probably do that. Programmed subconscious tendencies to steer me where they want me to go—or a sleeper personality ready to take over in the right circumstances." She looked at him with those fathomless eyes. "Of course, if a Machine has been rebuilding you and altering your memories for several decades, it would be very simple for it to do the same thing to you, as well. You could be a puppet without realizing it."

"We both could be." He found himself wondering if his visceral dislike of the Psthao-psthao was something the badger had put in his mind. What else? Was there *any* real Arkad? "At least we know Ree's mind isn't under anyone's control."

"Whenever she encountered one of the Elmisthorn exiles, her heart rate and respiration increased, her body temperature rose, and her pupils dilated. It was very much like the way you respond when we are close together."

"Maybe she's scared."

"Her fear reactions are different. The Elmisthorn on Earth have been trying to engineer instinctive loyalty in their human servants."

"Jacob said it didn't work!"

"I am only telling you what I observe."

He didn't say anything for a while. There was something very important he wanted to ask her, but finding the right way to ask it turned out to be very difficult. Finally he just asked, "Baichi, do you like me?"

She took her time answering. "Yes," she said at last.

"I mean, do you *like* me? You can tell how I feel about you, right? From my pupils and stuff. Do you...feel that way about me?"

"Yes," she replied. "But we cannot act upon our desires."

"Why not?" he asked, and then blushed as a thought struck him. "Oh—I'm sorry. I should have guessed. I'm really sorry."

"No," she said. "It is not a physical problem. I can even have children, if I wish. No, I cannot fall in love with you because I am afraid of what will happen if I allow it. Love and desire make humans behave irrationally. I must remain in control of myself. It would be dangerous if I did not. So I am actively suppressing my attraction to you."

Arkad didn't know how to answer that. None of the stories in WOL had prepared him for this. What would John Carter or the Monkey King do in a situation like this?

Suddenly he couldn't stand to stay there with her. Without a word he got up and went off downstream past the pile of crystal slabs to forage.

There was a cluster of tubeworms attached to one of the rocks in the river, their cone-shaped shells anchored at the tips to the downstream sides of the rocks. He pulled a couple loose and then tried to crack one open with a fist-sized stone. His first blow split the shell, but he went on pounding it harder and harder until it was an unrecognizable mash of pulped flesh and fragments. He swept the whole mess into the water and threw the stone as far as he could.

He didn't need her, he told himself. So what if she didn't like him? There were thousands of other humans—millions, if you counted Earth. As soon as he got to one of the human enclaves, he'd be able to meet dozens of girls his age, and none of them would have Machine-tech implants to keep them from liking him. Baichi wanted to stay in control of herself? Fine, let her do it, then. Let her stay in control without him. If she thought it was so dangerous, she could stay perfectly safe and alone.

She wasn't real, he thought. And then he thought that he wasn't real either. All of this could be just an illusion being piped into his brain as he floated in a tank. Or maybe he was a simulation, existing as nothing but data in the badger's mind. Arkad felt the sun-warmed rock under his hand, then the water flowing past. If nothing was real, what did it matter? He could just lie here forever. It was comfortable and peaceful.

After about ten minutes he got bored. Real or fake, live or simulated, he wanted to do more than just lie on a rock. Somewhere beyond this canyon was a spaceship holding treasures of human civilization. Somewhere in space were planets with human colonies. The whole vast universe was out there, and Arkad wanted to see it all.

He washed his face in the warm river water, dried it with his shirt, then went back to where Ree was sleeping and prodded her gently with a finger. "Let's get moving," he told her. "We're just wasting time here."

As soon as she was ready he began moving upriver, setting his own pace, not looking back to see if either of them was following. None of them said anything; Baichi was her usual expressionless self, and Ree looked almost smug as she packed up her gear.

The closest settlement was about an hour's walk upstream. It was a Kchik village, with a central mother plant extending vines along the river and up the sides of the canyon, a few dozen workers clearing weeds and maintaining a stone floodwall, and a single squad of warriors on guard. Fortunately the town also housed some Itooti—Arkad found himself wondering if there was any place on Syavusa they didn't live. One of them had a boat, and was willing to take the humans upriver on the condition that they provided the motive power.

"The graceful boat lacks a powerful motor," said the boat owner, a male named Tatiatut. "To sail against the steady current, wise Tatiatut must wait for a favorable breeze. Three muscular bipeds can easily pole the swift boat up the placid river."

The boat was flat-bottomed, nearly as broad as it was long, with a sail that folded like a dragon's wing from a picture. Baichi took the starboard pole, and Arkad took up the portside one while Tatiatut steered and shouted encouragement. With two of them poling, the work was more tedious than hard, and they managed a fairly steady one kilometer per hour against the current.

The three humans didn't speak much during the voyage, at least not to each other. Arkad chatted with Tatiatut about the river, fishing, and the conditions in the storm belt to the west.

"This obscure route is still the safest way to reach the inaccessible Black Land," said the Itooti. "By approaching that uninhabited country from due east, the intrepid traveler passes through the weakest part of the fearsome storm belt. On the distant western side, the violent weather is so bad that only a massive ground crawler could withstand it."

"Unprotected Arkad wonders if travelers can make it through the dangerous storm belt on the weakest side."

"Candid Tatiatut admits that he has never attempted to pass through the gusty storm belt. Mystified Tatiatut wonders why three freakish bipeds wish to do so."

"Discreet Arkad cannot discuss his valid reasons for wanting to make the risky journey," he replied.

As they poled upstream, Tatiatut pointed out the occasional faint surge in the current, accompanied by a slight rise in the water level. "Brief rains pass over the branching headwaters of the deep-cut river. Roaring floods in the narrow canyons become tiny ripples in the broad main stream."

They reached a section with steeper walls, where the cliffs came right down to the water's edge and the center of the channel was too deep for their poles. Arkad and Baichi switched to paddles, and by the time they were past the narrow section, Arkad was ready to pass out from fatigue.

After more than fifty hours of poling with frequent rest breaks, they came to a wide spot in the canyon where two subsidiary streams joined the main channel and created an oval basin a kilometer across. Arkad could tell at a glance that the flood-control dams blocking each stream, notched by V-shaped spillways so that they looked like rows of huge teeth, were Vziim work, as were the towers that clung to the canyon walls and rose to the level of the surrounding plateau. But the tunnel mouths that dotted the cliffs lacked the obsessive precision of Vziim work, and Arkad recognized Psthao-psthao livestock browsing in the brush that covered the level bottom of the basin and the lower slopes of the sides.

He felt a shiver of fear and revulsion at the thought of them. Was that real, he wondered, or something the badger had done to him?

"This remote town is the final stop on the life-giving river," Tatiatut announced. "Canny Tatiatut will trade here for shiny silver, attractive hides, and useful tendons while the muscular bipeds must disembark."

The weather in the basin was noticeably windier than it had been downstream. Irregular breezes constantly tossed Arkad's hair about, and from time to time a powerful gust came howling down one of the canyons. A fine layer of dust began to accumulate on his skin.

According to the map, this town was called Zayaziya, though in smaller text it was also labeled Tsayo-Tsiyo. Two Vziim clans inhabited towers on opposite sides of the canyon, and the Psthao-psthao tunnels were all over. The place was too small and out-of-the-way to support any inns, but while Tatiatut haggled with a Vziim matriarch over the exchange ratio between copper and silver, Arkad approached one of the old female's senior daughters to ask about a place to stay.

"You tell me if we can pay to rest in a room," he said to her.

She recoiled in surprise. "I did not know you could talk," she said. "I thought you were a beast the small one brought to do work."

"I did work on the boat to get here," he said. "Now it will go back down but we three go on to the west. We need to rest where there is no wind and dust."

"You tell me why you want to go west from here," she said. "That way leads to storms, heat, and the Black Land with no life."

"We wish to go there. You tell me if we can get a room."

They worked out a price, and the three humans were allowed to camp out in a storage area at the bottom of the cliffside tower on the north side of the canyon. The space was blessedly dark and cool, and half of it was taken up by sacks of cement mix, which the Vziim presumably calculated the humans could neither eat nor steal.

The three of them washed off with river water, then simply collapsed onto the cool stone floor without even bothering to eat first. Even Baichi wanted to lie down for a time. Arkad found the dark and stillness of the room very soothing after the glare and dust outside, and was asleep as soon as he closed his eyes.

When he woke he wasn't sure how long he had slept. Ree was still curled up in her bag. Baichi was gone.

He caught a scent in the air and suppressed a shudder. Psthao-psthao. Had one of them come here in the dark as he slept? Or had he simply not noticed the odor before?

Arkad got up. Past the stacks of cement was a low door, which proved to be unlocked. He hesitated only a second, then pushed it open. Beyond was a broad passage lit by patches of electric paint. He turned right, more or less at random, and wandered along it. After about a hundred meters the construction of the passage changed. The precise Vziim vaulting gave way to a smooth, rounded tunnel which looked as though it was carved by water or perhaps some chemical. The scent of Psthao-psthao was stronger there.

He forced himself to go on. If he stopped now, he'd certainly turn and run back out, and he didn't want that. So he made himself take a step, and then another, into the tunnel. He wanted to find a Psthao.

The rounded tunnel curved to his left, going deeper into the cliff, and then abruptly opened into a broad, disk-shaped chamber. One of the herd animals lay in the center, and he could just make out the long, shiny black bodies of a couple of adult Psthao-psthao crouched beside it. Their faces were pressed to its flanks, and Arkad realized with horror that they were drinking blood from it.

Arkad froze as one of them turned and scuttled toward him. "You tell me if you come to get a meal," it whispered through its spiracles in pidgin.

"No," he whispered back, then cleared his throat and spoke more firmly. "I do not eat your food. I have a thing to ask one Psthao."

Another Psthao joined them, and Arkad could see two or three more had entered the room.

"You are *Arkad*," said the newcomer, brushing him with a pair of feelers. "I know of you."

"That is my name," he replied, fighting the urge to run. He made himself sit on the floor. That brought his head down to the same level as the two Psthao-psthao. A second one tickled his forearm with its feelers, then spoke to the others in their own language.

"The thing that was here first of all took you from us," whispered the one who recognized him. "It has done that in the past."

"You tell me if you were the one with me," said Arkad. "You tell me why you would help me die."

"You did not need help for that," it replied. "All your parts were hurt. All we did was stop your pain and wait with you for the end."

"You tell me why you did that."

"It is our way. All life must end in death. All life must come from death. We did not wish you to die with no new life."

"You tell me if you took the one who gave me birth."

"That was a long time past. I was not yet born then, but I heard of it. Her flesh did hatch a fine clutch of young, and all were good Psthao. A few live still, if you wish to meet those in whom her life is now. They are far from here, though."

"I go to the Black Land now," said Arkad. "You tell me if you folk would come to get me if I die there."

"The thing that was here first of all will take you if you die there. It will keep your flesh in a deep place and no new life will come from you. It will be a sad death."

A thought struck him. "You tell me how far you can go to the west in the ground from here," he said. "I need to go past the land of wind."

"Our ways go part of the way," it said. "You would be safe."

All of a sudden Arkad realized he wasn't afraid anymore. He wasn't speaking with a monster that wanted to eat him or drain his blood. It was just another one of Syavusa's interesting inhabitants—with a different idea of how to honor the dead.

"You tell me if you can show the way," he said, scrambling to his feet. "I can get my team and we can go soon."

"I can lead you through the dark," it whispered, and Arkad didn't shudder at all this time.

CHAPTER 17

"I DON'T LIKE THIS," SAID REE, NOT FOR THE FIRST TIME.
The five of them—Ree, Arkad, Baichi, and two Psthao-psthao—were making their way through a very narrow passage in complete darkness. The humans were up to their knees in rushing water and had to stoop because their heads would otherwise bump into the ceiling.

The Psthao in the lead whispered to Arkad, and he translated for the other two. "He says that if the water rises to fill the passage, take a deep breath and let the current push us back to where there is air. The streams come and go." Arkad was grinning in the darkness. It sounded like fun.

He didn't get to try the Psthao's suggestion, though, because as they reached a place where the passage started sloping upward very steeply, the flow began to diminish, and by the time they had reached a narrow vertical chimney, there was just a steady seep down the walls. A strong air current moving past them made the chimney give off a low moaning noise.

Apparently the Psthao-psthao didn't actually dig many passages of their own, preferring to connect and enlarge natural caves whenever possible. Since their method of excavation relied heavily on dissolving rock with chemicals, it was hard to tell where their work ended and the natural formations began, which was of course the whole point.

The moaning chimney took them up to a broad, low-ceilinged cave with just the faintest hint of light seeping in. The Psthao led the way up a shallow slope until they all could see a bend ahead lit by genuine daylight.

"We stop here," the lead Psthao told Arkad. "Too much wind and heat out there. West from here you cross hills where storms pass, then you are in the Black Land."

"I thank you for your help," said Arkad.

They had to approach the exit slowly, to give their eyes time to adjust. Gusts blew in and out of the cave, keeping the air constantly full of dust. Finally the three humans emerged from the side of a hill to look out at the surface again.

The land in front of them was a broad valley, deeply cut by steep-sided gullies. Almost nothing grew on the surface, but the gullies were full of lush plants. The wind was strong but irregular, an endless assault of powerful gusts laden with grit, coming by surprise from random directions. Overhead the sky was dusty blue, with clouds sweeping across it shockingly fast.

For the first time he could remember, Arkad had trouble figuring out which way to go. Until now they had simply walked toward the sun, but now it was high in the hazy sky. He finally had to wait for a clear moment and look down at his shadow to see which way was west.

"This doesn't look so bad," said Ree, as the three of them went down the hillside. "I thought it would be like a constant typhoon."

"I've heard that it's much worse over on the other side of the Black Land. Something about the weather patterns," said Arkad.

"I can put up with this," said Ree.

The first storm hit shortly after they reached the bottom of the hill. One moment they were walking in strong sunlight, with random gusts blowing. Then the sky turned yellow-green and darkened. The wind shifted suddenly to the west and strengthened from a gust to a blast. The windblown dust stung Arkad's exposed skin. For an instant the darkness flashed blindingly bright and a clap of thunder drowned out the roar of the wind.

"Down!" he shouted, and threw himself to the ground as the other two did the same. He clung to the bare dirt and squeezed his eyes shut as the wind tore at him. Another lightning flash lit up the insides of his eyelids, and the boom hit at the same instant, loud enough to leave his ears ringing. He could smell the ozone in the dusty air.

Then something hit him. It was warm and heavy and it took him a second to realize it was rain. He couldn't even feel individual drops; this felt more like a heavy blanket pressing him down. The wind shifted around to the south, and it felt even stronger. Lightning flashes and ear-splitting thunder came every couple of seconds now, and the noise made Arkad whimper and try to flatten himself into the dirt even more.

As the wind shifted to the east, its fury reached a crescendo, but the rain and lightning trailed off. Sunlight broke through the clouds as the wind finally came from the north and began to weaken.

And then, as suddenly as it had come on, the storm had passed them by. Arkad raised his head to look around. All three of them were covered with a layer of caked-on dirt, almost like stucco. The surface of the ground had changed from bare dirt to a slick layer of silty mud.

For a couple of minutes none of them said anything. Then Ree abruptly got to her feet. "We'd better find some shelter before the next one comes along."

They hustled across the valley, slipping and stumbling a bit at first until the sun could bake the surface dry again. When they came to a gully it was half-full of churning brown water, and they had to wait until the stream was low enough to wade across.

Another storm caught them in the center of the valley, where shallow canyon channels braided and twisted, half-choked by a tangle of plants with massive roots. They had time to scoop out a little shelter in the side of a low hillock, and they huddled in the hole as wind and dust lashed at them again. This storm had no rain at all, but the barrage of lightning was intense. Claps of thunder and the echoes off the sides of the valley blurred together into a steady, deafening rumble.

As the storm reached its peak, Arkad felt a strange tingling sensation run through his entire body just before lightning struck the top of the rise less than twenty meters away. He felt the concussion of the thunder more than he heard it, and for a few seconds afterward, he couldn't breathe.

Once that storm had passed, the three humans adopted a new way of moving across the valley. There was no thought of stopping to rest; they jogged along at the fastest pace they could maintain, constantly watching the sky to the northeast, where the storms came from. Whenever a dark cloud came in sight, they immediately sought shelter.

They weathered two more storms before reaching the hills on the west side. Wind and rain had scoured the rocks bare of topsoil, but in the crevices between the exposed rock layers, Arkad could see clumps of wiry plants. The humans found a deep overhang where soft rock between two harder layers had been eroded away, and wedged themselves into the deepest part of it to rest and eat.

Ree's self-cleaning suit was still pristine white, and Baichi's cloak had turned silver to keep her cool. Arkad's clothing was just dirty. His skin inside his shirt was caked with dust, and he could even feel dust inside his pants. His hair was stiff, but he was too tired to care. He slept until another lightning storm passed by. That one had rain, so Arkad got up and crawled to the edge of the shelf to let the deluge wash him. He slept more after that, and the passage of another storm woke him only briefly.

When all three were awake they discussed their next move. "According to the map, there's another valley beyond this ridge, and then more hills, and then the Black Land," said Ree. "About forty kilometers. If we really move, we can make it across the valley, rest in the hills, and then push into the Black Land."

"I don't see any water in the next valley," said Arkad, looking at the map on maximum detail.

"There are hollows in these rocks holding water," said Baichi. "I can smell it."

"All right, you find water and fill up the filter bottles," said Ree. "As soon as we get a long clear spell, we'll go over the ridge. I absolutely don't want to get caught by a storm while we're on top of these hills."

Once again Arkad was struck by how much Ree had changed. She seemed very determined, almost reckless. To his own surprise, he found that he had to be the cautious one. "Forty kilometers with only three liters of water?"

"I don't need any," said Baichi.

"Even so, that's not much."

"Don't forget the bottles can recycle our urine, too," said Ree.

"We still have to go into the Black Land—and we have to get back. I don't see any water sources west of here on the map," said Arkad.

"I've come too far to turn back," said Ree. "Just get me to the *Rosetta* and we'll be all right."

What could he do? Ree seemed hell-bent on reaching the ship, no matter what the risk. Baichi could ignore most physical dangers. He could let the two of them go on without him. He could probably make it back across the valley by himself, maybe find his way to the canyon...

But then he would be all alone again, with no other humans for company. Arkad had been alone too long. "Okay," he said to Ree.

They stayed under the rock ledge for a few more hours until another storm passed by. That one tracked down the valley they had already crossed, so that Arkad had a good view of it from the ridge. He could see the cloud wall and the funnel reaching down to the ground, all shrouded in veils of rain. From that distance the lightning was just a series of flickers inside the storm.

As soon as that system was a kilometer to the southwest of them, they began scrambling to get over the ridge before the next one arrived. The distance to the top was a hundred meters, and the hillside was all big chunks of bare rock. They climbed up tilted slabs, then jumped to the next across narrow gaps which might have been bottomless. As always, Baichi climbed without any sign of effort or clumsiness, but even Ree seemed to have found new energy, and she surged ahead of Arkad to reach the summit first. He struggled grimly along at the back of the party, unwilling to complain.

From the top of the ridge they could look back across the valley, with no storms in sight at the moment, and then across the next basin, which was broader and shallower, with a very flat bottom. The ground was a uniform pale gray, with no gullies and no plants in sight. The wind from the west buffeted them on top of the ridge, and it was hot and dry.

A storm caught them as they worked down the other side. The western slope was less steep and had stretches of loose smaller stones instead of giant slabs. They were halfway down one long stretch of scree when the wind began to shift and strengthen. Arkad saw a whirlwind beating its way right along the crest of the ridge, and the three of them crouched down among the sharp, hot rocks.

They crossed the basin at a near sprint, as the floor turned out to be a mathematically level plain of salt, with no cover or protection at all. The heat was merciless, and the only reason they didn't drain the filter bottles was that they were terrified of stopping to drink.

They almost made it.

The three of them had crossed twenty kilometers in a little over four hours when a storm cell appeared in the northeast. It was a big one, filling the valley from ridge to ridge and looming into the upper atmosphere.

"We've got to get to cover!" Ree shouted over the rising wind and dug in her bag for a medical patch which she slapped onto the side of her neck. Then she turned and began to run faster than Arkad had ever seen her go. He summoned his last energy for a final sprint to the ridge ahead.

The air was soon full of dust and salt until Arkad could see nothing any direction but a milky haze. He put a hand on Baichi's shoulder, since her eyes could penetrate the murk while he could barely open his own. Ree was somewhere ahead of them. He thought he saw her stop and turn toward them.

As the haze turned dark and the wind's roar rose to a scream, Baichi suddenly stumbled and fell. Arkad, surprised, took a spill himself and then crawled back to her. She lay on her back, and her face bore an expression of utter panic.

"Come on," he said, trying to help her up. "We've got to get away from here." He had to shout to make himself heard.

"Can't!" she managed to get out. "Can't move!" She feebly lifted one arm and then it fell back to the ground.

"You've got to get up!" he shouted. He tried to lift her. Baichi was slender and no taller than Arkad, but she was solid. He could barely raise her torso off the ground, and her limbs and head sagged like those of a dead thing.

Something hard and cold thwacked Arkad in the face, then two more. He saw pea-sized white balls bouncing off him, and it took him a second to realize they were hailstones. Ice was falling on him in the desert.

He managed to get Baichi draped over his shoulder and then got his legs under him as he strained to stand up. Once on his feet Arkad began to stagger in what he hoped was the right direction. The only guide he had was the wind. The sky was greenish-black, lit by purple flashes of lightning, and the air was so full of dust and hail he could barely see the ground. But the wind was steady, so steady that he could almost lean against it as he staggered westward as fast as he could manage.

When lightning hit nearby the noise made him fall, which was probably for the best as more bolts struck all around. He lay flat, holding Baichi close to him. The only way he could tell she was still alive was that she was trembling all over. He put his face right up to hers and was startled to see that she was crying. The tracks of windblown tears through the dust on her pale skin were plain to see.

"We'll be all right!" he shouted over the wind. "Don't be afraid!"

But inside he was pretty terrified himself. Baichi was stronger than human, invulnerable, probably immortal. If she was scared, things must be worse than he knew. He couldn't lift her again, couldn't even tell which way to go anymore. The world was a swirling, roaring chaos of flaying wind, dust, lightning flashes and rain. All he could do was huddle close to her, trying to protect their faces, and endure.

Arkad had no way to know how long the storm lasted. It could have been a few minutes, or a dozen hours. When the wind finally died down enough for him to open his eyes, he found that he and Baichi were half buried in dust. On that perfectly flat valley bottom, two human bodies were enough of a windbreak to create a small dune of salty dust on their leeward side, behind Baichi. More dust had piled up in the narrow space between them.

"Can you move?" he asked her.

She struggled and began to cry again. "Nothing *works*! I can't move, I can't tell anything about my internal state, I can't even regulate my emotions. I keep *crying*," she wailed.

Arkad didn't say anything. He managed to get her over one shoulder again, got painfully to his feet, and then staggered off toward the westward ridge.

"This isn't so bad," he said, trying not to grunt with the effort. "I've carried much heavier loads. Back in Ayaviz I stole a broken compressor once. No Pfifu or Itooti could lift it, and no Vziim could move while holding it up, so nobody locked it up or watched it. I got a kilogram of copper for it."

"Now I'm just a broken machine, too," she said, and he heard her sniffle. But then she laughed. "How much copper will you get for me?"

"You? Well... you're about eighty kilos, and I bet you're made of pretty rare stuff, so I'd guess you're worth two or three hundred grams of palladium. Maybe more. There's just one problem: we're going the wrong way. Nobody in the Black Land to buy anything. I guess I'll have to keep you."

She didn't answer, so he slogged heavily on in silence.

The next storm passed mostly to the east of them, so Arkad just squinted to keep the salt dust out of his eyes and kept going. Stopping out here would be suicide. He had to keep walking. The muscles in his back and legs weren't just aching, they were burning. Just keep walking, he told himself. He repeated it inside his head, with a silly tune he remembered from a video about fish.

As gusts of wind stung him with salt and dust, he felt Baichi shift on his shoulder.

"I think...I think something's coming back!" she said. "I can sense things about myself again. My blood chemistry's all messed up. Full of cortisol, oxytocin...I can't regulate anything yet."

"Can you walk?" Arkad managed to gasp out.

"Let me try."

He tried to set her down gently, but lost his balance and both of them landed heavily on the hot salt flat.

She got to her hands and knees by herself, took a breath, and then stood upright. "I still feel weak," she said. "My cells are still just working on chemical energy." She took a couple of steps. Arkad could see that she hadn't recovered her old superhuman grace. Her steps were jerky, hesitant—like an ordinary human. Like him.

She walked a few more steps, then realized Arkad was still kneeling on the ground, trying to will himself to stand up again. When she took a step back toward him, Arkad waved her off and stood up. "Just a little tired," he said, and the two of them staggered ahead together, holding each other for support.

They got to some big fallen rocks at the edge of the salt flat before the next storm hit. This one carried a little rain, and Arkad scooped salty mud into the filter bottle to extract a few milliliters of water for them to drink.

As they huddled between two boulders, he asked her, "Do you know what happened to you? Was it like that time back in the mercenary camp?"

"Yes," she said. "It was exactly like that time, and now I know exactly what happened. Ree did it."

"What? How?"

"I could see her through the dust," said Baichi. "She reached into her bag, turned, and pointed something at me. I felt an energy discharge, and then everything just shut down."

"Are you sure? Maybe you got struck by lightning or something."

"I would have felt the static charge before a lightning strike, and the current would have burned and damaged me. This was more like a signal. An off switch. Ree has something that can shut down my Machine parts."

"That thing in her bag we couldn't figure out?"

"Possibly. It looked like Machine technology. I wonder where she got it."

"Jacob said she used to work for the Combined Forces, and they're friendly with the Machines. Maybe..." he hesitated for a second, afraid of hurting her feelings, but then plunged ahead. "You said after Bharosa the Machines gave the Combined Forces weapons to stop your brothers and sisters. Maybe Ree has one."

"In case I ever started to kill and destroy. Yes, that makes sense." She had regained much of her old masklike calm.

"But why did she do it?" said Arkad. "It doesn't make any sense at all!"

"She does not like me. She was always nervous around me."

Arkad couldn't think of anything to say. He sat leaning against the warm rocks, resting his stiff legs and aching back. At some point he fell asleep. When he woke Baichi was gone, along with the filter bottles. He climbed up on the rocks and looked out over the salt pan, but couldn't see her. "Baichi!" he shouted.

"Here!" she replied from behind him. He turned to see her jump lightly from boulder to boulder, holding a bottle in each hand. She landed right next to him. "It all came back!" she said. "My cells switched over to fusion again. I can monitor and control everything inside me. I can remember everything and sense everything. I'm *alive* again!"

She danced across the boulders, alighting precisely atop each one, and twirling in midair when she leaped. She looked so joyous Arkad forgot for a minute how sore and thirsty he was.

"I found some water," she said. "I had to dig for it. The bottles are full." She looked more serious and said, "Which way do you intend to go?"

"I don't know," he admitted. "Would you come with me if I turn back? We could get across the storm belt to the canyon lands, then downriver to the sea. There's food, water, people—we can find a place somewhere. The other choice is for us to push on past this ridge, *hope* we don't run out of water in the Black Land, *hope* we find the *Rosetta,* and then . . . do you think it would still be in shape to take off?"

"It has spent fifty years without maintenance or protection from the elements," said Baichi. "We can only be sure if we locate it ourselves and examine it."

The sensible course would be to turn back. Baichi was watching him without expression. "Let's go see," he said.

They sheltered among the rocks for another couple of hours, then climbed the ridge in an interval between storms. These hills were less rocky than the ridge to the east, with steep slopes of bare dirt that quickly turned into landslides when Arkad tried to climb them. In the end it proved easier to find old slides with exposed cliffs above them, and scale the cliffs.

When they reached the top, he looked west and saw the Black Land spread out below him. It was truly black, with no surface detail and no way to get a sense of scale. The air was startlingly clear, with no windblown dust or haze at all.

The western side of the ridge was a gentle slope of hard-packed bare dirt, and as they descended, the wind vanished. The air was hot and still. Ahead, the black surface seemed to ripple in the heat.

The Black Land began very abruptly at the bottom of the slope. Arkad stopped about half a meter from the edge of the black surface and knelt to get a better look. Beneath his knees the ground was bare dirt and gravel. Ten centimeters beyond his knees it was perfect black.

He put his face right down to the surface to see what it was. With one eye closed and his nose touching the ground, Arkad could make out a dense pattern of tiny branching black fibers covering the dirt. The pattern was regular and seemed to have infinite levels of complexity. He poked at it, but the fibers must have had deep roots because he couldn't budge the black covering at all.

"That surface is cooler than it should be," said Baichi. "Much cooler. Most of the energy reaching the surface is being absorbed rather than reradiated."

"Is it some kind of plant?" asked Arkad. "Something that doesn't need water to grow?"

"Or a power plant. This kind of self-propagating structure is not uncommon in Machine technology. The output must be at least a hundred gigawatts."

"Do you see any big yellow rocks sticking out of the black stuff?" Arkad asked her.

"How big?"

In Arkad's memory the rock had loomed as big as a mountain, but then, so had his mother. "Maybe . . . ten or twenty meters?"

"I can see something that way, about that size. Ten kilometers away."

They set out across the black surface. It wasn't bad to walk on; considerably more pleasant than the desert they had crossed. The surface was flat and even, and the air was coolest around Arkad's feet. At his head it felt like the inside of a furnace, but his feet were barely sweating. The two of them made good progress and reached the rocks in just a couple of hours.

"Is this the rock you remember?" Baichi asked.

Arkad walked slowly all around the outcrop, trying to decide if it was. The rocks rose out of the dark surface as if they were half submerged in a calm black lake. The color of the stone was right, he was sure of that. The size, the shape . . . he wasn't sure. Finally he found a spot where a tilted boulder created a patch of shade and sat down out of the sunlight. It was comfortably cool there, but the rock was still absolutely dry. Arkad closed his eyes and breathed. The little hollow smelled of dust and cool stone, and there was a very faint scent of metal which was strongest when he rested his head on the black ground.

"Yes," he told Baichi. "I've been here before."

"So has Ree," she said.

"How do you know?"

"There are wipes and human feces hidden between those two stones."

Arkad nodded. He had seen the droppings of all the other sentient beings on Syavusa, and none of them looked like human waste. Pfifu rinsed out their internal cavity with lots of water, Itooti excreted dry pellets, Vziim voided long gooey strands which they used in construction or hoarded up to sell as fertilizer, and Psthao-psthao produced almost no waste at all. None of them would use scented wipes.

They crawled into the little patch of shade for a rest, and

Arkad allowed himself a little water from the filter bottle. He was determined to save half for the trip back.

"Do you remember how far it is from here?" Baichi asked him.

He shook his head. "I don't remember leaving the ship at all, but it can't be far. I was very little. My mother must have carried me most of the way. How far can an ordinary human woman walk if she's carrying a toddler?"

There was just enough room for the two of them to lie down. To Arkad's surprise, Baichi rested her head on his chest and draped her silver cloak over the two of them. The underside of the cloth was deliciously cool, and Arkad could see the air over it ripple as the fabric pumped heat away from their bodies.

She put one arm across Arkad, and it seemed only natural for him to put his right arm around her shoulders. Baichi seemed so small and fragile when he held her. Even though he knew she was stronger than he was, he couldn't help feeling protective. Arkad had never felt that way about anyone before. His world had been full of enemies, allies, neutrals—and prey. There had never been anyone he felt the urge to take care of.

He must have fallen asleep like that, and he dreamed of holding her close, feeling her body pressing against his. When he opened his eyes her face was right in front of his, her dark eyes gazing into his, and he leaned forward to kiss her. But she pulled back before their lips touched.

"I will go up and look around," said Baichi, springing to her feet. Her usual impassive calm was gone; she looked . . . flustered? Arkad had read the word but now he thought he knew what it meant. After a moment of wordless hesitation, she darted into the sunlight and began climbing the rocks.

Arkad stayed in the shade and rested a bit more. There was no way he could go back to sleep, but his muscles were stiff and he was getting sunburned in spots. He was just wondering if he should go after Baichi when she dropped to the ground just outside their refuge.

"A spacecraft just landed near here," she said. "I think Ree has found the *Rosetta* and called for some help."

"Is it a Combined Forces ship?" he asked, scrambling to his feet.

"No," she said. "It is an Elmisthorn craft."

CHAPTER 18

AICHI'S CLOAK COULD ALMOST MATCH THE PERFECT BLACK
color of the ground—but that meant it absorbed all of the
intense sunlight, which made the fabric hot enough to scald
Arkad if he brushed against it. Baichi could tolerate the heat,
but her own body soon began radiating the excess away, so that
she was almost as hot as the cloak. They had to move in short
sprints, punctuated by periods when Arkad lay flat on the black
ground, trying to cool off in the baking sunlight, while Baichi
shielded him from view with the cloak.

Eventually they were close enough for him to see the spaceship.
Baichi identified it as a medium freighter, a standard Family of
Species design. The ship looked like an upside-down rowboat a
hundred meters long, with guidance fins at the front and back.
To Arkad's eyes the shape looked like Pfifu work, which made
sense since the Elmisthorn had conquered the Pfifu home world.
The really amazing thing was that they had somehow prevented
the Pfifu who built the ship from decorating it.

Four climate-controlled bubble tents, luminous white against
the black landscape, were grouped just outside the ship's forward
cargo hatch, and Arkad and Baichi could see individuals from
four different species moving around between the camp and the
ship. There were at least three Elmisthorn, including one wearing
an elaborate garment of golden ribbons and jewels, who must
have been a very high-ranking Alpha.

The Elmisthorn were accompanied by some immense centaur-
shaped beings which Baichi identified as Gustrogin, one of the

273

first species forcibly inducted into the Family of Species. Two of the Gustrogin wore armor and carried fearsome-looking plasma guns; the other two wore survival suits and were busy moving big cargo containers into the ship. Arkad could also make out a pair of Pfifu wearing spacesuits to protect themselves from the dry air and fierce sunlight.

And he could see Ree, hovering near the high-status Elmisthorn Alpha. Now he understood why she had been so reckless about the final stretch of the journey: she must have known they were already here, waiting for her.

About fifty meters away from the Elmisthorn ship was what looked like a low hill, completely covered by the same dark material which coated the ground. The more Arkad looked at the low hill, the more curious it seemed. It was steep-sided and topped with three low ridges which ran exactly parallel to one another. On the side facing the alien ship there was an opening in the hill, and he could see pale-blue rock.

Then it all snapped into focus for him. The hill was a ship. The bluish rock was metal with a faded coat of paint. The perfectly black ground cover had grown up over the triple hull of the *Rosetta* since it had landed, and the dark fibers draped away from the sides of the ship as though it was covered by a blanket. The Elmisthorn and their workers had cut away the black fibers at the nose of the ship, where the *Rosetta*'s cargo ramp was open. They were looting the ship.

"You need shelter and water," Baichi told him.

Arkad agreed. It was so hot it was hard to think. "Maybe we can sneak aboard the *Rosetta* without them noticing," he whispered back. "There might be some water there."

The two of them moved slowly until the bulk of the *Rosetta* was between them and the Elmisthorn camp, and then approached the black mound. Up close he could see that the steep sides were really a canopy of black fibers, branching into ever thinner filaments to create a completely opaque covering. The filaments were incredibly tough, but Baichi was able to force her fingers into the mass and then pulled her hands apart until there was a rent big enough for them to wriggle through. The effort made her skin shimmer with heat.

Under the canopy it was cooler than any place Arkad had been since leaving the tunnels of the Psthao-psthao. He stood in the darkness, letting his eyes adjust and savoring the sensation. When he could see again they moved along the hull, past the gaping mouths of the fusion motors, to the aft docking hatch between the engines. From the front end they could hear the clatter of the Elmisthorn team using power equipment.

The ship was resting on its belly, with no landing gear extended, and in a couple of places Arkad could see where the exterior plating had buckled or torn. That didn't look good.

The aft docking hatch was circular, with four flanges spaced evenly around it like a Vziim's hands. The hatch itself was bare metal with a small control panel and a handle in the center. It had a keypad and a fingerprint reader.

More out of curiosity than anything else, Arkad touched his index finger to the reader. To his surprise a small green light came on, and he heard a faint *kachunk* from the edge of the hatch. He pushed on the handle and the hatch swung open. Red emergency lights came on in the airlock inside.

Beyond the airlock was a long tunnel between the engines, lit by a few more emergency lights. It had ladders running along the sides, and the two of them had to stoop to walk through it. A flash of memory struck Arkad: he had once run down this tunnel, but it had seemed to stretch into an infinity of darkness dotted with red, and in a sudden panic he had turned and run back to his mother.

At the end of the tunnel, another hatch opened into a room filled with controls and machinery. It smelled familiar. The arrangement of things in the room seemed odd and confusing—until Arkad realized that the wall they had just passed through was supposed to be a floor. Many cover panels had been removed, exposing tangles of wiring, pipes of all sizes, valves, and pumps. A toolbox sat on the floor/wall with its contents scattered around it.

Baichi looked at the giant coils of the hyperspace drive. "This unit is badly damaged. Look! You can see where the windings have melted."

"Could we fix it?"

"No," she said without any hesitation. "It must be replaced, or at least rebuilt. We lack the supplies and tools."

He had known it was a foolish idea to expect to be able to sneak aboard, power up the *Rosetta*, and fly off. But that foolish idea had kept him going across the desert. Now Arkad had no plan at all.

The only exit from the engine room led through another hatch and another long tunnel, which was big enough for them to walk upright. Eventually it opened into a room Arkad recognized.

"This is the common room," he told Baichi. "That's the kitchen over there, and the bathroom across from it. And that passage..." he hurried forward and opened the next hatch.

The passage beyond it had three doors on either side; they were more like stiff curtains than actual doors and could be switched from horizontal to vertical depending on whether the ship was in space or sitting on the ground. Arkad counted three on the right-hand side and slid that door open.

"You left your room a mess," said Baichi. Arkad knelt on the floor among the toys and blankets. The fuzzy yellow blanket, the stuffed plush llama, the three wooden boats, the plastic astronaut in the green and gold spacesuit, the elephant-shaped cup—those had once been his entire world, and then he had forgotten all about them until now. They were dry, dusty, almost crumbling.

Everything felt old, much older than Arkad. The badger had been telling him the truth, then. How many times had it repaired him and brought him back to life? How old was he, really?

Arkad put down the llama and almost ran across the hall to his mother's room. She had left it clean and orderly, but the faint scent that lingered brought tears to his eyes.

"Whose things are these?" asked Baichi. She had opened one of the cabinets under the bed and lifted out a set of coveralls.

"I think those must have been my father's," said Arkad. He spread them out on the bed. They were big, made for someone tall and broad-shouldered, and they had obviously seen a lot of use. But the sight of them stirred no memories at all in Arkad. He folded them again and put them away. "I want a drink."

He went back to the kitchen and found the potable water tap. The water tasted coppery, and he could feel little flecks of something as he swallowed, but it was water, and he had drunk far worse. First he began to sweat, then his eyes teared up, but he didn't stop drinking until Baichi put a hand on his arm and said, "That's a liter. Stop. You can come back for more. I have made contact with the ship's data net. Most of the onboard systems have failed."

"What about the cargo?"

"The cargo containers were sealed and self-contained, with their own environment controls and power. But all of the monitor links are disconnected and I cannot sense them. That could mean the containers failed, or simply that the Elmisthorn and their servants have removed them."

With a bellyful of water Arkad didn't feel as fuzzy-headed anymore. "Let's see how much they've stolen," he said.

The corridor—or tunnel—that ran past the crew quarters ended at a six-way junction. Up led to the flight deck, down led to the ventral docking port; while right, left, and ahead led to the cargo holds.

He opened the hatch to the forward hold. The space was brightly lit by sunlight streaming in from outside—and was empty. The portside cargo hold was also picked clean. As they approached the starboard hold, both Arkad and Baichi could hear the sound of machines and Gustrogin laborers moving cargo containers.

"We don't have much time. They're almost done," he said.

"I think we have snuck aboard the wrong spacecraft," said Baichi.

For a second he didn't understand what she meant, and then he did. They crept back to the central corridor. "I want to check the cabins again. There might be something we can use."

He searched through drawers and cabinets. In one of the drawers under his grandfather's bed was an olive-green metal lockbox adorned with the white silhouette of a pistol. Baichi wrenched the box open, and they took out the weapon.

"This is an M50 automatic pistol. I'm keying the palm reader to recognize your hand. Do you know how to use it?"

Arkad shook his head.

She loaded the magazine, showed him the safety catch, and then handed Arkad the pistol. "Don't put your finger on the trigger until you want to fire it, and don't point it at anything you don't want to shoot."

"Maybe you should take it."

"I will not fight them," she said. "Ree knows that. You probably should not fight them either. I don't think this weapon can penetrate the Gustrogin battle armor, but I suppose it is better than nothing."

Arkad drank more water, but failed to find any food. They rested in his grandfather's cabin and devised a plan. Arkad would provide a distraction by emerging from the black desert and entering the Elmisthorn camp to surrender and beg for water. Baichi would slip aboard the other spaceship. At her signal, Arkad would sprint for the cargo hatch, she would fire up the main drive, and they would leave Ree and the others behind on Syavusa.

"Do you think it will work?"

"It is risky, but at least it plays to our strengths," said Baichi. "I am quick and silent, and you are good at lying."

He remembered something from an old video. "For luck," he said, and gave her a kiss. To his surprise, she returned it, and a long time went by before the two of them separated.

They slipped out of the aft docking hatch, paused for one more goodbye kiss, then Baichi moved in the direction of the Elmisthorn ship while Arkad headed straight out into the desert, away from both the *Rosetta* and the alien camp.

He walked until he started to feel hot, then turned left and went a kilometer, doing his best to stay hidden behind low hills and folds in the black surface. After about half an hour, he turned toward the camp and abandoned his attempts at stealth. By this point he was authentically hot and tired, so he had no trouble staggering convincingly as he approached the cluster of bubble tents. The pistol tucked into the waist of his trousers was heavy, and the metal was hot against the skin of his back.

One of the armored Gustrogin guards spotted him when he was about a hundred meters from the camp. After a moment the guard and Ree hurried out to meet him.

"Arkad!" said Ree, and she sounded genuinely glad to see him. But then her voice took a suspicious turn. "Where's Baichi?"

"Back in the desert," he said, letting some of his real anger out when he cried, "Why did you leave us?"

"I lost you in the sandstorm," she said, now with a look of concern that was almost convincing. "Once I got clear, I waited for the two of you, but you never turned up. Finally I decided to push on while I still had some water. And look"—she gestured at the ships and the camp ahead of them—"You're safe now. We've got food and water and a medical unit. We'll take good care of you. You are among friends."

"Who are these people?" he asked.

"They're friends," she repeated with a big smile. "We're all on the same side here, Arkad. They want to recover and preserve the treasures from the *Rosetta*, just as Jacob did. We're going to take them all back to Earth where they belong."

One of the lower-ranking Elmisthorn trotted up to them, and this time Arkad could see the look of unrestrained adoration on Ree's face as she and the Gustrogin knelt to speak with it face to face. Arkad remained standing.

"Question: is this the male feral," it asked in oddly accented English.

"Yes, it is," Ree replied with the same accent.

"Question: where is the female cyborg."

"The male says it is back in the desert." Ree looked at Arkad and spoke in the way she had done during their journey. "Was she alive when you left her?"

"No," he said, and let himself feel even more angry this time. "You left us and she died! I couldn't help her! I tried to carry her but she was too heavy."

The Elmisthorn looked up at Arkad. "Question: do you know anything about that ship." It nodded toward the *Rosetta*.

He shook his head. "No. I was just a little kid when my mother and I left. I don't remember anything."

"There is no need of it," said the Elmisthorn to Ree.

"Request: may I give it food and medica?" Ree asked.

"Yes, you may. Use your own supplies." The Elmisthorn turned and trotted off toward the camp. Arkad followed with Ree and the guard. He kept his face forward, but his eyes kept darting to the Elmisthorn ship, and the open cargo door in front. The Gustrogin workers were using a robot tractor to move a container up the ramp.

He judged the distance and then looked around. Could any of them stop him? He knew he could outrun Ree, and the Gustrogin looked so heavy he didn't think they could move very fast. But the Elmisthorn were very swift runners—and the Gustrogin guards had guns. He couldn't outrun a plasma blast.

Just then Ree patted the side of his neck. "Time to give you a checkup," she said. He felt a faint tingle under her fingers and reached up to feel the drug patch she had stuck to his skin. Then he passed out.

Arkad awoke in a bed with raised sides and a battery of folded robot arms above him. His head nestled in a U-shaped headrest which held it comfortably immobile. When he tried to sit up, he found that there were restraints on his shoulders, wrists, knees, and ankles.

"Hello?" he called out.

Ree appeared, looking down at him. "Sorry about that," she said. "I wanted to get you into the med unit as quickly as possible." She looked at a screen above Arkad's head. "You were pretty dehydrated, and you're still a little banged-up—though frankly I'm amazed you weren't hurt worse when the balloon crashed. By rights that should have killed you."

"Why am I tied down?"

"Oh, that's just to immobilize you for the med unit," she said, but did nothing to remove the restraints. "I do have a couple of things to ask you. Where's Baichi?" she asked, sounding casual. She was still watching the screen above his head.

"I don't know," he said.

"You said she died in the desert."

"I don't know where she is," he repeated, since it was true.

"Mm. Do you trust me, Arkad?"

"No," he said. "You lied to Jacob. You lied to all of us. I think you even lied to the people who helped you get off Earth."

"I make no apologies. I serve the greater good. Did you leave Baichi in the desert?"

"I don't know where she is."

Ree looked at him, then nodded and tapped her wrist device. "Warning: the female cyborg may be nearby." She looked down at Arkad again. "These medical monitors can tell when you're lying—and *I* can tell when you're trying to avoid answering a direct question. What were you two planning? And where did you get that pistol you were hiding?"

He glared back up at her but said nothing.

"I wonder if you have any value as a hostage," said Ree. "Do you think she's programmed to value human life at all? Doubtful. Ah, but I've got something she *does* care about, even if she thinks you're expendable." Ree moved out of sight and he could hear her murmuring something, but couldn't make out what she was saying. After a couple of minutes she returned. "All right, I'm going to release you, but not all at once. If you fight or resist, I'll just close the lid on the medical unit and knock you out, understand?"

"Okay," he said.

She freed his wrists and taped them together in front of him, then released the rest of the restraints and helped him out of the couch. Ree led Arkad out of the medical bay, and he realized they were aboard the Elmisthorn ship. He followed her through the ship to the main cargo bay, which was packed with big sealed containers. Each container had a thick plastic inspection window in the center of the square side facing the walkway, with a simple touch screen.

Ree tapped the screen on the closest container. "Here's Jacob's treasure, all safe and sound." The screen said:

CROWN JEWELS AND ROYAL REGALIA

BRITISH • BOURBON FRENCH • BONAPARTE FRENCH
• SPANISH • PORTUGUESE • SWEDISH • NORWEGIAN
• DANISH • AUSTRIAN • HUNGARIAN • LOMBARD •
ROMANIAN • RUSSIAN IMPERIAL • IMPERIAL GERMAN
• SAXON • PRUSSIAN • BAVARIAN • BOHEMIAN •
GREEK • PAPAL • OTTOMAN IMPERIAL • MOROCCAN
• ETHIOPIAN • SAUDI • JORDANIAN • IRANIAN
• HYDERABADI • TRAVANCORE • MYSORE •
JAIPUR • THAI • JAPANESE • QING CHINESE

Across the walkway Arkad saw EGYPTIAN NATIONAL MUSEUM ITEMS. Next to that was DA VINCI PAINTINGS. Stacked on top of them was JAPANESE CALLIGRAPHY AND TEXTILES.

"This is the one Jacob was particularly obsessed about," said Baichi, pointing to the label:

POLITICAL DOCUMENTS

U.N. CHARTER • MAGNA CARTA • DECLARATION
OF THE RIGHTS OF MAN • DECLARATIONS OF
INDEPENDENCE • CONSTITUTIONS • CHARTERS
• TREATIES, LETTERS, AND DIRECTIVES

"They must have emptied out every museum on Earth!" said Arkad, overwhelmed by the thought of all those containers packed full.

"They only got away with a fraction. Do you know some people actually killed themselves because some things had to be left behind? They digitized and scanned as much as they could, of course, but for some things they thought the actual physical objects were irreplaceable—which is why they make much better hostages than you," she added triumphantly.

The Pfifu technicians were attaching domed objects, like the pointy ends of giant eggs, to some of the containers.

"Shaped charges," said Ree. "The Elmisthorn brought them in case we had to breach the *Rosetta*'s hull. I've thought of a new use for them: with the blast confined inside one of these airtight, armored shipping containers, they'll blow the contents to dust and ashes. It's too bad we don't have enough for all the containers. We could save ourselves all the bother of hauling this junk back to Earth."

"If you want to destroy it all, why not just leave it here?"

"Because I'm afraid Jacob was right. This stuff has power. Those criminals who call themselves 'free' humans can use this as propaganda against the Family of Species. Manipulate people by appeals to obsolete ideologies and myths. Appeal to imaginary past glories. Remind them of what humans could do on their own. There's still enough unmodified humans on Earth to make that a problem. Until they all die out, this stuff is too dangerous to leave lying around. Now come along; it's time."

The little expedition had gathered in the front of the cargo bay: four Pfifu, two Gustrogin in battle armor and two more in survival suits, three Elmisthorn, and Ree and Arkad.

Ree handed Arkad off to one of the unarmored Gustrogin, who clutched his right arm in a massive hand, then she knelt before the high-status Alpha Elmisthorn. "Request: may I speak to the female cyborg?"

"Yes, you may," said the Elmisthorn. Arkad watched it with interest. The Alpha didn't act like the ones he had met on the plains of Syavusa. They had been graceful and swift, strong enough to knock him down, and curious about things. This one's neck had an exaggerated curve, its limbs looked far too delicate, and it seemed awfully passive and dull. If all of the ruling class of the Family of Species was like this one, Arkad began to understand why the exiles on Syavusa were afraid their civilization was doomed to collapse.

The Elmisthorn and Pfifu retreated to the back of the cargo hold. The two Gustrogin soldiers took up firing positions at the front of the cargo ramp, with the workers and Arkad just behind them. Ree strode down to stand at the foot of the ramp. She spoke into her wrist device, and the ship's speakers sent her voice booming across the black land outside.

"Baichi!" she called. "I know you're not dead. Arkad told me everything. I know you're out there, and I know you can hear me. Come out and show yourself! Whatever scheme you were planning has failed. I've got him, and I've got all of *Rosetta's* cargo. Show yourself now or I'll start blowing up the containers. Understand? All your precious cultural treasures gone. The new Earth doesn't need that garbage anyway. You have one minute."

To the soldiers she added, "Order: wait for my word to fire."

"Ree, don't!" said Arkad. "Just let me go. We'll go away. You can take the stuff."

"Yes, we can, and we will," she said to him over her shoulder. "I'm going to give my master an even better gift: a Machine hybrid being and the weapon that can stop her. That's probably worth more than all this junk Jacob was so desperate to recover."

She turned back to face outside. "Ten seconds!" she said into her wrist device. "Don't waste my time, Baichi!"

"I am already here," said Baichi from behind everyone.

CHAPTER 19

ARKAD TURNED TO SEE BAICHI STANDING BEHIND EVERYONE, at the hatchway leading from the cargo hold into the flight deck of the Elmisthorn ship. She was holding one of the Elmisthorn Betas over her head, gripping it by the neck and one rear leg. It struggled and clacked its mouthparts but she ignored it and stood perfectly still.

"Set down all your weapons and release Arkad or I will pull this being apart," said Baichi in her usual calm tone.

The Gustrogin relaxed its grip on Arkad's arm, and he quickly stepped away from it, and tried to tear at the tape on his wrists with his teeth. The Elmisthorn Alpha and its companion cowered behind the Pfifu technicians.

"Order: do not fire!" said Ree in Elmisthorn English, then switched to the older language and adopted a friendly, reasonable tone. "I know you won't do it, Baichi. You aren't like that. Just put it down. There's no reason for us to fight, dear. In fact, I'd like to make you the same offer I made to Arkad: come to Earth with us. Let it go and everything will be all right."

Arkad ignored what Ree was saying. He had learned that much about her. Instead he watched her hands. Her left hand, with the wrist device, was raised in front of her. Her right hovered in the vicinity of her hip pocket. The wrist device controlled the charges on the cargo containers, and he guessed the pocket held the weapon which had paralyzed Baichi's Machine parts. Which would she choose? Carry out her threat—or try to cripple Baichi?

285

"You're an outcast among humans," Ree continued. "They hate and fear you. The Machines despise you. Only the Family of Species will welcome you in. The Family welcomes everyone. If you help us fight against the Machines, you'll earn respect and acceptance."

As she spoke, her right hand rested on her hip, then slid into her pocket.

"Don't do it!" Arkad shouted.

Several things happened very quickly at the same time. Ree pulled the oddly shaped little device out of her pocket. Arkad hurled himself at Ree. The nearest Gustrogin soldier raised its weapon to fire at Arkad.

And Baichi, moving fast enough that Arkad could hear her passage through the air, dropped the Elmisthorn she was holding and launched herself like a missile at the Gustrogin. The plasma blast aimed at Arkad caught her instead, washing her in blue flame and setting her cloak on fire. She shattered the rifle with her left hand, and with her right she struck the hulking Gustrogin soldier in powered armor a single blow which cracked its helmet and knocked it tumbling down the cargo ramp.

Arkad only got a peripheral view of all that because he was struggling with Ree. His leap ended with both of them lying in a heap at the foot of the ramp. The little device flew from her hand before she could activate it, bounced once, and clattered to the black ground.

Arkad scrambled to his elbows and knees and tried to get past Ree to grab it, but she got a fistful of his shirt and pulled herself ahead. Their reaching hands were both a few centimeters short of the device.

The Gustrogin soldier Baichi had punched crashed to the ramp just behind them, with one foreleg resting heavily on Arkad's ankle. Arkad held onto Ree's arm for dear life, and with the Gustrogin's weight pinning him in place, he was able to pull Ree's hand away from the device.

Behind him, the second Gustrogin soldier fired at Baichi with a laser built into one of its armored forearms. She punched it in the center of its chest, splintering the armor there, then used her hands to pry the entire breastplate apart. That shut down all the armor's systems, and Baichi lifted the massive being and hurled it bodily down the ramp past Arkad and Ree.

"She's out of control!" said Ree. "We have to shut her down or she'll kill us all!" She followed that up by kicking Arkad in the face so that he let go of her arm. She lurched forward, snatching at the little device.

But before her fingers could close on it, a small foot as pale as paper came to rest on top of the device.

Baichi glared down at Ree. Arkad had never seen her angry before. He had never seen *anyone* that angry before. Her expression and the still-burning remnants of her cloak gave her the look of a wrathful angel. The air around her shimmered with heat. "You may not harm him," she said.

Ree grimaced and stabbed a finger at her wrist device. Arkad closed his eyes, waiting for the sound of the charges destroying the treasures inside the cargo hold.

Nothing happened. He opened his eyes. Ree pressed the touch panel of her device again and again until Baichi lifted her by the collar of her expedition suit and tossed her into one of the inflated tents of the campsite.

At the back of the hold, the Elmisthorn and Pfifu were trying to open the hatch, but it remained shut.

"Are you doing that?" Arkad asked Baichi.

"Of course," she said, calm again, and then raised her voice and spoke in the same form of English Ree had used. "Order: all of you leave the ship now."

When they hesitated, she picked up one of the plasma rifles from the unconscious Gustrogin. "Now!" she repeated, and her voice made the metal of the hull ring.

The Elmisthorn Alpha, retaining some dignity, led the others out of the cargo hold, down the ramp to the ground. Baichi covered them until they were past, then led Arkad onto the ramp, which began to close as soon as he stepped onto it. From somewhere in the interior of the ship, Arkad heard the sound of pumps and turbines whirring to life. The locked hatch at the back of the cargo compartment opened as they approached.

"Come on and strap in," said Baichi, leading the way up to the flight deck. "I took over the ship's data net as soon as I got aboard. I think I can fly it."

Arkad tumbled onto one of the cushioned couches on the flight deck. It was cup-shaped, built for Pfifu rather than humans, but he managed to get the safety harness around himself once Baichi removed the tape from his wrists.

For a moment the ship didn't move. Then . . . another moment went by. Arkad glanced over at Baichi, who was staring into the middle distance. Her normally impassive face had a very slight frown.

"Something is interfering with my control," she said. "Possibly a security override or—"

She stopped. Motes of dust in the air were coalescing into a furry black-and-white face hovering in front of Arkad.

"I'm sorry, my dear boy, but I can't let you go. That cargo's too important. I can't let the two of you take it. It's simply too risky." The familiar gruff voice was clear, but somehow Arkad had the sense that he was hearing it only inside his own head.

"You promised you wouldn't interfere!"

"Hmm, yes. Well. I didn't think you would actually get this far, if you see what I mean."

"This is unethical behavior," said Baichi quietly. "The higher-order minds will not approve."

"If they find out," said Mr. Badger.

"I will tell them."

"Don't be foolish, child. I can shut you down and kill your biologicals with a thought. If anyone asks why, I can simply replay your recent display of irrational anger. You are a hazard."

Her face went blank again, but this time Arkad sensed that Baichi was actually shocked.

"Forget about any higher minds," said Arkad. "I don't even know what those are. The stuff in the cargo was made by humans, and that's who it belongs to, not you. What you're doing is wrong. You're stealing. I know all about stealing—I've done it all my life, to stay alive. But I never stole anything just to have it, and I never took from anyone worse off than I was. So never mind about Baichi telling anyone. *You'll* know. If you take this ship, then every time you look at it or think about it, I want you to remember that a dirty little street thief like me despises *you* for stealing it!"

The mask floating in the air was suddenly just a puff of drifting dust again. "I've got control back," said Baichi, and from below them came a loud humming sound as the ship lifted on a cushion of air and began to move. The treasure-laden spaceship gained speed across the desert until its nose lifted and it soared into the sky. Then the main engines lit and it blasted upward on a tail of blue fire, accelerating brutally to orbital speed. Arkad felt himself pressed back into his seat until black spots appeared in his vision, and then he passed out.

When he woke they were in free fall, and Syavusa was a vast crescent against the stars. Arkad let himself float up to the windows for a better view, and hung there, watching the sunlight shine off water, the swirls of cloud, and the cluster of lights on the night side that marked the spaceport.

As he floated there, he saw the bright disk of the sun touch the edge of Syavusa's atmosphere. It appeared to sink through the layers, each adding a different color, until the last red edge vanished behind the curve of the planet and the *Rosetta* flew on in darkness.

"I've never seen a sunset before," said Arkad.

"We will have to boost into a transfer orbit soon," said Baichi. "I am afraid there may be other Elmisthorn ships nearby. We have to get away from this world."

"We should check the whole ship," said Arkad. "Make sure nobody stayed behind."

"I am in control of the ship's data net."

"I know—but it's an Elmisthorn ship. They might know places they can hide from the sensors, or maybe ways to fool them. I'm sure the Pfifu would have figured that out."

Arkad had another reason for the search, which he didn't want to admit to Baichi: he wanted to inspect his new domain. He was now the master—well, maybe the first mate—of an actual starship! He had never before owned more than he could carry and now he had a whole *ship* of his own!

Moving about the Elmisthorn spaceship in orbit was tricky. Arkad had never been in zero gravity before, and even his years of experience climbing and swinging around the rooftops of Ayaviz were scant preparation. The interior of the starship was all rounded-off and soft to the touch, as if the designers expected passengers to go clumsily launching themselves around and crash into things.

Baichi showed Arkad how to unlock the compartment doors, and he began to work his way down from nose to tail, searching each deck completely before moving on.

It was easy to tell which quarters were for which crew. The Gustrogin soldiers had a whole deck to themselves, a single room furnished at their giant scale. He was surprised to see that each soldier's locker contained a musical instrument as well as space for weapons and armor.

The Pfifu deck was a riot of color, with individual cabins custom-fitted by their occupants. Arkad was amused to notice subtle mockery of the Elmisthorn and Gustrogin worked into the artwork on the walls. He felt a pang of worry for the Pfifu left behind in the parched heat of the Black Land. But they had survival suits and supplies, and Ree could show them the way to safety. They might even decide to stay on Syavusa.

He didn't feel sorry for Ree at all, though. She could die of thirst in the desert for all he cared. Arkad found her quarters and the medical lab where she had questioned him on the deck below the Pfifu quarters. That was one compartment he absolutely didn't want to return to, but he checked it all the same, looking into all the storage lockers where a Pfifu might hide.

On the Gustrogin deck, Arkad had begun picking up small items which looked as if they might be useful—a filter bottle, a tube of smart glue, a cloak like Baichi's—and he continued on the Pfifu deck until he found himself trying to manage a bundle almost as massive as himself. Items kept escaping from the cloak he was using as a sack, and when he reached the hatch between the human-configured deck and the Elmisthorn quarters he stopped and broke out laughing. For the first time in years, he didn't have to pack up everything he wanted to keep and carry it around all the time. He could put something down and *nobody would steal it*. Arkad wedged his bundle into a storage bin and continued without it—but old habit kept nagging at him, and he kept having a what-have-I-forgotten feeling.

The Elmisthorn had as much space as the Pfifu crew and Gustrogin troops combined, safe in the middle of the hull. Their quarters were paneled with mirrors, which somehow were still soft to the touch. The air was delicately scented and hidden speakers played a soft crooning. Arkad found the mirrors a little unnerving, as his every movement was echoed by a whole army of Arkads. It reminded him uncomfortably of what the badger had said about reconstructing him over and over.

The storage lockers behind the mirrors in the Elmisthorn cabins were full of gaudy ornaments and luxuriously soft clothing. Arkad was surprised to see how much of the fabric was hand-woven or even stitched of animal skins, and then he reflected that the rarity and work required were probably what made the garments appeal to the Elmisthorn in the first place. He had no idea why they would have brought such luxuries on an expedition to a remote world like Syavusa. Were they afraid someone would steal their lovely clothes if they left them unguarded at home? Perhaps the universe wasn't so different from Ayaviz after all.

He did pick out one garment, a kind of decorative ruff made of red and black feathers woven with gold. It would look good on Baichi, he thought. The idea of being able to give her a present was very exciting.

Below the opulent Elmisthorn decks he found the comfortingly utilitarian engineering decks, with access tubes leading through the fuel tanks to the drives. He was particularly careful to search those areas, as even an unskilled saboteur could probably cripple the ship.

"It's all empty," he told Baichi when he got back to the flight deck. "The ship is ours. Look, I found this for you." He handed her the feathered ruff. She looked at it impassively for a moment, then smiled and put it on. The black and red feathers against her chalk-white skin were very striking.

She was smiling. That made Arkad smile, a ridiculous goofy grin he couldn't suppress. "What do you want to do?" he asked her. "We've got a ship, we can go anywhere we like. Do you want to be merchants . . . or explorers? Maybe privateers against the Elmisthorn!"

"There are only two of us and this ship is not armed."

"Well, are there any other lost treasures we can go looking for?"

"We must deliver this cargo to the humans at Invictus."

"Is it far?"

"It will take this ship eight hundred and twenty-nine hours to get there. A month. Thirty sleep cycles for you."

Thirty sleeps—and waking thirty times to see Baichi. He looked at her pale face, lit blue and green by the cockpit screens, framed by the dark ruff. His mouth felt dry. "You said you wouldn't fight anyone. But—"

"I couldn't let them hurt you," she said. "Back in the desert, when all my systems failed and I was left with just my human brain and body—I couldn't keep it from happening. I love you, Arkad."

"I love you, too," he said, and as he spoke he knew it was true. He touched her hand and the cool pale skin seemed to make his fingers tingle. His heartbeat was very loud.

She pulled away her hand. "And that is why I cannot stay with you," she said.

"Why?" he asked, baffled. "We love each other! We've got a ship and all the historical stuff Jacob was looking for. We've won! We can be together forever now."

"It is too dangerous."

"I'm not scared of the Elmisthorn."

"They are not the danger. I am."

When Arkad only looked at her in bafflement, Baichi continued. "Back on the surface I was angry enough to kill Ree—to kill all of them—because I love you. If they had harmed you, I don't think I could have stopped myself from destroying them all. The badger was right: I became irrational—and dangerous. Love is too dangerous for me. We will have this voyage together, and we can make the most of it. But when we reach Invictus I must leave you, and keep myself from loving you or anyone ever again."

"No," he said, trying desperately to think of some way to argue her out of it. But just looking at her calm implacable face told him that was impossible.

She held out Ree's little device to him. "You should have this. In case I go wrong somehow."

Arkad closed her fingers over it and pushed her hand gently away. "No. Keep it, or throw it out of the airlock. I don't want it. I still trust you—I'll always trust you. I love you, and I can't control my brain the way you do. I'll always love you."

He looked away so she couldn't see the tears in his eyes.

A long time later he cleared his throat. "You said we can make the most of this voyage. All right, then. Show me how to fly this ship. And how do we figure out where we're going?"

She gave what might have been a chuckle. "Don't forget you need food and sleep. There will be plenty of time after you've had a rest."

"I don't want to wait for anything. I'm done with waiting. Let's *go.*"

On the western edge of Syavusa's daylit side, where the sun hung eternally on the eastern horizon, never rising, a wiry human boy woke on the beach, just beyond the reach of the breaking waves. He was naked and couldn't remember how he had gotten there. Nearby on the sand he saw a neatly folded blanket and a knife.

Arkad wrapped the blanket around himself, toga-fashion, and tucked the knife into a fold where he could reach it quickly. He looked around. To the north he could see a dark thread of smoke against the sky. North, then. He shook his head to clear it, trying to remember how he had come to be on this beach. The last thing he could recall was... Ayaviz. He'd been scavenging on the Ring. Everything after that was a blank.

Except... there was something about a pale, narrow human face with great black eyes. He didn't know whose face it was, but that ghost of a memory seemed intensely important. She (how did he know it was a she?) was someone he wanted to find.

Very well, Arkad decided. He would find her. He started walking.